AGRIPPINA

AGRIPPINA

THE MOST EXTRAORDINARY WOMAN
OF THE ROMAN WORLD

EMMA SOUTHON

PEGASUS BOOKS
NEW YORK LONDON

AGRIPPINA

Pegasus Books, Ltd.
148 West 37th Street, 13th Floor
New York, NY 10018

First Pegasus Books paperback edition October 2020
First Pegasus Books hardcover edition August 2019

ISBN: 978-1-64313-610-3

10 9 8 7 6 5 4 3 2

Printed in the United States of America
Distributed by Simon & Schuster
www.pegasusbooks.com

To all my Difficult Aunts

'Who gets to speak and why is the only question.'
Chris Kraus

Contents

Introduction: History and Fiction

This is the story of an extraordinary woman. She is extraordinary because she saw the limits placed upon her by her world as a result of her gender and simply decided that they didn't apply to her. She saw clearly the spaces where women could not go, stormed into them anyway and was murdered as a result. This is the story of an empress, who was the sister, niece, wife and mother of emperors. It has incest and murder, wars and conquest, plots and prayers. It has a little of everything a good story should have because it is, importantly, a story.

Agrippina the Younger was born Julia Agrippina and lived from November 15CE to March 59CE. Her life spanned, and was intimately bound up in, the reigns of four of the first five Roman emperors – Tiberius, Caligula, Claudius and Nero – known as the Julio-Claudians. Which all sounds great for source material on her; after all, the Julio-Claudians appear to be pretty well covered in sources. They're the emperors everyone can name. Except that 'well covered' in Roman terms generally just means more than one fragmentary source, and Agrippina is a woman in a world where women are considered to be staggeringly uninteresting, if not totally irrelevant. As a result, we have just three major literary sources that mention Agrippina with any detail, and a total of seven literary sources from the entire corpus of Latin literature that think she was interesting or significant enough to deserve a single line; one of which is a play.

The three big sources, with which you will become familiar over the course of the book, are Tacitus's *Annals*, which is doomed to be defaced by sniggering Latin students for the rest of time, written around 116CE; Suetonius's biographies of the emperors from Julius Caesar to Domitian, collectively known as *The Twelve Caesars*, from just a little later, about 121CE; and Cassius Dio's Greek language, but culturally Roman, *Roman History*, from about 230CE. Conveniently, each of these slips into a different genre of Roman literature, but each has its own glaring, crippling problems when it comes to reconstructing the life of Agrippina. As you will have noticed for a start, each is published between 50 and 180 years after Agrippina died. Reading Tacitus therefore is, to us, essentially the same as reading a recently published history of the Second World War, while reading Dio is like reading a new history of the Georgians: they may be excellent but they are describing different times. Secondly, two of the sources are incomplete. Tacitus is a great read but was not very popular in his time so he survives in just two fragmentary manuscripts, the fragments of which do not overlap, so there are some big chunks missing, including the whole of Caligula's reign. This is a loss I shall never get over. The relevant books of Dio, on the other hand, are lost entirely and all that we have left are epitomes made by the much later writers Zonoaras and Xiphilinus, who cut down, paraphrased and supplemented Dio's words for their own purposes. These are, in essence, fragments of Dio's work and they are more fragmentary and confused than they appear when bound in a pretty translation. This leaves just Suetonius's biographies, which would be fine if they were biographies of Agrippina; but they're not. They are the biographies of the men that Agrippina was attached to. Suetonius is interested only in the motivations and actions of the subjects of his biographies and so the women in their lives, like our Agrippina, slip silently into the background to be brought out only when her presence could tell the reader something interesting about the more important man.

Trying to pry a Roman person, let alone a Roman woman, out of these fragmented, scattered sources is hard enough but, on top of the holes, the bits we do have are moralising in the extreme. Virtually the first thing that Tacitus tells us in his *Annals* is that he will 'write without malice or partisanship', a sweet promise this his history is merely the dispassionate recitation of objective facts. At the same time, though, he also tells us that he picks and chooses what to tell us about any given year because he believes that the historian has a duty to tell history that is moral and instructive: a historian should actively praise good behaviour and condemn wickedness. In the same sentence he tells us that the Julio-Claudian period of which he writes was 'a tainted and wicked age', which, although I strongly suspect that he did indeed believe this was a dispassionate and objective fact, is an opinion. Of course, the reader of Tacitus will have noticed that he's not being as objective as he claims as soon as he starts telling us what his characters were thinking. This happens for the first time in Book One, Chapter One of the *Annals* when Tacitus insists that Augustus gave his grandsons the made-up title 'Princes of Youths' with 'pretend reluctance.'[1] For the general reader, this is all the better as Tacitus is hilariously catty and tells a brilliant anecdote, as we shall see. For the historian or biographer, though, it is a pissing nightmare, because it means that every fact that Tacitus gives us is twisted and manipulated and carefully presented to tell a story that fits his overall narrative of moral decline and Roman degradation. And quite often, Tacitus's narrative includes mind reading to make his story work. Within that narrative, Agrippina looms large as a symbol of everything that is wrong with the imperial system.

Suetonius is equally moralising, but in a less sophisticated way. He is simultaneously more and less useful to the biographer than Tacitus because, as one of the emperor Hadrian's freedmen,[2] he had access to an awful lot of letters and documents and liked to show that off. This means that we all get to read Augustus's letter to Livia in which he tries to decide whether her grandson Claudius is mentally incapacitated or merely externally revolting, and that's obviously great. On the other hand, he also liked to throw every single thing he heard, read or thought about the subjects of his biographies down on the page and present rumour, letters, personal experience, narratives taken from histories and things he read written on walls as equal facts, often without telling us what is what. At the same time, he threw all these things on the page in a thematic fashion, rather than a chronological one. So, the good deeds of Caligula from his whole reign are crammed into the first 20 chapters of his biography, while the bad deeds then take up the next 36 chapters, giving the strong impression that Caligula was good for a while and then went bad. Meanwhile, the family members of the imperial subject float around in the back-

---

1. Tacitus, *Annals*, 1.1

2. Freedmen (and freedwomen) were emancipated slaves. As part of their manumission they were usually granted Roman citizenship but were bound by ties of obligation and formal gratitude, and sometimes affection, to their former owner and their families. In the early Imperial period, they formed an informal nouveau riche business class. In case you forget, though, there's a glossary at the end for terms like this.

ground of these context-free thematically linked anecdotes, appearing and disappearing as the narrative of each chapter demands. In essence, Suetonius's biographies have a tendency to read like a badly cited off-brand wiki page for Barack Obama; one littered with 'citation needed' notes and a references list that treats White House publications and the Above Top Secret conspiracy forums as sources with equal weight.

This is an important point: not one of our ancient literary sources would pass even the most basic Wikipedia test. Every one of them would be, at the very least, subject to a strongly worded header that warned the reader that a lot of this was drawn from a single source. Barely a sentence would survive even the most lax demand for citation and support that underpins the modern Western understanding of what history and biography are. They absolutely cannot be treated as texts that are truthful in the way that you or I might conceive of truth, where they discuss something that actually happened. A much more useful way to look at the way that Tacitus, Dio and Suetonius constructed their writing is to think about the story that David Cameron fucked a pig.

In case you don't remember, this story emerged in 2015, when David Cameron was the prime minister of the UK, before he set fire to his reputation with the Brexit referendum. A Conservative ex-minister, Lord Ashcroft, who was embroiled in a personal feud with Cameron over a job, published an unauthorised biography of Cameron (*Call Me Dave*) in which he recounted an incident that had allegedly occurred while an 'unnamed MP' and Cameron were at university together, as part of a private dining club for extremely rich, extremely un-self-aware, male students.[3] At one meeting of this dining club, says the book, they had eaten a whole pig with attached head, just like Henry VIII might have done, and the teenage David Cameron had been peer-pressured, while a little drunk and flushed with attention, to get his dick out at the dining table and put it in the

3. Michael Ashcroft and Isabel Oakenshott (2015) *Call Me Dave: The Unauthorised Biography of David Cameron.* London: Biteback. 'Drugs, debauchery and the making of an extraordinary prime minister'. The original article was Michael Ashcroft and Isabel Oakeshott (20 September 2015). *Daily Mail.* London.

dead pig's mouth. One imagines that, if this happened at all, which it probably didn't, at worst a flaccid penis would have been flopped into the dead, cooked boar mouth for two seconds. However, when the aggrieved Ashcroft decided he needed a hook to get people to buy his book, the anecdote was irresistible.

And so, one night in September 2015, the story was broken by British newspapers that David Cameron had fucked a pig. And we all know that, on the level of objective, real-world, capital T Truth, the story is not True. David Cameron did not have sexual relations with that pig. But as a story, as a narrative, it's too funny, too perfect. It encapsulates everything that the social and political opposition to Cameron hated about him and his government: it has the exclusive university dining club setting, a dining club where they had a pig's head like medieval lords; it has the image of the braying, drunk mob of red-faced posh boys, the peer pressure, and the notion that Cameron would do anything for approval; it has a literal penis going into a dead pig. To make the situation almost too perfect, there is a pure intertextual joy in the fact that the writer Charlie Brooker had spent years accusing David Cameron of looking quite a lot like a ham and had written a TV show in which the British prime minister was forced to fuck a pig. David Cameron fucking a pig had so many facets that encapsulated everything that was unpopular about the Conservative leader that the public couldn't resist it either. So they wrote think pieces and made puns on Twitter about it, hashtags were invented and people talked about it seriously in broadsheets and on the news. But all that was done in the knowledge that it probably didn't technically *happen*. People are smart; they know the story is – at absolute best – a wild exaggeration about the antics of a drunk kid. At best. Most likely it was a half-truth woven by a man who we know had recently and publicly stopped supporting Cameron after Cameron denied him a job. PigGate was widely believed, and reported, at the time as being an act of revenge by Ashcroft, to hurt Cameron personally. We know this. We don't really, truly believe that David Cameron had sex with a pig. But still, there's a PigGate Wikipedia page, it was in all the papers, it was in *Time* magazine. The prime minister of the United Kingdom of Great Britain and Northern Ireland was forced to publicly deny on television that he had ever had sexual contact with an animal. It's part of Cameron's reputation, his legacy, even though it's just a silly story no one believes. In 1,000 years, it's just possible that this is a thing people will know about him: Brexit, phone hacking and the pig fucking. Which brings me back to the sources for Agrippina and her life. So much of what we have about Julio-Claudian emperors and their families is stories just like this – stories about sex, about private habits, about things happening on islands that no one ever visited, behind closed doors and even inside emperors' heads. Take this classic line about Caligula, for example, probably one of the best known 'facts' about him:

> '...it is also said that he planned to make Incitatus [his horse] consul.'[4]

This is written by Suetonius, about 80 years after Caligula died, and Suetonius is pretty clear that the level of chat we're talking about is the level that David Cameron fucked a pig fits into. It's a rumour, a story, something no one really believes but everyone thinks is funny because it fits what they think about Caligula: he's a deranged, uncontrolled lunatic who likes his horse way too much and has no respect for the institution of the Senate. But another 50 years after that, 130 years after Caligula had a favourite horse, we get this from Cassius Dio:

> 'He swore by the animal's life and fortune and even promised to appoint him consul, a promise that he would certainly have carried out if he had lived longer.'[5]

The rumour, the 'it is said', has become fact. Today, it's in *Horrible Histories* books with FACT! written next to it.

That's an extreme example, of course. But it's indicative of all the sources and the difficulties of trying to get a person out of them. Essentially, everything that we know about Agrippina comes from these three sources and is a blur of misogyny, genre tropes, moralising

4. Suetonius, *Caligula*, 55.
5. Dio, *Roman History*, 59.14.7.

grand narratives and unsourced rumours. It is my job here to peel back layers of rumour, narrative and lies and find out if there is anything at all underneath. But what criteria do I use to decide which stories are 'true' and which are 'rumour'? I mean, some are seemingly obvious, like the Caligula horse one. Others are, in context, obviously bollocks, too. Almost any accusation of incest can be disregarded because incest was a bizarrely common accusation in the first century CE; there are numerous examples of people openly making accusations of incest in order to take out their enemies. So, either the Romans were constantly fucking their siblings, or it's a strange cultural quirk of the period to accuse your enemies of fucking their siblings. Dealing with the rest, however, can be a problem.

All this also works to explain why this book has the chapter headings it does. If you are eagle-eyed you will have noticed that Agrippina is presented here only through her relationships to other people. Those other people are all men, with the exception of her mother, who is also called Agrippina. Both Agrippinas are named after a man: Agrippina is merely a feminine version of Agrippa, as Julia is a feminised version of Julius. As a woman, Agrippina exists only when her actions impact on the lives or actions of men in the political or military sphere because in the ancient world, as a woman, she exists only through her relationship to men. She can be seen only through the distorting lens of her relationship to other people and how well or badly she performed the ideal form of that relationship. It's mostly badly, which is why we get to see so much of her. If she had been performing well, she'd be as invisible as her sisters. Even so, as we shall see, there are big chunks of her life – years of it, including while she was empress – where we have no idea what she was doing because she wasn't impacting politics or men's public lives. She could have been spending her days murdering girls and bathing in their blood and the sources wouldn't record it because that's women's stuff and, therefore, very boring. As an individual, as an empress and as a member of the Julio-Claudian family in her own right, Agrippina is just not important in Roman eyes.

When Agrippina is not standing next to a man, she slips back into the darkness of history. History is mostly darkness. All we get to see in our sources are the very few men and women who managed – through luck or hard work or ingrained privilege – to burst into the tiny spotlight that historians hold and be seen by doing something very, very good, or very, very bad, or simply being emperor. For every little head that blinks in the glare of the historian's spotlight there are 100,000 more whose important, significant lives have been untouched by it. Go to Highgate cemetery in London, for example, and you will see the graves of Douglas Adams and Karl Marx, and you will walk past a further 169,998 bodies of women, men and children whose names and stories will disappear with their gravestones, whose lives have vanished in the darkness. You'll step over their graves to get to the famous ones. Those who stand in the spotlight reflect a little light, though, and with the reflected light we can see the people standing next to them: their wives and children and close friends. We see Agrippina in history only because she was the daughter, niece, wife and mother of powerful men. The sheer multitude of her relationships with famous men means we can see her a little better than most women, but we can still only see fragments.

What this all means, beyond me having a moan about how hard it is being a Roman historian, is that there is no objective, capital T Truth about Agrippina. There is only a series of stories, drawn from other people's stories about men. The only way through is to be honest about that. This story is as much mine as it is Agrippina's, because I have chosen how to present the information I have. But it is a good story about a woman who deserves her own place in history. It is about a woman so important that men do everything they can to hurt her by accusing her of incest, adultery, murder and child abuse. It is about a woman who ran the Roman Empire for longer than a lot of male emperors, and about how the men who controlled the world reacted to that. It is about, at the centre of it all, power.

A Very Brief History of Rome

Before we leap into the life of Julia Agrippina, we need some context. Agrippina lived in a culture that is quite alien to our own, and which valued its history and its religion very much. Romans in every stage of Roman history, from the second that Aeneas stepped onto the shores of Italy to the moment that Romulus Augustulus was deposed in 476CE, felt themselves to be the very modern point of a history that stretched back thousands of years. The tendrils of their history were real, living things that entwined their way around their everyday lives, mostly through their family histories. Romans were a collective. Each individual existed primarily as part of a family and then as part of the Roman state, and those identities were considerably more important than any individuality. This is why about a third of the men and women in this book share the same names and why daughters usually take a feminised version of their father's name (Claudius/Claudia, Drusus/Drusilla, Agrippa/Agrippina, Octavian/Octavia and so on): their familial identity is the most important thing about them in a cultural sense. Without having a little bit of knowledge about Roman history, and the history of the Julian and Claudian families, virtually nothing about Roman culture in the first century CE makes sense. At the same time, a tiny bit of background about Roman history tells you an awful lot about how they saw women in a big-picture sense, and what they thought the purpose and function of women was. So, let's take a whizz-bang tour of nearly a millennium of Roman history up until the birth of Agrippina's parents.

Rome has two founders: Aeneas and Romulus. Aeneas was a child of Troy who escaped when it was sacked by the Greeks bearing the Trojan horse, carrying his father and household gods out of the ruined city but abandoning his wife. He travelled about a bit and eventually arrived in Italy and, long story short, became king of Alba Longa. A few royal generations later and a princess was raped by the god Mars, resulting in twins. The princess was also a Vestal Virgin, and had therefore taken a vow of chastity. Rape was considered a violation of that vow (this is a theme we shall return to) and so her sons, Romulus and Remus, were condemned to death as punishment. She tried to feed the twins to a wolf, which raised them instead (just keep going with me here). When they grew up, because they were demi-gods, the boys decided to found a city of their own, had a fight about which hill would be the best hill and Romulus killed Remus over it. So, Rome was named Rome and Romulus seemed pretty happy with the Capitoline Hill as the capital/best hill.

Romulus now needed to populate his city, so he rounded up some random men from the area and all was well and good until they realised that a city of exclusively men was both horrible and wouldn't last long. They needed women. To get some women, the new Romans, led by Romulus, pretended to throw a party for their nearest neighbours, the Sabines, and while the Sabine men were distracted at the party, the Romans sneaked off and stole all their wives and daughters. This was the Rape of the Sabine Women. The Sabine men, surprisingly, weren't happy that all their wives and daughters had been kidnapped, so they started a war. However, the Sabine women were soft-hearted and had very quickly become attached to the Romans because the Romans hadn't literally raped them, just kidnapped them. Women had low expectations of men in myth. The women wanted neither their fathers or their new husbands to die so they flung themselves between the two armies and stopped the war. As a result of this action, the Sabines and Romans became united as one people under the dual kingship of Romulus and the Sabine king, Titus Tatius.

Immediately in the foundation myths you can see the crystallising of some of the most important parts of Roman culture: respect for one's father, respect for one's gods and the role of women as conduits and connectors between families. Women here function as links that tie peoples together, who bring peace and continuity in opposition to death and war. Men, on the other hand, are mostly violent. Easy, right? Good. Because there's more and, to be honest, it's all as gruesome as this.

For the next few hundred years, the kings ruled happily. There were lots of good kings, like Numa, and everything was grand.

Until the kings started to go bad, as kings do, culminating in 509BCE with the reign of Tarquinius Superbus (if you're going to be an evil king, you may as well have an evil king name). Superbus's son, Prince Sextus, developed an obsession with a woman named Lucretia, a woman of high rank and higher morals who spent her evenings weaving woollen cloaks for her husband and being quiet. Sextus, being a depraved prince, was so aroused by Lucretia's modesty and weaving skill that he raped her (literally this time), assuming that she would keep quiet about the violation to her honour because rape was indistinguishable from adultery. However, Lucretia was also a woman of great moral strength and she immediately told her father and husband and then killed herself to spare them the pain of having to do it. Her father and a sort of family friend who was invited for no real reason took her body, displayed it in the Forum as evidence of the despotism of the king and thus incited a revolution, led by the family friend, which overthrew the kings forever. That friend's name? Lucius Junius Brutus.

This story, while exceptionally grim, also tells us an awful lot about the place of the female body in Roman culture. A woman's body is a private space, invaded by the king. We also learn that even though Lucretia was assaulted, and told everyone that she had been assaulted, and everyone believed that she had been a non-consensual actor, she still bore the shame of adultery and had to die. Her consent was irrelevant. Her suicide was an act of masculine moral strength because she knew that her honour as a woman could never be restored. This is important: remember it for later. Finally, we learn that things that happened to women that were out of the ordinary could cause massive social and political upheaval. Women drove historical narratives, but ideally by dying.

Back to the story. The kings were overthrown in 509BCE and the Republic was instituted by a collection of ancient aristocratic families known as the patricians. The Republic was specifically set up to control both religion and politics, those things being inseparable. Two consuls took the place of the kings at the top of the political ladder and split the kingly duties between them. The rest of the political system was divided into offices, carefully set up to divide powers and stop anyone from gathering too much individual control over anything. Two consuls, for example, meant that one could veto the other, preventing anyone from doing anything too terrible, and all terms were limited to a year. No one was really supposed to be consul twice. The consuls were the head of the Senate, initially made up of the patricians, who ruled through consensus. Men obtained a political office through a very direct form of sort-of democracy that involved elections but is irrelevant here. You just need to know they existed. The structure of the Republic was the crowning glory of the Romans and the thing they were most proud of.

These themes of republic, of shared power and of consensus and agreement are key to understanding the early emperors. Without knowing how violently Romans were repulsed by the idea of hereditary monarchy, and how absolutely core the notions of shared rule were to the image that Romans had of themselves, the actions of the early Roman emperors look bizarre and inexplicable. At the same time, take note of the idea of the patricians: these were ancient families who granted themselves authority purely on the basis of their antiquity and basically everyone agreed that they were the best because they were older. That's important, too.

The Republic ticked along all right for some centuries. There were some fights between the patricians and the plebeians that were irrelevant by the time of Agrippina but which caused lots of waves of trouble that continued to simmer. Then the Romans started expanding their territory and their armies started to grow. At this point, we leave the world of myth and enter reasonably well-documented military and political history. Now, the Romans granted men who won great military victories a big parade called a triumph and an enormous amount of personal prestige and authority. This was fine when wars were fairly small and great victories were rare, but during the Punic Wars against Carthage in North Africa[1] and the destruction of that city in 146BCE, massive victories became more common. The Punic Wars brought the Romans into contact with a lot of new people they

---

1. Modern-day Tunisia.

thought they might like to conquer, and so it brought certain men a lot more personal glory – and personal power – than had previously been possible. The first two to emerge from this milieu and cause trouble were Marius and Sulla. Marius got so much personal power that he ended up being consul a terrifying seven times, so Sulla was sent to bring him down a peg or two by replacing him as general in the east. Which is how the first civil war started in 88BCE. This bit is complicated and not very important but basically Marius died, there was a second civil war involving Sulla, Sulla won and became dictator for a few years, reorganised the state then retired. At Sulla's retirement, normal politics was reinstated. Everyone expected that the Republic would settle back to normal and recovery from the civil wars would start.

Apparently, however, no one predicted that a lot of young men would see Marius and Sulla as idols to be imitated, young men like Pompey, who came up through Sulla's armies, and Julius Caesar, who was a supporter of Marius. The conquest of the known world was still going on and Pompey was enormously successful in the east, defeating Mithridates in modern Turkey. Caesar, meanwhile, conquered Gaul and wrote books about it in the third person. In the middle was Crassus, who defeated Spartacus and became the richest man imaginable. Everyone was killing a lot of people and being praised a lot for it and there wasn't room in the empire for all their egos. You all know what happened here. There was another civil war, Caesar defeated everyone and followed in Sulla's footsteps by making himself dictator. Except, unlike Sulla, who understood that the dictatorship was a short-term emergency position, Caesar decided that he would like to be dictator in perpetuity and made his decision to be in charge of everything forever a bit too obvious. Mainly by telling everyone repeatedly that he was going to be dictator forever and letting Mark Antony offer him a crown in front of people. No one liked that, so Brutus and chums gave Caesar twenty-seven stab wounds and declared, once again, that the monarch had been overthrown and the Republic restored.

Again, somehow, no one accounted for the ambitions of younger men. So, when 19-year-old Octavian, Julius Caesar's posthumously adopted son, appeared from nowhere and started calling himself Caesar, demanding revenge and threatening people with swords, everyone was quite surprised. When Octavian turned out to have a friend named Agrippa who was a military genius and actually started defeating his elders in yet another civil war, everyone was even more surprised. And a bit upset. Octavian defeated Brutus and company, and then allied with Julius Caesar's best friend Antony to unofficially rule the empire. Except that was never going to last, because the empire was still not big enough for two giant egos. Octavian started another war with Antony, defeated him at Actium and was finally the last man standing, effectively king of the world. But not in name. What Octavian, who was a very smart young man, learned from his adoptive father was that when men made their power explicit, other Romans got stabby. What he did instead was continually insist, until the day he died, that the Republic was fine, that he wasn't in charge, that everyone could do exactly what they wanted. He just happened to have the best ideas and everyone agreed and stop looking at that sword over there.

Octavian defeated Antony in 31BCE, after almost 200 years of continual war and almost 100 years of civil war. Rome was exhausted and had gained an enormous amount of territory to rule, an effort that required a lot of paperwork. So the Senate let him have his illusion of not being emperor because they were just happy that there were no more young and ambitious men left to threaten Octavian and continue the terrible cycle of war. They gave him laurels and called him Augustus and pretended that he was just like them but the best of them. He was the Princeps: the First Citizen.

Which just about brings us to where we begin. Agrippina's parents were born in about 14BCE and 16BCE respectively. Octavian was granted the name Augustus, which solidified his position, in 27BCE. What you will have noticed (hopefully) is that the second we slipped into history rather than myth, all the women disappeared. That was about 1,000 words of men doing war and politics. Awful stuff. That's because Roman history as told by the Romans is all about men doing war and politics while women are quiet. There are a few women who appear in these stories for some dramatic purpose. Cornelia Africanus, the mother of the Gracchi, was a powerful character from the very beginning of the civil wars: a widow who raised her children right. Cleopatra is a figure who has resonated through the centuries as a beautiful, decadent, powerful queen, presented by Octavian as everything a Roman woman should not be so that Antony's liaison with her was reason enough to destroy him. Fulvia was Antony's second wife who raised an army for him and was abandoned by him as a result. Octavian's sister Octavia stood as a modern Sabine woman between her brother and her husband Antony until she was also abandoned in favour of Cleopatra. A litany of near forgotten women were married off to create alliances and divorced when they fell apart. Women are quiet, private and do as they are told by their brothers, fathers and husbands for the most part, so they were not worth mentioning unless they were exceptionally bad (Cleopatra and Fulvia) or exceptionally good (Octavia and Cornelia).

This is our final lesson from this tour of Rome: it is perfectly possible to tell a history of Rome after Lucretia that does not mention women at all. War and politics only involve men on an official level. Only men wrote histories. So, if a woman is included in the narrative of the original sources, it is because the male author has made an explicit and definite decision to include her and has a reason for it. Women in the Roman world are never a neutral. They can never simply exist in the public eye. When they are held up to be looked at, they always mean something. That's our most important lesson as we turn to look at Agrippina, who is missing from most of the beginning of her own life.

Chapter One: Daughter

Julia Agrippina Minor

The story begins with a baby, a Roman baby, born to the imperial family, and the first girl to be born after four boys. Her mother was used to childbirth by now. This one was born on 6 November 15CE. In Roman custom, the baby is taken from the mother and placed on the floor in front of the father. If the father accepts the child as his own, he picks her up. The father was Germanicus, remembered as one of the greatest generals of his age. The mother was Vipsania Agrippina, named after her father Agrippa, and she was the granddaughter of the emperor Augustus, who had been dead for a year now. The baby, being swaddled by a nurse, was named after her mother and became Julia Agrippina Minor. The Romans never were very inventive with their names. In the years to come, this baby will have an extraordinary life. She will be the sister, niece, wife and mother of emperors. She will stand in a cloak made of gold before adoring crowds as an empress. She will spend years in exile fearing for her life. She will die violently. She will look at the world she lives in and try to shape it around her and she will do things no Roman woman did before or after her. But all that was yet to come. At the beginning of the story, it was 15 November 15CE and she was a tiny newborn, wrapped up tight in swaddling clothes, in an army camp on the edge of the Rhine where her father was making his name as one of the most important and beloved men in the empire.

Julia Agrippina, who will be Agrippina the Younger for this chapter,[1] was born in a town called Ara Ubiorum rather than in Rome because her father had been sent by the reigning emperor Tiberius to oversee the Roman legions that were permanently stationed on the German borders of the empire. Tiberius was the second emperor proper of the

1. In this chapter, there are two Agrippinas and it gets confusing, so the subject of this book will be referred to as Agrippina the Younger, and her mother will be called Agrippina the Elder. You can refer to the list of characters if you forget which is which. But don't worry, only one of them makes it out of this chapter alive.

Roman Empire. He inherited his throne from his stepfather Augustus,
who had created the concept and role of Roman emperor and called
it the Principate. Tiberius had two sons: one biological, called Drusus,
and one whom he was forced by Augustus to adopt. This second
son is Germanicus, who was also Tiberius's biological nephew. The
family tree of the Julio-Claudian emperors is a living nightmare of
incest, borderline incest and adoption so settle in for some confusing
relationships. Agrippina's mother exemplifies the confusion. In 15CE
Agrippina the Elder was simultaneously Tiberius's ex-stepdaughter,
niece and daughter-in-law. When Agrippina the Younger was born,
Tiberius had been emperor for a little over a year and was already less
popular than cholera. Germanicus, on the other hand, was more popular than honeyed wine. Across the empire, Agrippina the Elder and
Germanicus were basically the Prince William and Kate Middleton of
their day. They were young, beautiful, effortlessly royal and charming
to be around. They managed to embody every possible virtue that was
required of them. Agrippina the Elder had had several adorable babies;
she eventually had nine children of whom six survived past infancy.
These six were three boys – Nero, Drusus III and Gaius – and three
girls – Agrippina the Younger, Drusilla and Livilla II – so they even
managed to have a perfect balance of babies.[2] The ability to have loads
of babies and be devoted to a single husband were the main virtues
required of a Roman woman so Agrippina the Elder was doing brilliantly.

Germanicus did even better. Germanicus was the grandson of Mark
Antony, through his mother Antonia Minor. She is known now as
Antonia the Younger because her older sister was also called Antonia (the Elder). As I've said before, we're going to have to deal with
a lot of this. Germanicus was probably named Nero Claudius Drusus
at birth after his father, Nero Claudius Drusus, but became known
as Germanicus after his successful campaigns in Germany. And Germanicus was adored by the Romans, especially by those Romans who
never met him, like historians and biographers writing 80 years after

---

2. As with Agrippinas, there are also several people called Drusus and Livilla. I've differentiated them with numbers, but you can check the family tree or the list of characters if you
get confused or forget. It's okay. They're confusing.

his death, and the general population of Rome. The people who met him were, to be honest, rather more split on how much they liked him. But historians worshipped him, and he is remembered in writing as near enough a demi-god. His limited actual success deterred no Roman writer, as these tended not to be limited to mere truths, and Tacitus tells us that people believed that Germanicus 'outdid Alexander the Great in clemency, self-control and every other good quality' even though he provides only evidence to the contrary.[3]

Suetonius, meanwhile, half-dehydrates himself so furious is his adoration, and six of the 60 chapters in the emperor Gaius Caligula's biography are dedicated to spunking praise on his father. That's a full 10 per cent about his dad. Germanicus was handsome, smart and funny, he killed men in hand-to-hand combat like Achilles but was so desperately modest you'd never know it, everyone fell in love with him where ever he went, except those who were jealous of him like mean old Tiberius, and to them Germanicus was kind and tolerant. He had bandy legs, but he worked every day after dinner to strengthen them by riding horses. He never knobbed his slaves and he only had one wife and he fathered loads of children for the empire. To our sources, he was literally a perfect man. According to both Tacitus and Suetonius, when Germanicus came to town people would follow him around and run up to 20 miles outside Rome to meet him. Indeed, he was 'in danger of being mobbed to death whenever he arrived at Rome'.[4] Basically, Germanicus was the Beatles. And much like the Beatles, he insisted upon being a real-life, quite disappointing person rather than the cipher that teenage girls and grown historians want him to be.

Germanicus and Agrippina had been married to one another on the orders of Augustus. Agrippina was the youngest daughter of Augustus's only biological child, Julia. Both Julia and her eldest daughter (also called Julia, infuriatingly) had been exiled for improper female behaviour like getting drunk with loads of lads and weeing on the rostrum in the Roman Forum. Agrippina also had three brothers, two of whom had died in their twenties. The third brother, Agrippa

3. Tacitus, *Annals*, 2.73.
4. Suetonius, *Caligula*, 4.

Posthumous, had been exiled for being a bit weird and scaring every-one. It was quite easy to get exiled by Augustus. He was not a man who tolerated difference. Julia the Elder, Julia the Younger and Agrippa Posthumous had all died mysteriously and violently within days of Tiberius inheriting the throne in 14CE, because Tiberius was petty. By 15CE Agrippina the Elder was the only member of her immediate family left alive, which meant she was the only person of her generation left who had the blood of Augustus in her.

This was a really big deal. The Romans were obsessed with family lines and lineages. Apart from the city of Rome, the family was the most important thing in a Roman's life. Your family name was the most important thing about you by far. Your great-grandparents' achievements were equally as important as your own. If you were a Julian, you were one half of the imperial family and could trace your bloodline back through Augustus to Julius Caesar and then to Aeneas and the goddess Venus. The other side of the family was the Clau-dians, an ancient but not divine family and therefore very much the poor relations. The Julians and the Claudians initially came together into one Julio-Claudian clusterfuck when Augustus married Livia (a Claudian) and then adopted Tiberius, her biological son from a pre-vious marriage. The marriage of Germanicus (Claudian) to Agrip-pina the Elder (Julian) was meant to hold the families together for another generation. And it worked. Against all the odds, Germanicus and Agrippina the Elder were compatible in a lot of ways and seemed to genuinely love each other. The nine pregnancies that Agrippina had, some coming mere months after giving birth to the previous child, suggest that they never stopped bonking for a start. They were constantly at it. Agrippina the Elder followed Germanicus to every grim misery pit that he got sent to for their entire marriage, and usu-ally had a kid while she was there.

Germanicus made his name and reputation in a war with various German tribes between the Rhine and the Elbe immediately follow-ing the death of Augustus in 14CE. Germanicus arrived in Germany about 15 minutes before the news that Tiberius had decided not to decommission any soldiers who had been enlisted for less than 20 years. The length of service was supposed to be 16 years. Tacitus points to some soldiers who had served for 30 or 40 years. Instantly, the troops mutinied. And quite reasonably. Many of them had been in service for decades, and in service meant marching about in Germany, a place the Romans feared and loathed, in the cold and constant rain, with very limited rights and very low pay. Their conditions were also horrendous. As Tacitus puts it, the mutineers showed 'their lash-marks, their white hair, their tattered clothes... their limbs bent and bowed with old age'.[5] It's not hard to empathise with them. Germanicus struggled to put down the mutinies, partly because his power to meet their demands to get paid for their service and be allowed to go home was non-existent, and partly because he was bad in a crisis. His first approach to dealing with the mutiny began with a long and tedious speech about loyalty, went through some weeping and ended with him faking a suicide attempt in front of everyone in the hope that they'd stop him. Except one soldier offered him a sharper sword, so Germanicus went off in a huff. At this point, Germanicus had three kids, was in his late twenties, commanded a huge army, was first in line for the throne if something happened to Tiberius, and was acting like the protagonist in a very low-quality YA book.

Despite this initial failure, he did stick around – with his wife, who was heavily pregnant with Agrippina the Younger, and three-year-old son Gaius by his side. He did some more crying in his room and some more bombastic speeches, which was his slightly pathetic best, until Agrippina the Elder took things into her own hands. She set up a very conspicuous leaving party, taking herself and her children very loudly out of the Roman camp and into the township of some friendly Germans, telling the troops that they couldn't be trusted around the granddaughter of Augustus and so she had to get some foreigners to protect her from them. This triggered a shame mechanism in the highly loyal troops, who adored her and her son, and weren't about to have the granddaughter of Augustus feeling safer with Germans than with them. After this, the mutiny died down. Germanicus took all the credit, gave some more speeches and then made the troops themselves kill the mutiny leaders to teach everyone a lesson. And then he cried

5. Tacitus, *Annals*, I.33.

about that, too. He cries a lot, to be honest. Historians have opinions about it, but they're not important here.

This was when our Agrippina the Younger was born, in farthest, darkest Germany when her parents had just put down a mutiny by the very skin of their teeth. Quite reasonably, they probably decided to send their newborn child to Rome, out of harm's way, where she could be looked after properly. Agrippina the Elder and Germanicus spent the next year campaigning in the Teutoburg Forest and righting old wrongs in the name of the Romans while shagging all the time, because Agrippina the Elder became immediately pregnant again. She had another daughter ten months after giving birth to Agrippina the Younger; Julia Drusilla was born in September 16CE. Agrippina the Elder's pelvic floor must have been wrecked. But Germanicus was taking revenge on some Germans and she wasn't about to miss that. The Teutoburg Forest is in the region of Osnabrück, near the Weser River and was important to the Roman army and to the family of Augustus because in 9CE it had been the site of a brutal massacre of Roman soldiers by an alliance of Germanic tribes led by a Roman citizen, Arminius. The Roman general Quinctilius Varus had inadvertently led three legions to their deaths. That's approximately 15,000 men slaughtered in a forest. Augustus had never quite recovered from the trauma of the loss. The day of the massacre was held as a day of mourning by Augustus, and two of the three legion numbers were never used again, such was the psychological impact of the massacre for the Romans.

For Germanicus to reach the forest again was a pretty big deal symbolically, and he was able to finally raise a funeral mound for the soldiers who had died there, which was a very big deal indeed. He also had a bash at taking revenge on Arminius, and Tacitus claims that he won two minor victories and got Arminius on the run but was recalled to Rome before he could catch him. Tacitus is very clear that the only reason Germanicus failed to fully exact a Roman revenge on Arminius was because a jealous Tiberius didn't want Germanicus getting any more glory than he already had. This is probably true. Tiberius didn't trust our beloved hero one bit and didn't need him winning too many victories and taking the attention away from the emperor. Tiberius was also an extremely conservative old man who hated the idea of having to deal with the administrative headache of adding new territory to the empire.

Tiberius has a generally very bad reputation, some of which is deserved (he killed Julia and Agrippa Posthumous, officially killed the Roman Republic), and some of which probably isn't (accusations of pederasty). One of the primary accusations levied at him by Tacitus is that he lies about everything. Now Tacitus loathed – *loathed* – Tiberius with the kind of passion that makes one suspect that Tacitus was not fun at parties. Like he might just start going on about obscure bits of Tiberius's reign in a slightly mad-eyed way when everyone else just wants to eat some more seafood and impress one another with hilarious epigrams. He gives off a slight air of conspiracy theorist uncle, mostly because, like all conspiracy theorists, he forces all apparent 'facts' to fit his narrative regardless of logic or sense. So, while some 9/11 Truthers like to think that the planes that hit the Twin Towers were, in fact, missiles disguised as planes through the use of holograms (I wish I had made that up), Tacitus insists that everything Tiberius did that was good or honourable was, in fact, just a lie. For reasons. Tiberius's documented reactions to Germanicus's successes in Germany were to give him the name Germanicus, grant him a triumph and deliver a probably quite tedious panegyric to him in the Senate. In Tacitus's telling, however, Tiberius's celebrations were 'so ostentatiously elaborate, they did not ring true'. Which seems a tiny bit unfair. Tacitus's claim that Germanicus was only prevented from crushing Arminius because of Tiberius's malicious jealousy is also, in context, just a lie. Tiberius was extremely cautious with his troops and was clear throughout his reign that he saw the borders of the empire as something to be maintained and protected, not expanded. Indeed, such an order was part of Augustus's will. Moreover, Germany offered nothing tangible to the Romans as a territory and certainly wasn't worth an extremely risky war against a foe known to be very dangerous indeed. The idea of allowing Germanicus to prance around Germany on a semi-personal journey of revenge and glory, to gain some pointless territory that would be expensive and difficult to defend, was not a particularly attractive one. And it especially wasn't attractive to Tiberius, whose main loves seem to have been being quietly where other people weren't and not being hassled by anyone. That was suspicious to Tacitus, too, who saw it as yet more evidence of Tiberius's mendacious nature. What kind of Roman didn't like hanging out with other Romans? Only a bad one.

The symbolism of Germanicus's victories was significant, though, and Tiberius didn't even pretend that it wasn't. So when Germanicus returned to Rome he got the greatest of all possible Roman honours: he was hailed an Imperator and granted a triumph. Imperator is the Latin word from which our word emperor derives. It originally just meant general, but after Augustus began using it as a part of his name (calling himself Imperator Caesar) it became an imperial epithet, and eventually became an imperial title and then, a long while later, Charlize Theron got to be an Imperator in a desert. But for Germanicus, being hailed an Imperator was a huge honour. Many years after his death he would be remembered primarily and with enormous respect as an Imperator. And on top of that, he was granted a triumph.

A Roman triumph was a pretty great thing. It consisted of a parade through the streets of Rome up to the temple of Jupiter, led by the man of the hour, in a luxury purple robe and the classic laurel crown, borne in a four-horse carriage. The streets of Rome would be lined with thousands and thousands of citizens and visitors cheering and singing. Behind the general marched his troops, who shared in the glory their leader brought them. They tended to sing bawdy songs about the general. Behind them marched captives and any spoils that he brought back with him. It was to avoid this spectacle that Cleopatra and Antony killed themselves when they were defeated by Augustus. The procession itself was surrounded by several days of feasting, public games, religious sacrifices and general partying. This all sounds pretty amazing, and probably was when men were conquering massive swathes of eastern lands and bringing back 50,000 prisoners and several tonnes of gold looted from a city. Germanicus had just ridden through a foresty bit of Germany and no one records what he brought back, so it was potentially eight men and some branches. But that's okay. It's not the spectacle that matters as much as the symbol.

Germanicus got one of the first triumphs in many, many years and it was a great party afterwards and, more importantly, it meant that Agrippina the Younger's first true experience of her parents was that they were adored in the streets by screaming crowds and followed by adoring soldiers. That's the most significant bit of all.

Her parent's time in Rome was brief, though. Within a year, they were off again. This time they went to Syria where Germanicus was sent to sort out some diplomatic stuff. The older two boys and the younger two girls were again left behind but, weirdly, they took their favourite kid, Gaius, along with them. Agrippina the Elder also managed to have the last of her children during the trip, giving birth to Julia Livilla in Lesbos in 17CE. I'd say that she had officially banned shagging, but this was only really her final child because of what happened next. After a nice holiday in Dalmatia (modern Croatia), some sightseeing in Greece, the baby thing in Lesbos and some more hanging out in Asia Minor, Germanicus finally popped over to Syria to do his job. He actually managed his most significant lifetime achievement in negotiating the coronation of a Rome-friendly client king who ruled for an impressive 16 subsequent years, an achievement he was so happy with that he went on holiday again to Egypt. A holiday in Egypt sounds fine, because who doesn't want to see the pyramids and go on a Nile cruise? Except Egypt was a forbidden territory for Roman senators, and especially for powerful ones. This was because pretty much all of Rome's grain supply came from Egypt and so anyone who controlled Egypt had the power to starve Rome to death. News therefore of the much-beloved, high-on-success consul of the Roman Senate and heir to the throne Germanicus skipping around this fragile territory wasn't received terribly well and Tiberius told him off. And then things got worse. When Germanicus finished his holiday, he returned to Syria where his troops has been left, only to find that the governor of Syria – Gnaeus Calpurnius Piso – had started interfering with his troops and making decisions that Germanicus felt he had no right to make. Germanicus and Piso already hated one another and seem to have been in conflict over their clashing powers in Syria for a while. This incident simply made things worse. Everyone started threatening to go and set Tiberius on the other and tensions got quite high. And then, in the middle of it all, Germanicus got ill. And died.

During his illness, Germanicus became convinced that he had either been poisoned, or cursed, or both. The difference between cursing and poisoning in the Roman telling of these events seems to be negligible as they wholeheartedly believed in the efficacy of magic and witchcraft. Both Tacitus and Suetonius describe Germanicus finding a number of spells and curse-related objects around his house at the time of his illness, the kind of objects you'd be surprised to find in your house. Tacitus gives some delightful details, describing human remains, bloody ashes, spells, curses and lead tablets inscribed with his name hidden in the walls of his bedroom. To Germanicus, the originator of these bits of cadaver was, of course, Piso. His last words to his wife were widely reported and highly dramatic. He demanded, 'Even strangers shall mourn Germanicus. But if it was I that you loved and not just my status, you must avenge me! Show Rome my wife, the daughter of the divine Augustus!'[6] And then he passed on.

The belief that Tiberius got Piso to murder Germanicus was common and became embedded in Tiberius's reputation. Tiberius did like killing people that he didn't like, ideally while they were very far away from him. And Germanicus was causing a lot of trouble by being so successful and popular and wandering into places where he wasn't allowed. But it seems a little unlikely to me that Tiberius murdered Germanicus, given that he was Tiberius's best familial asset and that Tiberius gave no actual, tangible indication of having any ill will towards Germanicus outside of Tacitus's mind-reading tricks. Whether Piso murdered Germanicus is a murkier question. He certainly had more reason to. But what we have to remember is that Germanicus had just spent time on a Nile cruise through Egypt where tropical diseases were rampant and water purification processes weren't so great: malaria, diphtheria, hepatitis A, typhoid, yellow fever and any number of tropical parasites were significant health risks. There's a reason European soldiers dreaded being sent in that

6. Tacitus, *Annals*, 2.71.

direction before penicillin was invented. The idea that Germanicus picked up – as a semi-random example – typhoid fever in either Egypt or Syria is not a totally fantastic possibility. The fact that his wife was also very ill, and that the alleged witch Martina also died of illness before getting back to Rome, serves only to highlight the health perils of the east. But as with so many things in history, literal truth is not necessarily important. What is important is how easily Germanicus's immediate family and the people of Rome believed that Piso had murdered Germanicus because Tiberius told him to, and there was no convincing them otherwise.[7]

Germanicus died aged about 33, and Agrippina the Younger barely met him. She would be around three when her father died, having only really seen him for those few months when he was back in Rome. The thing about the Roman obsession with family, though, is that no one ever really dies. Death masks are made, and famous ancestors loom large centuries after they die. Stories are told and retold again and again, and reputations are rarely dented by something as prosaic as mortality. Germanicus would be one of the most important figures in Agrippina the Younger's life until the day she died. In part, that's because of how her mother maintained his reputation once she returned to Rome, and Agrippina the Younger learned a lot from her mother.

---

7. Piso and his wife were formally prosecuted for the murder after significant pressure from senators who supported Germanicus and Agrippina the Elder. Piso killed himself before the trial could commence. His wife, Placina, was saved from prosecution by the intervention of Tiberius's mother Livia. From Agrippina the Elder's perspective, justice was not served.

Return to Rome

Do you remember when Princess Diana died in 1997 and half the country broke for a while? I remember my dad taking me, aged 14, up to Kensington Palace to see the flowers people were laying because he thought we'd never see anything like it again. I was a small 14-year-old, and the sea of bouquets that had been laid was to me, no exaggeration, waist-deep and seemingly endless. Hundreds of thousands of people travelled to lay a bunch of flowers. Even if you didn't see it, you've probably seen pictures of the funeral and the princes walking behind a hearse that was drowned in flowers being thrown by the crowds. That moment in British history when people simply couldn't cope with what had happened is probably the closest analogy to what happened when Germanicus died in October 19CE. The empire mourned and Rome itself was the centre of that mourning. Suetonius describes people taking to the streets, pulling statues of the gods to the ground and throwing stones at temples in their rage that their Germanicus had been taken from them. Others threw their household gods out of their front doors and smashed them.[1] People rejected their babies, shaved their heads, and grieved deeply.[2] Tacitus, interestingly, directly opposes Suetonius and claims that there were no big public demonstrations but that people were so moved and bereaved that they just went home and left the city empty, 'a town of sighs and silence', filled with nothing but a sad winter gloom.[3]

Agrippina the Elder insisted on bringing Germanicus's ashes home to Rome immediately, despite it being October and a treacherous out-of-season sea journey. News of her coming preceded her and on the day of her arrival back in Italy she pulled off one of the most spectacular visual stunts since Augustus's time. She was truly her grandfather's granddaughter. In American politics the term 'optics' is used

---

1. Household gods are called *lares* and are represented by little statuettes which lived in every house to protect it and the family.
2. Suetonius, *Caligula*, 6.
3. Tacitus, *Annals*, 2.82.

to describe the visual impact and public perception of an event. Good optics means that something will look impressive or pleasing to the public, and Agrippina the Elder gave amazing optics. Agrippina the Elder and her party arrived at Brundisium (Brindisi) in southern Italy. Word had spread that she was drawing near and Agrippina the Elder had deliberately waited just off the coast to ensure that people were ready for her arrival. Accordingly, thousands gathered at the harbour to greet her, crowding the port and the streets, and hanging off the city walls to get a good view. As her boat drew into the harbour, the crowd fell into a respectful, awed silence. And then she appeared, stepping slowly out of her boat. She was young, but exhausted by mourning and travelling. Her hair was loose in mourning. She stepped down, her eyes downcast, clutching the urn to her chest, the perfect image of the grieving, wronged princess. Behind her tottered little six-year-old Gaius with his head covered and the still infant Livilla II. At the sight of them, the crowd broke its silence and cried out as one in mourning for her lost husband, their widowed princess, their fatherless princes. The cries continued as she walked through them and into a waiting carriage surrounded by the almost 1,000 soldiers who had been sent to accompany her back to Rome. The event was short but powerful. News of it spread like wildfire across the empire and the image of Agrippina the Elder, bowed and humbled, carrying her husband's urn, would ripple through the history of the Julio-Claudians. Little Gaius, in particular, would never forget it.

Brundisium is about 600km from Rome, and during the days of travelling they passed through many towns and cities in the same way, drawing crowds of mourners who followed them for miles. Eventually, when they were about 95km from Rome, they were met by the rest of the family. Agrippina the Younger, her brothers Nero and Drusus III and her sister Drusilla were reunited with their mother and siblings, meeting Livilla II for the first time. Tiberius's son Drusus II, Drusus II's wife Livilla I, who was also Germanicus's biological sister and was heavily pregnant with twins, and Germanicus's brother Claudius all accompanied the children on the trip. They met at Terracina in what must have been quite the reunion. Agrippina the

Younger was just four years old and, probably even more than her father's triumph, this would be a powerful moment for her. Meeting her grieving, sick mother in these extraordinary circumstances.

The good optics didn't stop there. The family returned together to Rome, where they were again met by thousands of onlookers as they processed down the main road into Rome – the Appian Way – a group of grieving men, women and children, still with their 1,000 soldiers. The whole imperial family, except Tiberius and his mother. They were conspicuously absent. The group marched down the Appian Way and into the city. Agrippina the Elder continued to clutch her husband's urn. A few days later, they walked to the Mausoleum of Augustus in the centre of the city and she placed the ashes where they belonged. There was no proper Roman funeral for Germanicus because his body had been cremated in Syria, so instead the Roman people lit up the Campus Martius with torches all night and wept and prayed and gave speeches. They hailed Agrippina the Elder loudly as their only hope, calling her 'the glory of her country, the last of the blood of Augustus, the peerless model of ancient virtue!'[4] The crowds raised their arms to the sky, though they were essentially standing outside Tiberius's house, and called for the gods to protect Agrippina the Elder and her children from the persecution of the emperor. Agrippina the Elder believed with all her heart that her husband had been murdered on the orders of Tiberius, and his failure to make even a token appearance at the enormous semi-funeral of his adopted son was taken as proof of his guilt. Tacitus agreed with her, citing a number of his 'elders' as first-person witnesses. Tacitus even accused Tiberius of forcibly preventing Germanicus's mother from attending his interment as yet more evidence of his guilt. Tacitus's beliefs are academic, but Agrippina the Elder's were not. She believed that her husband had been murdered and that she and her children had had their rights as Julian heirs to Augustus stolen from them.

From Agrippina the Elder's perspective, Germanicus had been murdered as part of a dynastic feud that was only partly imaginary. The Julio-Claudians were two families, connected by marriage into one. But the two halves of the family never stopped being suspicious

4. Tacitus, Annals, 3.4.

17

of one another. Livia was accused of poisoning Agrippina the Elder's brothers so that Augustus's throne would pass to a Claudian (Tiberius) instead of them (Julians). Germanicus was technically a Claudian, but his children were Julian because their relationship to Augustus was so powerful that it overrode any other connection. Germanicus becoming emperor, therefore, would mean that the throne would pass back to the Julian side for at least two generations, condemning the Claudians to relative obscurity. With Germanicus gone, however, Tiberius's Claudian son Drusus II would inherit the throne and the Claudian claim would be safe. This is, of course, pragmatic thinking but there's no way of knowing whether Tiberius or Livia ever thought like this. Agrippina the Elder certainly did, though. She saw her husband's death as treachery, as theft of her children's rightful inheritance by usurpers to the Julian throne. She possibly even believed that she had a better right to it than Tiberius. When Germanicus died, his last words to her demanded she get revenge, but he also told her 'forget your pride, submit to cruel fate, in Rome, do not provoke those stronger than yourself by competing for their power'.[5] Recognising the contradictions in his demands, she didn't listen.

If Germanicus was a bit overrated as a general, Agrippina the Elder was underrated in general. She had survived an awful lot; although by Julian standards her childhood and younger years were about average, the loss of an entire family before the age of 30 was still horrifying. She had then given birth to nine children in army camps and other people's houses across the empire, and had buried three of them. While very pregnant, she put down the mutiny in Germany. While pregnant again (with a child who died), she had saved her husband's life and those of a legion when she intervened to stop a bridge being destroyed by panicking soldiers in the middle of a battle, riding a horse through chaos and comforting the troops. She was an extremely proactive, competent woman with a strong sense of brilliance, and when she returned to Rome with her husband's ashes she was filled with fire. She was in her early thirties when her husband died and she had grown used to a lifetime of being adored by everyone. More importantly, she had got used to being obeyed, respected and treated

5. Tacitus, Annals, 2.72.

like the princess she was. She had a very firm belief in the status and importance of her family and nothing could take it away from her. Not that the people, armies or Senate of Rome wanted to: they hailed her as a daughter of Rome and adored her as the last descendant of Augustus. This was to cause her and her children a lot of trouble over the next few years. We need to talk about the trouble a bit because Agrippina the Elder was perhaps the most significant influence in our Agrippina the Younger's life and what happened to her and her two eldest sons was hugely important. And really complicated.

Agrippina the Elder

Agrippina the Elder returned to Rome in 19CE with two symbolic middle fingers raised in Tiberius's direction, while Tiberius sulked in his palace. The atmosphere went slowly downhill from here. But they were family, and – like Michael Bluth – the Julio-Claudians always put family first. They couldn't just avoid one another and get on with their lives, and Agrippina the Elder didn't want that anyway. Agrippina the Elder wanted revenge. She wanted Tiberius off the throne. She wanted the power back in her hands where she felt it belonged and she absolutely wasn't going to step back and wait for that to happen. Agrippina the Elder had no time for gendered bullshit like not legally being able to engage in politics because she was a woman. She had spent her entire life as a Roman princess, had grown up with no knowledge of the Republic, and brushed aside any conservative or traditional hand-wringing about how she should behave. And so, Agrippina the Younger grew up with a mother who scorned tradition, was furiously proud of her lineage and was a stubbornly public figure in a constant battle with an emperor who was stubbornly traditional, grumpily smug and painfully private. Naturally, and even without the belief that Tiberius murdered Germanicus, the pair loathed each other.

The drama between Tiberius and Agrippina the Elder would take 15 years to play out fully: the whole of Agrippina the Younger's childhood was coloured by this feud, with peak drama coming in 29CE after a decade of misery. To make the situation more complicated, there was a third actor, whose main joy in life was shit stirring. This was Sejanus, Tiberius's Praetorian Prefect.[1] You might remember him as Patrick Stewart with hair in the 1970s BBC version of *I, Claudius*. Sejanus adds an extra layer of complication to the events of this decade because what he really, really wants in life is to be emperor. Had he been around during the civil war

---

1. The Praetorian Prefect was the head of the emperor's private army, the Praetorian Guard. The Praetorian Guard were a significant force, the only force stationed in Rome, and were under the personal control of the emperor via the Praetorian Prefect. The Praetorian Prefect was appointed by the emperor and was one of the most powerful and trusted roles in the Roman court.

period, he would have been truly dangerous. It's interesting that he wanted to be emperor because he wasn't of senatorial rank, obviously, he was an equestrian, which is basically the business class of Rome. The senators are the aristocracy, while the equestrians are the Philip Greens of the Roman world.[2] Sejanus apparently thought that if Tiberius could be emperor, anyone could, and so he did his best to wiggle his way into Tiberius's affections, cut him off from his family, make Tiberius reliant on him and then become his heir. He was basically Tiberius's abusive boyfriend. As a result, he saw Agrippina the Elder and her children as rivals and he did his damned best to destroy them.

Agrippina the Elder's family was Sejanus's third target. His first was Tiberius's only biological child, and sole remaining child after Germanicus died, Drusus II. Drusus II and Sejanus loathed each other on a personal level. At one point, Drusus II punched Sejanus, which is a serious escalation for a Roman, because Sejanus had become the guy that Tiberius asked for help and Drusus II felt sidelined by his dad. In response, Sejanus fucked Drusus II's wife and plotted with her to kill him. Allegedly. At the very least, Drusus II died very suddenly not long after the punching incident and, not long after that, Sejanus asked Tiberius for permission to marry Drusus II's widow. Tiberius said no. This was the second of Sejanus's plans to become a member of the imperial family to fail. He had previously betrothed his four-year-old daughter to Germanicus's nephew, Claudius's eldest son, but that fell apart when the boy accidentally choked to death on a pear. Sejanus was furious and he turned on Agrippina the Elder with a new plan: if he couldn't get into the family by any legitimate means, he'd just destroy every one of them so there'd be no one left standing but him when the time came for Tiberius to choose a successor.

Agrippina the Elder was singled out immediately, both as a very prominent member of the imperial family and because Tiberius looked to be considering her eldest sons as his successors rather than Drusus II's sole surviving son Tiberius Gemellus. Agrippina the Elder's eldest sons were Nero and Drusus III and, almost immediately after Drusus II died, Tiberius began drawing them closer to him and into the public eye. They were aged

2. In this analogy, Cicero is the Roman Lord Alan Sugar as the first of his family to be allowed to enter the Senate after he was a very, very rich equestrian.

16 and 17, respectively, in 23CE, which was the ideal age in the imperial family to start taking on some responsibility if you were going to be expected to rule in the future. But where Nero and Drusus III went, their mother went. Her influence was first demonstrated on New Year's Day 24CE when the priests gave the annual prayer for the safety and health of the emperor. This was a solemn occasion and an important one, so everyone was blindsided when the priests prayed not just for Tiberius, but for Drusus III and Nero, too. Including Tiberius. Tiberius's instant reaction was anger with Agrippina the Elder for arranging this, though I have to say I think it's quite impressive. She obviously gave no fucks about causing a stir and somehow got the priests to surprise the emperor – the emperor – by putting her sons on his level in front of everyone. I assume that she did this partly because she genuinely believed that her sons deserved this honour, and partly because it manipulated Tiberius into either having to tell everyone to stop praying for these hugely popular kids or just take it. It seemed like a win-win for her. Except Sejanus took full advantage of Tiberius's fury and Agrippina the Elder's presumptuousness.

Sejanus had always hated Agrippina the Elder, both as an uppity woman and as someone with more power than him. He hated her even more because she fought him on everything she could, using male proxies in the Senate. Agrippina the Elder built for herself a faction, a group with overlapping aims who worked together to protect and advance Agrippina the Elder's family over everyone else. They were a loose political party within the constant fluctuations of Roman politics. Sejanus took a two-pronged approach to attacking Agrippina the Elder: first, he abused her friends and the members of her faction with lawsuits, accusations and criminal proceedings that were expensive, time-consuming and bad for the reputation. Secondly, he spent all his time whispering in Tiberius's ear about all the terrible things that Agrippina was allegedly up to and how mean she was about him. Sejanus kept Tiberius suspicious and constantly on edge, constantly prodding at his insecurities and worries. Like an abusive boyfriend.

This needling came to a head in a couple of dramatic scenes that are recorded by Tacitus. They all happen between about 25CE and 27CE, when Agrippina the Elder is around 40 and Agrippina the Younger is somewhere in the region of 10 to 12, and beginning to be aware of the world she lives in. We know she was becoming at least slightly aware of her world, because she is the source for the first of the scenes. She wrote about it in her own memoir to show how cruel Tiberius had been to her mother. She wrote that, at some point in these years, her mother fell ill. Nothing serious, just a flu or some bug, but she was ill enough to be confined to her house for a while and so Tiberius came to visit her. Maybe they sat in the atrium of Agrippina's house, which was always a nice place to receive honoured visitors. Maybe somewhere else. But unlike any other time they met, when they might argue or be cordial on a good day, this time they sat awkwardly while Agrippina silently cried. At last, she took a deep breath, looked at the emperor through her tears and asked him for permission to remarry. She maybe had someone in mind, but perhaps she was just lonely. She had been a widow for a decade, she was raising a family of six, she wanted a man to share the burden of her fight. But she was a woman and she couldn't marry without permission, so she had to ask the one man who would never say yes. The very man she was fighting. Tiberius sighed, put down his cup and left without answering.[3] She would never be allowed to remarry. She would remain alone. Agrippina the Younger saw this, her mother becoming so ill and sad and desperate that she showed her most feminine and vulnerable need to her greatest enemy. Decades later, when she was in her forties herself, Agrippina the Younger wrote it down so that the world would remember how her mother had suffered, how women suffered. This picture of Agrippina the Elder is an image of a woman old beyond her years, tired by the constant fight that is Roman politics, exhausted by being a Roman woman in public, lonely and pitiful. This is not a common image of her. She is presented almost exclusively as an arrogant lioness, roaring at the slightest provocation. This was Agrippina the Younger's attempt to humanise her mother and perhaps even herself.

The second scene comes from the same time and shows a completely different side of Agrippina the Elder. Agrippina had endured months of Sejanus's allies abusing her friends and allies and finally lost her temper. She wasn't an idiot and she knew that association with her was causing trouble for her friends. The prosecution that tipped

3. Tacitus, Annals, 4.53, quoting Agrippina the Younger's memoirs.

her over the edge was her cousin Claudia Pulchra being accused of magic, trying to poison the emperor and adultery – she was a busy woman! When Agrippina heard about this accusation, she went to find Tiberius and have it out with him. She stormed into the palace, flinging doors open until she found him in a small chamber making a personal sacrifice to a statue of Augustus. Agrippina demanded that he stop the prosecution and that he stop listening to Sejanus's ridiculous attacks and start protecting his own family. Her blood was up, and her fury was only stoked by the sight of Tiberius sacrificing to Augustus. She growled, imperious and cold in her anger, that the divine blood of Augustus did not flow in mute statues. 'I, born of Augustus's sacred blood, am its incarnation,' she declared, which is gloriously imperious! She spat that no man should sacrifice to the Divine Augustus while allowing his grandchildren to be persecuted, making clear her power and her prestige, and her true belief in her own right to rule, and outright accusing the emperor of hypocrisy. Tiberius, to his credit, took the onslaught, and implied insult to his own lineage, well in the moment. He replied with a Greek epigram: 'it is not an insult that you do not reign.'[4] Sadly, it is not recorded how Agrippina responded, but I doubt it was politely. Especially not as her speech did nothing: Claudia Pulchra was condemned to death.

The final scene came a little later. After almost a decade of fighting and failing, under constant attack from Sejanus, believing that Tiberius wanted to kill her, of being alone, Agrippina the Elder was becoming a bit wobbly. But, still, family came first, and so she still presented herself to dinner with the emperor like clockwork. In her fear, though, she had stopped eating with him. She sat and refused food. She had stopped eating because Sejanus had taken a new tack and had started whispering to her that Tiberius would kill her as he had killed her husband, that Tiberius was planning on poisoning her at the dinner table, that she was unsafe. Tiberius, unaware of this, believing wholeheartedly that Sejanus was his loyal and beloved friend, saw only Agrippina the Elder sitting cold and distrustful at his table. One day, he tested her. He threw her an apple to eat. Agrippina the Elder caught the apple and, without changing expression or saying a word, placed it on the table and ignored it. This was, effectively, a direct accusation that

4. Tacitus, Annals, 4.52.

Tiberius had attempted to kill her. This really marked the total breakdown of any relationship they had.

Sejanus's plan, therefore, was going brilliantly. It got even better in 28CE when Tiberius got completely fed up of Rome, of the Senate, of court politics, of Agrippina the Elder, and his mother, and the aristocracy, and all the drama, and just quit Rome. He went to the island of Capri and never came back. He put Sejanus in charge of Rome in his absence and relied entirely on Sejanus's reports on what was happening in the city. Sejanus was now the only non-family connection between the emperor and the Senate. All he had to do now was completely destroy Agrippina the Elder and her sons.

At this point, infuriatingly, there is a big hole in the surviving manuscripts of Tacitus's *Annals*, so it all gets a bit confusing. Just before it cuts out, Sejanus was setting Nero and Drusus III against each other, persuading each of them that their mother preferred the other. Nero, the elder, is presented as sort of a harmless dote who let his words run away with him sometimes and was easily influenced by pals, seeded by Sejanus, into saying thoughtless things. Drusus III, the younger, is set up as resenting his youth and being jealous of his older brother. Both were being incited against one another. Sejanus was continuing his quiet plot to discredit them. Then he was gifted another opening: Livia, the emperor's mother, died. She was 75, but remained a potent force behind the scenes in Tiberius's reign and she would have cut her son's bollocks off if he had made any official moves against his own family. Even if she did hate Agrippina the Elder. This is why Sejanus had been forced to make all these quiet sneaky moves. With Livia suddenly gone, Sejanus had nothing standing in his way. As soon as the funeral was over, Sejanus wrote to Tiberius, accusing Agrippina the Elder and Nero of 'unnatural love and moral depravity' – aka, incest.[5] When the Senate heard this letter, they sat in stunned silence. When the people heard, they instantly produced (from somewhere) effigies of Agrippina the Elder and Nero that they brought to the Senate house where they staged an impromptu protest to protect them.

5. Tacitus, Annals, 5.3–5.

Tacitus says that Agrippina the Elder and Nero survived this huge attack, but not by much. Here, we confront the first hole in the manuscripts of Tacitus's *Annals* and we do not know what happened next. All we know is that, when the *Annals* pick back up again two years later, Agrippina the Elder and Nero had been exiled, while Drusus III was imprisoned in a palace dungeon. No one knows why.

The exile of Agrippina the Elder and her sons apparently infuriated Germanicus's mother Antonia the Younger, with whom the younger kids had gone to live again, and she finally broke with her long-held habit of refusing to engage with politics. Antonia was strongly conservative about the role of women. She wrote to Tiberius and described to him exactly how Sejanus was abusing him, abusing the family and told him Sejanus had designs on the throne so would probably kill Tiberius next. This was the family intervention that Tiberius needed. He had Sejanus and his entire family executed. It was too late for Agrippina the Elder, Drusus III and Nero, though. Tiberius loathed them too much and had endured enough of Agrippina the Elder screaming at him in his own home. He took out his petty, cruel streak on them. Agrippina the Elder he had regularly beaten. One beating was so terrible, she lost an eye. Eventually, she couldn't take it anymore and she starved herself to death, which is an extraordinary way to go. Drusus III died the same way, but unwillingly. He was so desperate to live that he ate the stuffing in his mattress. Nero was given the choice to fall on a sword or be murdered with one. He chose suicide. By 31CE, they were all dead.

At the end of all this, our Agrippina was 16 and the second oldest sibling left. She was an orphan and a huge swathe of her family had been wiped out: her uncle, her aunt, her grandmother, both parents and a couple of cousins had all been put to death. She hadn't been left in the schoolroom while all this was going on, though. In 31CE, she'd already been married for three years.

The First Husband

The wedding is Agrippina the Younger's one and only mention in sources for the first two decades of her life. It was personally arranged by Tiberius, which was actually a significant honour, and she was married to a member of the family, which was an extremely high honour. Her chosen husband was Gnaeus Domitius Ahenobarbus, most commonly known as Domitius, and was almost 20 years older than his new wife. Domitius's grandmother was Augustus's sister Octavia and his father was Lucius Domitius Ahenobarbus. The Domitian family were as ancient as the Claudians and as distinguished. He was a nice match in terms of status for Agrippina the Younger. He had been consul, which meant he was of the highest possible rank, and he was extremely rich. His posthumous reputation, however, is appalling. There are no pleasant stories told about him. Suetonius describes him as 'hateful in every walk of life' and records numerous horrible anecdotes.[1] In one, Domitius got angry with an ex-slave and killed him because the ex-slave was more sober than he was. In another, he ripped out the eye of an equestrian in the middle of the Roman Forum because the equestrian was rude to him. He was also accused of deliberately running over a child playing in the street, just for fun. And all that is on top of accusations of cheating bankers, extortion, stealing, and fucking every woman he laid eyes on, with or without consent. If even a quarter of the stories about Domitius are true, he was a dick. Suetonius is uniquely undiscerning in his recording of every anecdote that comes his way, so we can probably tone it all down, but, as a general reputation, this is not great. And this is who Agrippina the Younger was married to.

Her wedding day appears to have been at the end of the year 28CE, just after her thirteenth birthday and at the same time Tiberius was storming out of Rome. In most cultures the wedding day is an exciting day and the start of something new for women, and Rome was no different. Much like the Anglo-American conception of weddings

1. Suetonius, Nero, 5.

today, the Roman wedding day was all about the bride. Technically in Roman law the groom didn't even need to be present for the ceremony itself because it was only tangentially related to him. He was gaining a wife, which was probably nice but didn't necessarily affect him much; but for the woman it was a full life change, especially for those like Agrippina the Younger who were getting married for the first time. The bit the groom was mostly involved in was the betrothal ceremony beforehand, where the nuts and bolts of the legal contract and the bride's dowry were worked out with her dad. Women in Roman law were perpetually minors and were not allowed to negotiate or sign contracts themselves, so their father or legal guardian had to do it for them. The level of involvement of the bride herself in Roman betrothals is a matter of infinite variation, but as Agrippina the Younger was 13 years old, and had probably been betrothed when she was a couple of years younger, we can assume she wasn't invited to participate much. Instead she was asked if she consented and given a ring to mark her new status as a bride-to-be until the day of the ceremony. The traditional Roman wedding ceremony had three main steps: leaving the bride's house, a procession to the groom's house, and then being received into her new home. Agrippina the Younger's wedding was basically a royal wedding, Tiberius was an absolute stickler for old-fashioned traditions and Agrippina the Elder was both brilliant at optics and in desperate need of some good publicity, so we can assume that the wedding of her oldest daughter would be a reasonably big and public affair in Rome and have all the bits. This is how it goes.

The day started at the bride's house, which for Agrippina the Younger was her mother's house on the Palatine where she has spent the previous few years. The bride wore a new dress, ideally one she wove herself the day before. Whether a princess weaving her own dress would be a sign of brilliant femininity or of doing work that was obviously beneath her is impossible to know. But Agrippina the Younger got a new dress. Once that was on, she'd slip on new yellow shoes – the yellow is important – and fasten the dress with a belt tied with a particular knot. She would then have her hair done in a very particular way, a bit like those up-dos you literally only ever see on brides, with plaits and flowers woven through it except this hairstyle was called (brace yourselves) the *sex crines* and involved a spear. She'd then have her make-up done and her jewellery put on. Agrippina was a royal woman, so all of this would be done by a small army of slaves dedicated to making sure that she looked the best she could look. She would be dripping in gold and jewels. For Agrippina the Younger this would probably be simultaneously thrilling and terrifying. These were her last hours in her childhood home, living with her mother and siblings, being a child. But she was being dressed as an adult, as a bride. Every little girl who ever put a tea towel on their head and stomped about in their mum's shoes pretending to be a bride knows what this is like. All these shoes and hairstyles and belts were particular to being a bride and made you the most special and beautiful person around for a little while and that was thrilling.

When it was all done and ready, the final and most important touch was added, I imagine gently and reverently: the veil was placed over her eyes. The Roman wedding veil wasn't the gentle white gauze of today. It was a large and brightly coloured piece of material, probably yellow or red, like a big shawl, which went over the head and shoulders and fell down over the forehead to cover the eyes, stopping at the nose. It would then be held on with a crown. The bride would just be able to peep out underneath it and see her own feet. The veil made the whole outfit incredibly striking in the same way that an enormous white dress is immediately noticeable to onlookers. It made the bride both the very centre of attention and slightly removed from it, as she saw the whole ceremony only through coloured cloth.

Once she was dressed, Agrippina the Younger left the house for the last time. The front doors were flung open and she appeared to the bridal party waiting in the street. The bridal party is quite a literal term here: this wasn't bridesmaids and groomsmen, this was everyone who wants to turn up to go on the lash together. So Agrippina the Younger, in her bridal outfit, perhaps feeling both very grown up and very small, stepped out into the crowd that had gathered to celebrate her wedding with her. This was important. This was the first time Agrippina the Younger herself had ever had a public appearance where she was looked at and celebrated, where she was the very

31

centre of attention because of who she was and what she was wearing. She would have shared many of these moments with her siblings, mostly as a focus for everyone's sympathy, but this was her first solo outing and her first taste of people celebrating her. Judging from the direction the rest of her life took, I think we can assume she liked it. Being the centre of attention lasted a while, as the crowd processed through the streets of Rome with the bride, being rowdy, ribald and rude. Agrippina the Younger was escorted by children, holding her hands and leading her because she was half-blind, while the crowd and her family sang her a wedding song, probably written specifically for the occasion about how wonderful Agrippina was and how lovely her marriage would be, while other people made a series of mocking jokes about the groom. Given Domitius's propensity for gouging out the eyes of people who irritated him, though, I suspect that this element was very low key at Agrippina's wedding. But, essentially, the parade was a hugely public occasion full of joy and excitement for the teenage bride, walking to her new home, a street party just for her.

Domitius's main house was on the Via Sacra, which wasn't far away and meant that most of Agrippina the Younger's walk was through the monumental centre of Rome, past the glorious temples and statues of her ancestors. When she arrived at the doorway of Domitius's house, the main ritual elements – the bits that are analogous to our vows and ring swapping – would begin. Before she could go into her new home, there were four rituals that were traditionally performed. These were all basically optional. You could ignore them all and just stroll in if you wanted, in the same way that you can get married in a council office wearing joggers if you want today. But most people don't do that. Most people want a party and for a wedding to feel special and different, so they do all the weird rituals like being given away by your dad even though you are a feminist, and getting married in a church even though you follow Richard Dawkins on Twitter. And this was a royal wedding arranged by Agrippina the Elder, a woman who would never skip a chance to make something dramatic. First, Agrippina the Younger anointed the doorway with fat and wool. Basically, she smeared some kind of animal fat onto the door frame and then strung wool between the door posts, sticking the ends to the fat. Obviously that sounds both disgusting and bizarre, which it is, but this is very symbolic and serious. Probably as these things were brought out, the party atmosphere would die down and everyone would watch reverently as this little girl covered the door in goo. There are a few sources that then claim there was a little vow here, where the bride would say something along the lines of 'where you are Gaius, I am Gaia' or 'since you are Gaius, I am Gaia'. This was supposed to be a kind of explicit statement of goodness and virtue and general praiseworthiness. The groom, as I say, didn't have to say anything back because he might not even be there. If the groom didn't bother to show up, obviously this didn't happen, but I'm pretty sure even Domitius was afraid of Agrippina the Elder, so I reckon he was there.

Once the words were said, the groom and some onlookers lifted the bride over the step. This is the most important bit, the bit where everyone would hold their breath and watch intently, and the bit that nervous brides would get anxious about. This is the bit that really mattered. If you Google this ritual, which I did, you'll find all kinds of lunatic wedding websites claiming various explanations for the lifting the bride over the threshold, including the assertion that it was to prevent demons getting in through the feet, which is quite silly and very funny. Basically, it's just Roman superstition about luck and their obsession with seeing signs in everything. Nothing was exempt from being given some significance if it happened at a significant time. If five bees landed on a statue of a man and then the next day that man's great-great-granddaughter fell over, the bees were a sign. If lightning touched anything at all, it was a sign. Comets, eclipses, particularly dark nights, birds doing anything at all and unusual birth by any person or animal were all signs of something; it was just a matter of working out what. Tripping on the door of your new house as you enter it for the first time is a very obvious bad sign. Imagine that you, dear reader, were at a wedding and, during the 'I take you [insert groom's name here]' bit, the bride suddenly threw up or fainted, or accidentally said someone else's name. You and everyone else in the church would look at one another and say, 'well, that doesn't bode well for the marriage'. And that is exactly what this doorway thing was. Fucking up the step into the house in any way is just bad luck, and no one wants bad luck. So the crowds hushed and Agrippina the Younger was gently lifted over the door jamb and into her new home. Once there and safely on her feet, in the little cramped hallway, Domitius gave her fire and water. Presumably a candle or torch and a glass of water, but who knows. Fire and water were symbols of life and citizenship and showed she lived there now. The acceptance of the fire and water meant that the marriage ceremony was done and everything had gone fine and the party could start.

We can assume that all this went smoothly for Agrippina and that, hopefully, she enjoyed the whole thing. It was followed by her first grown-up party: a big feast with herself in the most distinguished position, lying on a special dining couch with her new husband, in her yellow shoes, eating all the best foods and drinking all the best wine. Beside her would be her mother, her three brothers, her sisters, her aunts and uncles and her new family. She now had two sisters-in-law, both of whom obviously had the same name and both of whom would be her frenemies for the rest of her life. One tends to be referred to as Domitia Lepida. She was older than Domitius, so she was in her mid-thirties when she gained Agrippina as a teenage sister-in-law. She was married to a man named Gaius Sallustius Crispus Passienus, who will come up again later. She was pretty much dedicated to living a quiet life of being very, very rich, for which no one can blame her. The younger sister is known just as Lepida and was slightly closer in age to Agrippina the Younger, being, probably, in her twenties. When Agrippina the Younger was marrying her brother, Lepida had already had a child with her first husband, a little girl called Messalina, been widowed, married again and had a second child, a son called Faustus Cornelius Sulla. Lepida also has a bad reputation so from that we can deduce that she was less dedicated to quiet luxury than her older sister. These were Agrippina the Younger's new family, with whom she would spend an enormous amount of time in the coming years.

As the party wound down, the couple were supposed to retire to the bedroom. There was no sense that sex was required to consummate the marriage as there is in our notion of wedding-night knobbing. Marriages weren't quite connected to sex in the same way in the Roman world. They were the only legal way a woman can have sex, technically, but that didn't mean that the couple had to have sex for any purpose other than having some children at some point. They could reasonably have a long marriage where they rarely touched each other. There was, however, a general expectation that virginities would be lost, willingly or not, on the wedding night and that was certainly a theme of the dirty jokes, especially for first-time brides like Agrippina. There's no way to know what happened on the night of Agrippina and Domitius's wedding; there's no way of even speculating how Agrippina might have felt about the prospect of her wedding night. There is no speculative assumption that can be made that isn't made through my own cultural lens that a 30-year-old having sex with a 13-year-old is appalling, or that a 13-year-old would be afraid. These are, however, products of my own cultural conditioning, and yours, too. We barely know what virginity meant to a young Roman aristocratic girl; we can't begin to fathom what first-time sex might mean. All we can know is that, at some point, Domitius and Agrippina had sex because they had a child together, but not until several years after their marriage when Agrippina was well into her twenties. Everything else is pure guesswork, and sordid titillation at that.

Agrippina the Younger was now, technically, a woman. A married woman, who suddenly had access to the adult world of politics and gossip and backstabbing and obligation. However, as far as the sources are concerned, the next few years of Agrippina the Younger's life are almost as quiet as her childhood. Agrippina the Younger herself, though, was probably not that quiet. Agrippina the Younger took after her mother in more ways than just her name. Agrippina the Elder was described as 'knowing no feminine weakness', as lusting for power to be held in her own hands, not in the hands of a man who could hold it over her.[2] She failed, though, by being too confrontational, too abrasive, too arrogant and too open with her desires. Her daughter learned from that. She learned that confronting men with power only ever ended badly. Men with power can, and will, hurt you; only with power can you protect yourself. As a woman, though,

2. Tacitus, Annals, 6.24.

it was foolish to go head-to-head with power. Agrippina the Younger needed to forge her new path to take back her birthright. She learned that, too: that she was the descendant of divinity and she deserved to rule. She had an unassailable right to it. She just needed to find her way there. These lessons shaped Agrippina the Younger into the woman she would become.

For now, though, she was still living under Tiberius and the main thing she had learned about Tiberius was that she needed to deflect attention from herself. The most likely explanation for her absence from the sources at this time is that she just wasn't doing anything that was worth Tacitus paying attention to, and neither was her husband. She was invisible as far as the historians were concerned. Of course, she wasn't invisible in the real world; she was highly visible every day in Rome as a member of the imperial family. Have no doubt that, at the time, if ever she dropped a spoon or coughed or wore a dress or was slightly rude to a slave, everyone knew about it. But Roman historians don't care about women. They only care about politics and war. And there the main events were now outside Rome on Capri where Tiberius had sequestered Agrippina the Younger's only surviving brother, Caligula, and Drusus II's son, Tiberius Gemellus, where he was grooming them for succession in all the wrong ways.

The only glimpse we get of her during these years comes through her husband, of course. In 37CE, after six years of nothing happening, Domitius became embroiled in a court case, a kind of peak Roman court case, where a woman named Albucilla was accused of impiety and adultery and Domitius was named as one of her many, many partners in crime. The case ended up dragging in about half the aristocracy and the new Praetorian Prefect, Macro, took personal responsibility for the interrogations. The accusations kept growing, and Domitius was then charged with incest with his younger sister Domitia Lepida. Rome became tense again and it began to look like the prosecution of Albucilla was a sideways attack on Domitius, and that Macro was leading the charge. This is interesting for Agrippina the Younger, because Macro was a strong ally of Caligula's and was instrumental in negotiating his succession to the throne. It's even more interesting because, before the trial could begin, Tiberius died after long illness, aged 77. At this point, Agrippina and Domitius have as good a claim as anyone to the throne. The familiarity of the incest and adultery accusations, the timing of the accusations during Tiberius's illness, and Macro's intimate involvement with both Caligula and the prosecution come together to form a picture of Macro, maybe with the knowledge of Caligula, trying to clear Domitius out of the way as a potential rival to the throne before Tiberius died. Tiberius, for the first time in his life, accidentally fucked up the plans of one of his scheming sidekicks by dying. Thankfully, Domitius was uninterested in being emperor, and Caligula's ascension to the throne was relatively smooth. And so, on 16 March 37CE, Agrippina the Younger became the sister of the emperor and was launched from historical invisibility to being one of the most important women in the Roman world.

Chapter Two: Sister

Gaius Caligula

'Favour and good fortune attend Gaius Caesar and his sisters.'[1]

Gaius is better known as Caligula but I am going to continue to call him Gaius because Caligula just feels too cruel. Caligula means 'little boots' or 'bootikins' or 'bootsie'. It's a cutesy diminutive of the word *caliga*, which is the type of shoe Roman soldiers wore and it's a nickname he got when he was three. Calling him Caligula now feels like calling Queen Elizabeth II by her childhood nickname of Lilibet. It's just a bit insulting. There's plenty of people who think that Gaius was a true monster who deserves every insult one can throw at him, but I'm not one of them. So he'll be Gaius here. And we'll do a quick overview of Gaius's life up to becoming emperor, so we're all caught up.

We've seen him a few times in the previous chapter: he got his Caligula nickname in the German camps with his mother and father, where he acted as a mascot to the troops and his mother got him a tiny military uniform. He was apparently a bit of a favourite of his parents as he was the only one who got taken to Syria when Germanicus went to sort out the Armenian king situation and was with his parents when Germanicus died. He then accompanied his mother and his littlest sister Livilla II back to Rome with his father's ashes, and was part of the mournful parade from Brundisium to Rome. He lived with his mother until her imprisonment, but was too young to be suspected of anything when his older brothers were also thrown in jail. He then went, with Drusilla and Livilla II, to live with their grandmother Antonia Minor.

He stayed there until he was 19, when he was suddenly called to join his great-uncle and unceremoniously granted his *toga virilis*. The *toga virilis* ceremony was the most significant point in a boy's life, and it usually happened when the boy was about 14. It was the moment

1. Suetonius, Gaius, 15.

when they became an adult and a fully functioning Roman citizen. It involved a private and public ceremony and was their official entrance into public society. The boy got to wear an adult toga and surrender the visible signs of his childhood, most notably the *bulla* that he wore from his birth until this day. A *bulla* was the protective necklace that boys wore both to mark their status as children and protect them from the unique harms and illnesses that threatened small children in an age where medicine was strongly focused on humours. They were not small pendants either; they were about the size of a child's fist. These were dedicated to the *lares* when they were removed. After this ceremony, the boy was a man and was eligible for the Senate and could go to the Forum and be a real citizen who contributed to public life. But Gaius had been deliberately sidelined and kept a legal child for several years longer than he should have been, probably because of what happened with his mother and brothers and the suspicion that cast on him, and his legitimate claim to the throne. Tiberius kept him in the safe position of a minor, a sound political move but a cruel one. A reasonable analogy is that Gaius got forced to stay in middle school, being squeezed into his tiny uniform. While his peers grew up, left school, got jobs, wore suits and got laid, he was left still wearing a little school jumper in a primary colour and grey shorts and sitting on chairs he no longer fitted into as he grew a beard and manly urges. For reference, Augustus took his *toga virilis* at 15 and was a priest and prefect of the city by the time he was 16. Tiberius gave his first public speech when he was nine and was in the Senate at 17. Nineteen is really old. The humiliation must have been palpable for Gaius who was effectively being punished and hidden because of his immediate family. He wasn't stupid either, and he'd been raised by a smart mother. He must have known what was happening to him, and it must have burned.

But one day, weird Uncle Tiberius who, in Gaius's eyes, had murdered his father, his mother and his brothers, called for him. He was flung into adulthood in name alone, only to be torn away from Rome and stranded on a beautiful but boring island with a man who probably terrified and appalled him. And there he stayed, with just Tiberius and a few hangers-on and his little cousin Tiberius Gemellus for company for years and years. Until Tiberius died in 37CE, when Gaius was 27. The most formative years of Gaius's adult, male life as a Roman citizen, when he should have been learning how to deal with the Senate and people of Rome, making friends, leading armies and having adventures, were spent trapped on a tiny island with a bitter old man. This explains a lot about Gaius and his reign.

There are contradictory accounts of how Tiberius died, which is to be expected as it happened on a small island and there were no good gossips around. There were plenty of detailed rumours that Gaius had killed him in order to take the throne, but I have no real time for them. Tiberius was in his seventies when he died and that's a good long life for a man who lived in a world without antibiotics. Plus, Gaius had no understanding of how to be emperor or what it would entail, and his reign was short and terrible, and he must have known that he would have no idea what he was doing. If anyone killed Tiberius, it wasn't Gaius. But probably Tiberius died of old age.

So, in 39CE, Gaius finally escaped from Capri. He had left the city as a 19-year-old, barely a man, and returned a 27-year-old, somehow even more sheltered and inexperienced than before. But now he was emperor.

Gaius Caesar Augustus and his Sisters

When news arrived in Rome that Tiberius had died and that Gaius was now emperor, everyone was apparently delighted for three reasons. First, Gaius was not Tiberius – although, admittedly, a cat could have become emperor and everyone would have been thrilled that it wasn't Tiberius. Secondly, the people of Rome knew only one thing about Gaius at the time of his ascension: he was the son of Germanicus. The first six chapters of Suetonius's biography of Gaius are about how brilliant his dad was and how beloved he was, and that appears to be representative of how people thought of Gaius in 37CE. He was, for the moment, the last remaining son of the prince of Rome's heart. He was hope for a new and beautiful future. He was a descendant of the Divine Augustus. He was not Tiberius. There's a lovely bit of an essay written by a Jewish leader named Philo – who absolutely despised Gaius so he probably wasn't lying too much – in which he says that the entire empire was in a festival mood and threw parties in delight at Gaius's ascension.

That's how Suetonius presents it, too, to the extent that Suetonius fudges over a very real power struggle that happens as Gaius ascends to the throne and makes it look terribly smooth and happy. In fact, Tiberius wanted his own biological grandson and namesake Tiberius Gemellus to be at least co-ruler with his adopted child Gaius. Tiberius Gemellus was the only surviving child of Drusus II and his wife, Livilla I, and he had just as much of a claim to anything as Gaius. However, Gemellus had two flaws that made him reasonably easy to bump off the throne before he even got there: he was 18 years old, and he wasn't the son of Germanicus. Being the son of the army's favourite son, Gaius had also made friends with the head of the Praetorian Guard, Macro – who may or may not have been trying to pre-emptively prosecute Domitius to clear Gaius's path. All this means that Gaius returned to Rome with the ghost of his father on one side of him and the loyalty of a private army on the other. That's tough to argue with.

That doesn't mean that people didn't, though, because Romans were an argumentative people, and because there were plenty of other men lurking around who had perfectly good Julian or Claudian blood and who wouldn't have minded being the regent to an 18-year-old emperor. Such as Agrippina's husband Domitius. When her brother entered Rome on a wave of confetti and adoration, Agrippina was 21 years old and just about to get pregnant.[1] I like to imagine that Nero was conceived around about here as the result of a celebratory marital bonk as he was born nine months later and that's a fun image. Equally likely, though, is that Agrippina finally felt safe enough to have a child and fulfil her duty to the state. Under Tiberius's capricious reign, no one in the imperial family felt safe, least of all Agrippina whose family had been decimated by her great-uncle. Tiberius's Rome was certainly not a place into which anyone would have felt comfortable adding to the imperial family. With the change in emperor, to her own brother no less, Agrippina's threats had mostly disappeared. She was now on the winning side. To make matters even better for Agrippina, the precarity of Gaius's initial position among the Roman Senate meant that he felt he had to demonstrate to everyone that he was the best possible man for the job by strongly emphasising how noble, brilliant and Julian his family was, with particular focus on his beloved sisters.

A large part of Gaius's first few months as emperor was dedicated almost exclusively to rehabilitating his immediate family, making a massive show of how great they were and how dedicated to them he was. In fact, he explicitly emphasises how Not Tiberius they were by mostly honouring the Julian side that connected him by blood back to both Augustus and Agrippa. One of his first acts was to sail off to the islands that his mother and brother died on, retrieve their ashes and return them to Rome to be interred in the Mausoleum of Augustus with great pomp and circumstance. That he did this in about April, when the seas were dangerous and sailing wasn't really recommended, echoed his own mother's dangerous trip to bring her husband's ashes home and really highlighted how dedicated and great he

1. As Agrippina the Elder didn't make it out of Chapter One alive, I'm going to drop the younger epithet now. Agrippina the Younger will now just be Agrippina but if her mother appears again, she'll still be Agrippina the Elder.

was as a son. Like his mother's great return to Rome, his trip also culminated with a huge and solemn procession of the ashes to Rome where they were placed (at midday, so no one would miss it) in the Mausoleum of Augustus. Pleasingly, Agrippina the Elder's inscription in the Mausoleum survived so we can see exactly how her son wanted her remembered:

> 'Agrippina, daughter of Marcus Agrippa, granddaughter of the Divine Augustus, wife of Germanicus Caesar and mother of Gaius Caesar Augustus Germanicus, Princeps.'[2]

Subtle as a brick is our Gaius. At the same time, he lifted the stain that Tiberius had placed on his mother's birthday by making that day a business day again and instituted a set of games in her name, to which a statue of her was carried in a sacred carriage called a *carpentum*, which is basically a very, very special carriage. Just in case anyone missed all this, he also released a set of enormous gold and silver coins with his parents' faces on it, one of which has Agrippina the Elder's face on the reverse and an image of her statue in the *carpentum* on the obverse. Agrippina the Elder was Gaius's real legitimacy because she was his blood connection to Augustus. His father needed no rehabilitation so he simply renamed the month of September to Germanicus. Unlike August(us) and July(ius), that one didn't stick, which is a tiny bit of a shame. Celebrating my dad's birthday in Germanicus would have been charming.

Amongst all this, Gaius drew his sisters into his celebrations. They were elevated both by their parents being enormously honoured and by their brother being emperor, which was enough for pretty much every emperor after Gaius who saw where he went wrong here. For Gaius, in order to legitimise his reign, decided to do his best to bring his sisters into the public arena as extensions of himself. First, they were given the privileges of the Vestal Virgins, which was a lot of privilege. The Vestal Virgins were the only public women in Rome, the only women with a formal state role. Their official job was to tend

---

2. *Corpus Inscriptionum Latinarum* 6.886. Gaius Caesar Augustus Germanicus was Gaius's full name after taking the throne.

the sacred fire that represented Rome's power and continuity. They served for a 40-year term and took a vow of virginity for that period (though they were allowed to marry afterwards) and had a huge number of incredibly important religious duties as, essentially, the female counterpart to *rex sacrorum*, the priest of Jupiter who took on the king's religious duties when kings were overthrown. The meaning and ideological role of the Vestals is blurry and confusing, but also not too important here. What is important is that they were given a lot of good stuff for a woman in Rome in recognition of how important they were and Gaius gave his sisters this good stuff, too. First, they got to be free of a male guardian which meant they could make their own legal decisions, do their own business and make their own wills. This was personally important as it set them apart in law and business from other women. They were also given lots of very public day-to-day honours that ensured that they were constantly in the public eye. The most striking was that they were granted a lictor when they were out and about. Lictors were attendants, employed by the state, who carried the *fasces*: a bundle of sticks with an axe hidden in it that forms the basis of the word fascism and represented military power and the right to exercise state violence. They were basically the presidential convoy of their time and their main job was to walk in front of the official they were attending, clearing the path so the official would never be impeded. For a woman who was not a Vestal Virgin to have this was significant. The sisters also got reserved seats of honour at all plays, festivals and games. This means that they were both separated from the crowd and on display at all times. Finally, their bodies were sacrosanct. Touching or harming a Vestal Virgin was automatically punished with death. All this was granted to 21-year-old Agrippina and her little sisters in 37CE.

One might think this was enough. Agrippina was elevated above every woman in Rome bar a few priestesses and her sisters; she had become a sacred object and a public person. But Gaius wasn't even close to finished. His next step was to include them in the prayers given for the wellbeing of the empire and emperor. This wasn't totally unprecedented; Livia, Sejanus and their brothers Nero and Drusus II had been included in the prayers previously, but it was a decent honour. It emphasised that Gaius wanted them to be viewed as part of the Roman state. And Gaius kept going. He had his sisters added to the ritualised formula used when consuls introduced motions in the Senate. That makes this sound very archaic, but it is merely the pronouncement that makes a motion formal in the same way that in the British parliament a motion is formally introduced by a person saying, 'I move that...' and nothing counts unless they say it properly. In the Roman Senate under the Principate, a consul would describe a proposition by saying that it was for the good fortune of the emperor, because sycophancy got you everywhere in Rome. Gaius's little innovation was to add his sisters to that bit so that all consular propositions were completed with the line 'Favour and good fortune attend Gaius Caesar and his sisters'.[3] Suddenly, the sisters were dragged right into the heart of politics and were figuratively present in the Senate house every day. Then, they were added to the oath of loyalty to the emperor sworn by every citizen at the beginning of a new reign and during times of crisis. Previously, citizens swore just to Augustus or Tiberius but now the oath ran: 'I will not hold myself or my children dearer than I hold the emperor Gaius and his sisters.' This is bizarre and extraordinary. I don't know about you, but an empire's worth of people swearing that they consider me and my siblings to be more valuable than their children and their own lives would go straight to my head, especially if I didn't even have to be emperor and deal with all the paperwork to get it. Agrippina, Livilla and Drusilla were being held up as intrinsic to the Principate, as important to the state as the emperor himself. As part of that, they also got their own coins – coins are important propaganda – and again Gaius was revolutionary. He was the first to put living young women on a coin. His last quietly dramatic act of filial piety was to put their names on coins, too. This doesn't sound like much maybe, but have you ever seen Princess Margaret's name on a coin? Coin faces were for rulers, not for their family. This act made the three sisters the first living women ever to be identified by name on a Roman coin. The most significant surviving coin of this type is a *sestertius* with Gaius's face on the front and three women side by side on the back. In the middle is Drusilla dressed as

3. Suetonius, Gaius, 15.

the goddess *Concordia*, Livilla stands to the right as *Fortuna*, and, on the left, is Agrippina as *Securitas*. She is resting her hand on Drusilla's shoulder and gazing at her, while in her right hand she simultaneously holds a cornucopia and leans nonchalantly on an elbow-height column. She is, like her sisters, draped in fabric with her belly button peeping out. Down the left side of the coin is her name: Agrippina. This is the first image of our heroine in public and as part of the imperial family. It is our first real image of her at all: the tiny representative of a goddess in a group of tiny women.

Importantly, all these actions were incredibly popular and worked exactly as planned. The Senate and people of Rome were fully convinced by all this that Gaius had the most legitimate claim to the throne and were reminded just how much they loved his dad and mum and that Tiberius was horrid for killing such a wonderful woman. At the same time, Gaius uses his sisters to convey a sense of continuity. This is the major purpose of using his sisters because, at the time of his ascension, Gaius had no children and the only useful person of the next generation was the 18-year-old from whom he had spent months trying to draw people's attention away. Gemellus was a rival, not an heir.[4] His sisters, however, were young, pretty and fertile. Each was married to a useful cousin and it helped to remind everyone that their mother had one of Rome's most productive wombs. Maybe, he hinted with his coins, his sisters could produce a lot of Roman babies, too. So this is our first picture of Agrippina. Before this, we have séen her only in the shadows; we have had to guess at her presence. Before this she was as private a woman as women should be, but now her brother had brought her out into the glare of public gaze and given her symbolic power over the rest of the empire. She was gaining the first flickers of that reflected spotlight.

The second time we see Agrippina and her sisters in public is also in 37CE and is the dedication of the Temple of the Divine Augustus. The temple had obviously been started by Tiberius but somehow no one had bothered to finish it in the two decades of his reign and it finally got polished off in the first couple of months of Gaius's, just about at

---

4. Gaius did adopt Gemellus upon his ascension, and then did everything in his power to draw attention away from his adopted son and towards his sisters.

the time that he was doing his best to remind everyone of his blood relationship with the newly anointed divinity. Some may call that convenient. The same people might also say that the dedication falling on Gaius's twenty-eighth birthday was convenient too as it meant that the celebration ended up being a dual party for the god Augustus and his great-grandson Gaius. The dedication was the official opening of the temple as a place of worship and was a huge public event involving games, races and celebrations over a few days. Dio claims that there were 60 horse races and that 400 bears died in the arena.[5] Gaius himself arrived at the party in a triumphal carriage drawn by six horses and sat overseeing all the proceedings in the front row, flanked by his sisters. It's a nice image this picture of young Gaius, laughing and happy, with Agrippina and his sisters sitting at his side as they watch the chariots speed round the Circus Maximus and cheer for their team.[6] This occurred at the end of August in the year 37CE and was really the pinnacle of Gaius's political career and of Agrippina's public profile so far. Agrippina was also just a few months pregnant, maybe just starting to show a growing belly and feel her child kick, and the present and future could not have looked brighter in this moment. The hot summer sun beat down on the young siblings, all in their twenties and beautiful, who had achieved what their parents wanted for them. They combined Julian and Claudian blood in their veins, they had survived the regime that destroyed their parents and brothers, Agrippina was growing the next generation of Julians, and the children of Augustus were on the throne celebrating their own divine ancestor with their people. It was a perfect moment.

Of course, it could not last. In September 37CE, Gaius fell mysteriously ill. He disappeared from public, taking his sisters with him. A vacuum appeared into which some people tried to force poor Gemellus. Gaius, however, was apparently still well enough to recognise this was a problem and Gemellus was quietly killed. No other person with a claim to the throne as strong as Gemellus's lasted as long as six months into a new reign ever again. They were simply too

5. Dio, Roman History, 59.7.4 Dio is a bit obsessed with bears dying. I think he liked them.

6. Suetonius tells us that Gaius was an obsessive fan of the Green team, to the extent that he regularly hung out in their stables, checking out the horses.

dangerous. Gaius decided he needed a child of his own and married Livia Orestilla, a woman who was so good at being a woman in the public eye that we're not even entirely sure that was her name. She's called Claudia Orestina in another source, which isn't even that close to being the same. A sense of uncertainty hung over Rome for months and the people and Senate of Rome got antsy when they could not see their emperor. For a culture that appreciated its history and antiquity so much, they were remarkably short-termist when it came to their own times. They had a point, though. If Gaius died, there would be no smooth succession to a son or heir, especially once Gemellus had been dispatched. Instead, the icy threat of civil war began to loom again.

Agrippina Mater

It was into this atmosphere of uncertainty and illness that Agrippina gave birth to her son, who was given the traditional name of his paternal family, not his maternal Julio-Claudians. He was born on 15 December 37CE and was named Lucius Domitius Ahenobarbus. Having a grown-up Domitius and a baby Domitius is just confusing for everyone, and he had his name changed when he was 14 anyway, so here we will call him by his more famous name: Nero. He was born in Augustus's villa in Antium which overlooked the sea and had its own theatre. It was a beautiful place to be. Oddly, we know more about this birth than we do about most because Pliny the Elder recorded it as an example of a breech birth in his *Natural History*, and he knew about it because Agrippina wrote about the birth in her own memoirs. Both of which are interesting.[1] Pliny considered a breech birth to be quite literally unnatural and a sign that the child was going to turn out to be miserable, horrible and probably a curse on the world. He noted that Agrippa was born breech but that Agrippa was both the sole exception and had died young and had a bloody awful life. Of course, Pliny also thought that death during childbirth was a good omen for the child, but only if they were male, so I'm not sure we'll trust his judgement on this. That Nero was a breech birth, however, was excellent proof of his theory as Nero did turn out to be miserable, horrible and sort of a curse on the world. It's more interesting that Agrippina chose to record the nature of her experience of childbirth in her memoirs. It's an intensely female act and very much an act confined to the private sphere. Lots of modern men have speculated that maybe Agrippina recorded the breech birth in her memoir because it was so deeply traumatic for her, which is why she never had any more children. While I am sure that a difficult birth in the ancient world was utterly appalling, I'm also wary of writing Agrippina off as a woman traumatised by it or of passing anachronistic judgement on her decision to write about it. It seems just as likely to me that she would record

1. Pliny the Elder, Natural History, 7.46.

the breech birth to draw a connection between her son and his great-grandfather Agrippa, especially as Pliny tells us that people born of breech births were colloquially known as 'having an Agrippa'. Alternatively, she might have recorded it like men recorded war stories, to emphasise her physical strength and endurance. Whatever the context of her including it, it is telling that she drew attention to the fact that she had given birth and emphasised her womanhood and her motherhood when she wrote about herself in intensely masculine spheres. As soon as Agrippina became a mother, she was defined by it almost entirely.

The first days of a child's life in Roman culture were fraught with anxiety on a lot of levels. The greatest fear, of course, was that the child or mother wouldn't survive. Probably a third of women would die in childbirth in the ancient world, and the same percentage of children. The prevalence of stillbirths and infant deaths is obvious just from looking at Agrippina's own mother: nine births, but only six children. We see this fear of losing the child in any of a thousand ways in an exhausting list of gods and goddesses associated with childbirth and the first few moments of a child's life. There's a specific god of the first cry. There's a goddess of breastfeeding. Given that Agrippina's labour was breech and probably the kind of awful that would get it a Channel Four documentary with a freakishly specific title, combined with her enormous profile and importance to the state and the fact that the emperor was also ill, we can assume that a lot of these gods were invoked and prayed to. The second and third anxieties were that the child would not be the husband's biological child or that it would be disabled some physical way.

We see these anxieties in a ritual we mentioned right at the beginning, the *tollere liberos* – literally the lifting of the child because the Romans aren't great at metaphors – which is described in a brilliantly solemn and incorrect medical text by Soranus, simply called *Gynaecology*. Here we learn that the midwife would check the child all over for deformities or impairments and then lay the baby on the floor in front of its father. The father would then literally choose whether to pick the child up or not. When the father picked the child up and baby was lifted into the air, they were formally and legally accepted into the father's family. This is the moment when a man becomes a father. I can't imagine how charged this moment must have been in every room where a child was born for hundreds of years. As the mother is still dealing with afterbirth and blood and fistulae, they are also finding out whether their child would be accepted or abandoned. Suetonius tells us that Nero was born just as the sun rose and that, as he lay on the floor waiting for Domitius to pick him up, while Agrippina lay in her own blood, the sun's first beams burst through the window and touched him. As Domitius looked at his tiny new son, the first great-great-grandchild of Augustus, that ray of light must have felt like a powerful omen. Of course, he lifted the baby and accepted him.

Roman motherhood looks quite different from modern motherhood, starting with the fact that the chances of Agrippina breastfeeding her son were precisely zero. This was what wet nurses existed for. Like her mother before her and just about every aristocratic and middle-class woman who could afford a wet nurse, Agrippina had better things to be doing than getting up at 3am to attach a baby to her tit. There was, I like to imagine, a sort of proto-yummy mummy set in Rome who were breastfeeding their own children specifically so they could feel morally superior to their peers. I have absolutely no doubt that innumerable letters were shared between Roman women over the centuries in which one complained about sore nipples in a tone that managed to be both self-deprecating and smug. This being Rome, though, we only have men's opinions on the matter and they are all highly troubling to a modern female eye. Our old stalwart Tacitus, bang in the middle of a philosophical dialogue he wrote about how important oratory was, decided to tell his readers that the reason Rome was so terrible in his modern times (being around 100CE) was that women didn't breastfeed anymore. He terms it 'giving themselves to their children', which tells you everything you need to know about how Tacitus conceived of women and children and breastfeeding. Instead of 'giving themselves to their children', he laments, mothers hand their children over to 'some silly little Greek serving maid' and that was why the kids of his day didn't like 'higher things' but were distracted by gladiatorial games and actors instead.[2] I am not exagger-

2. Tacitus, A Dialogue on Oratory, 28.

ating this in the slightest. Some things truly never change and apparently moralising about breastfeeding and how rubbish young people are now are among these things. The point here is that Agrippina would certainly have handed her son over to a team of slaves and a wet nurse with good credentials while she recovered and got back to the important task of being a member of the ruling family of Rome. It's easy and lazy to roll our eyes at this, as modern people sometimes do to women who don't breastfeed now, and to see Agrippina handing her swaddled little baby over to slaves to feed as being somehow cold or neglectful. There's a certain tendency to think that maybe she wasn't that interested in motherhood because she was a go-getting career woman.

Such a view was expressed by the ancient commentators, as we see in Tacitus there, and by our 21st-century culture which stills tends to divide women into women who stay at home and are good mothers vs women who go to work and are bad mothers. Except that Agrippina, like her mother before her, proceeded to spend the rest of her life dedicating herself to advancing her son and appears to have defined herself by her motherhood, but in a very Roman way. Motherhood in our modern Western world tends to be very focused on the mother and baby as being the most important parts of the mother–child bond because growing up means, to us, moving away from our parents and taking personal responsibility for our lives outside of our parents' lives. Accepting our parents' help with our careers is seen as unethical nepotism and a demonstration of a lack of personal ability. Motherhood in the ancient Roman world was essentially the exact opposite of this. There was no growing up and moving on. No matter how far away a son moved, they were intertwined with their family name and the achievement of their parents completely inextricably. Their parents, grandparents and great-grandparents were always known and shaping the direction of their lives. Very reductively, in the Roman world, the best way that a mother could show her love was to work to make sure that their child entered a world where their family was rich, respected and well connected. Whether a boob goes into a mouth is more or less irrelevant to that mission.

It is undeniable that Agrippina pretty much immediately went back to working for that goal. She was already one of the three best-connected women in the world (especially as Gaius's marriage to Livia lasted less than a year), she was free from a male guardian, she could go where she liked and – unlike her younger sisters – she had proved her fertility and produced the first in the next generation of Julio-Claudians. She was 22 years old and entering the year 38CE with the world apparently at her fingertips.

The Incest

In the historical record, the year 38CE started very badly with a bizarre act of public suicide. A slave called Machaon walked into the temple of Jupiter on the Capitoline – one of the biggest and most sacred spaces in the city – carrying a puppy and a knife. Skip this next sentence if you are particularly squeamish. He climbed up onto the altar, screamed terrible predictions for the coming year at everyone watching and then killed the puppy followed by himself. I can only assume that he did this in an attempt to get himself in the history books, which was very successful as here I am in 2017 in my office thinking about him because he killed a puppy 1,979 years ago. Still, it's not a good thing to happen on the first of the year. It made everyone uncomfortable. It made everyone particularly uncomfortable because the emperor was still sick (although he was well enough to show up to Nero's christening and make fun of his uncle and get married and then get a divorce two months later, so make of that what you will). People had also started falling suspiciously on swords, often ones belonging to the Praetorian Guard, and that made everyone uncomfortable, too. In quick succession, Gaius had knocked off his adoptive son Tiberius Gemellus, his former father-in-law Marcus Junius Silanus, and the Praetorian Prefect Macro. All of this looked a lot like the removal of anyone who had been around before he ascended to the throne and had any kind of power – real or symbolic — or was too close to him.

Were I Agrippina I would probably be a little antsy about all this. Unfortunately, we know absolutely nothing about what she was doing for this entire year. All we know is that a series of very strange accusations emerged about all three of the sisters and Drusilla's husband Lepidus all being involved in a simultaneously adulterous, incestuous, homosexual and probably non-consensual series of affairs. Lepidus was Gaius's absolute best friend. He was Drusilla's husband which meant he was married to Gaius's favourite sister (although possibly she was his favourite sister because she was married to his best friend ever), and Gaius liked Lepidus so damn much that at one point he started including him in family group statues across the empire. You can still see them today. There's Gaius and his sisters, there's their parents Agrippina the Elder and Germanicus, and then there's Lepidus on the end, just hanging out.[1] None of the other brothers-in-law got to be in family groups, which maybe made dinners with Domitius a little awkward sometimes. Just as awkward was the fact that, when Gaius was sick and everyone thought he would die, he possibly made Lepidus heir to the throne. Suetonius, being not very smart, claims that Gaius made Drusilla his heir, which is just unlikely given that women weren't allowed to speak in a public setting. Lepidus, however, was sort of a member of the family and trusted by Gaius. What the world saw, therefore, was their emperor being young and sexy, hanging out pretty much exclusively with his equally young and sexy sisters and his young and sexy brother-in-law. People being people, it took about half a second before someone had come up with some erotica about the whole thing.

The entire passage of Suetonius on this is quite fun, and if you're ever thinking of reading some Suetonius it's a grand place to start. In summary, it says that Gaius regularly had sex with his sisters, sometimes one after another. Additionally, he would let his male friends have sex with Agrippina and Livilla just for the fun of it. Drusilla, on the other hand, he kept for himself and 'treated as a wife' having allegedly started banging her when they were living with their grandmother.[2] He was also banging Lepidus on the regular, and also the wives of lots of senators. Everyone was busy being nude and sexy all the time. Interestingly, no contemporary of the siblings has anything to say about these stories of incest, even though we have several first-person accounts of Gaius's many personality flaws and, as I said earlier, the accusation of incest is a disturbingly common one.[3] It seems

---

1. It is a relief at the Sebasteion in Aphrodisias, the site of a number of unusual images concerning Agrippina.

2. When he was 17–19 and Drusilla was 13–16, though in most modern versions of this event, like *I, Claudius*, they are presented as being about eight, which says more about modern people than it does the Romans.

3. One of the earliest accusations was Clodius and Clodia in the first century AD who were repeatedly accused of incest, most notably by Cicero in his defence of a young bratty kid called Caelius. The accusation is also the source of Cicero's best ever joke: 'If I had not a

more likely to me that this is a projection of the Roman commentators who were unable or unwilling to conceive of close relationships that didn't involve sex. In this way, they are a lot like a jealous boyfriend who thinks that you can't go to dinner with a male friend by yourself because that's basically the same as sex, isn't it.

The reason that Drusilla was considered to be the favourite sister, which is a strange way of conceptualising 'treated her like a wife', was that, on 10 June 38CE, she suddenly died of fever and Gaius did not deal well. In modern parlance, Gaius stopped functioning. He stopped cutting his hair and shaving his beard, fled Rome and instituted a period of public mourning for Drusilla. Public mourning meant that no one could conduct business and no one was allowed to celebrate public or private festivals. He gave Drusilla a big public funeral, at which he was so upset that he broke down while reading the eulogy and made Lepidus do it instead. He then had the Senate grant her a series of honours, including deification. Technically, Drusilla is a goddess named Drusilla Panthea, though no one honoured her much. She was the first woman of the imperial family to receive this honour and the first person to receive it after Augustus, as Tiberius had refused to deify his mother Livia and no one wanted to deify Tiberius. She was given a public shrine with 20 priests. In Egypt, they renamed the month of Payni (May–June) Drusilleios. A two-day festival was instituted around her birthday. Gaius really liked his sister. For Agrippina, this would all have been a significant time, although she appears absolutely nowhere in the sources. She was, however, grieving her sister, attending her funeral, watching as these honours were heaped upon her baby sister. With the benefit of hindsight, knowing that Gaius lasted only a couple more years as emperor and that every aspect of Drusilla's new cult was instantly abandoned, it is possible to see this whole rigmarole as hollow and false. They seem craven and pathetic on the part of the Senate and bombastic on Gaius's part. In the moment, however, there is no reason to believe that the grief was not real and painful for everyone, including the senators. Just as the woes of the family appeared to be over, her death at just 21 was

quarrel with that woman's [Clodia's] husband – I mean brother! I am always making this mistake.'

a tragedy. There's no reason to believe that the Romans didn't genuinely respond exactly as the British would if one of Kate and Will's
kids died suddenly. And there's certainly no reason to believe that
Agrippina wasn't just as affected by the loss as her brother.

The Plot

The next year, however, Agrippina came roaring back into historical narratives in the most confusing possible way. Here, more than ever, I would probably kill a puppy to get my hands on the books of Tacitus's *Annals* that describe what happened in 39CE because it is so badly recorded that most people have just done a massive shrug rather than think about it and no one can really agree on what is real. But those people have usually been writing about Caligula, and I am here to talk about Agrippina, so there'll be no shrugging from me. In bare bones, at the beginning of the year Agrippina was the honoured sister of the emperor, front row at every race and extra special right of way in the streets, and by the end of the year she was living on an island the size of a piece of paper in exile. Something went wrong. As with the previous year, everything began ominously with the restoration of the charge of *maiestas*, a charge that Gaius had abolished less than two years before. *Maiestas* was a complicated thing. It referred generally to an attack on the majesty of the emperor, and is often seen simply as treason in modern eyes. Treason sort of implies that someone is plotting to physically harm the emperor or the empire in some way, though, while *maiestas* encompassed much, much more than that. *Maiestas,* as with everything in the Roman world, had a religious connotation as it was originally applied only to the gods. It worked its way down to semi-divine emperors through priests and consuls and incorporated all kinds of ideas of disrespect, sacrilege and any subversion of the dignity of the emperor. And all that is much more insidious and easy to accuse someone of than treason. Tiberius, for example, had Cremutius Cordus executed for being too nice about Brutus and Cassius (Julius Caesar's assassins) in a book of history, and Votienus Motanus went the same way for insulting Tiberius in private. Others were tried for making a vague allusion to the fact that Tiberius hadn't deified his mother, changing clothes in front of a statue of the Divine Augustus, and carrying a coin bearing Tiberius's face into the loo. *Maiestas* was essentially whatever the emperor wanted it to be in order to get rid of a troublesome senator. To make things even more fun, there were incentives for accusing people of *maiestas*! If you, random senator or equestrian, accused someone and they were successfully executed, you got to keep all their money and all their houses as a reward! Isn't that great and not at all terrible! Abolishing *maiestas* trials was one of Gaius's most popular acts at the beginning of his reign because Tiberius used them particularly liberally when he was in a bad mood, which was always, and the flexibility of the law quite reasonably terrified people. Gaius reversed his decision because it turned out that having a catch-all law that banned anything the emperor found annoying or threatening was very useful indeed, both for keeping people in line and making them really, really hate you. However, it was still far too close to Tiberius's reign for anyone to have forgotten how horrifying *maiestas* trials were, so Gaius announcing that actually everyone would be permanently watched for any tiny slight that could possibly be perceived as disrespect, and that the nicer your house was, the bigger a target you were, was a particular trigger for everyone to get terrified. Including Agrippina and Domitius.

The reintroduction of *maiestas* came as a result of a dramatic showdown between Gaius and the Senate, in which he accused the senators of being snivelling clients of Sejanus and responsible for the deaths of his mother and brothers. He then vocally empathised with the loathed Tiberius, stating that he understood why the former emperor had gone so murder-y, because the Senate spent all their time sneaking up to him and informing on each other to curry favour and make money. Further, he was pretty sure that they were all probably plotting against him and, for all these reasons, he saw no good reason to try to work with them peacefully because they were both awful and irritating. He concluded that it would be better if the Senate just did as they were told and stopped trying to talk to him or treat him like he was their mate. In response, they proved his point by nodding vigorously as he abused them, voting happily to reinstate the *maiestas* laws they loathed and feared, and then spending a full day celebrating and praising him in an official capacity, culminating in voting for new sacrifices to his mercy and kindness, which were to be carried out after a golden statue of Gaius was built and carried through the city and up to the Capitol accompanied by children singing a hymn in his honour. It's a wonder Gaius didn't vomit on their shoes, to be honest. *I* want to vomit on their shoes. Clearly, the relationship between Gaius and the Senate had deteriorated significantly, and it got worse after Gaius decided to put on an enormous spectacle just for the fun of it and built a three-mile-long bridge made of ships across the Bay of Baiae outside Naples and then spent a couple of days having massive parties. We can assume that Agrippina was present at this, because who would want to miss the opportunity to frolic across a boat bridge. Also, Baiae was a delightful spa town for the mega-rich, a sort of Monte Carlo for the Romans, so it was probably a brilliant time. Unsurprisingly, the Senate weren't delighted by the spectacle. Quite possibly because Gaius seemed to be deliberately doing pointless and expensive things to annoy them.

At about the same time, Gaius gave Agrippina yet another new sister-in-law. In 38CE he had married Lollia Paulina, who will reappear later in our story, and then divorced her about 30 seconds later. This year's wife stayed a little longer. Caesonia was older than Gaius, already widowed and the mother of three daughters. She seems to have been already pregnant when she married Gaius, giving him his only child and a cousin for little Nero, a daughter named Julia Drusilla. Caesonia also has the honour of being played by Helen Mirren in the 1979 high-class porn film *Caligula*, which is a pretty great legacy. Caesonia was from the kind of family that people tended to avoid at parties. Her mother Vistilia had been married six times and had gestation periods so unusual that Pliny the Elder felt the need to comment on them in his *Natural History*.[1] Another woman of her family, also called Vistilia, though the relationship is unknown, caused a public scandal by finding a novel way to avoid an adultery prosecution: as Roman adultery was simply sex between a woman of

---

1. He claims that she had an 11-month pregnancy with one of her children, another pregnancy of seven months and that Caesonia was born after just eight months. Natural History, 7.4

high rank and a man she wasn't married to, women of low social rank and certain professions were excluded from the law. These professions included actresses, pub owners and, of course, prostitutes. So Vistilia registered herself as a public prostitute. It didn't work, unfortunately for her, though it is brilliant, and she was exiled for being kinda gross in the eyes of the Romans. Caesonia's mother's six marriages were seen as only marginally less revolting to senatorial Roman men who liked to glorify the image of a woman who remained devoted to a single man, even after he died, relentlessly praising women who maintained a chaste widowhood, while at the same time upholding laws that forced women to remarry two years after they were widowed. Caesonia was therefore already tainted by her female family members and thus tends to be described in books by men both ancient and modern as a low-class, fugly slut who deserves nothing but judgement. The kindest assessment I could find of Caesonia in modern books is that she looked 'severe... authoritative... and more mature than Caligula', where mature is a euphemism for old.[2] Suetonius and, bizarrely, Vespasian's pet Jewish historian Josephus, record that she was so aged and grotesque that everyone assumed she used love potions to win Gaius's heart. These love potions were then thought to have been what sent Gaius mad and made him so wicked. The best bit of these stories is not the overt misogyny, it's the unspoken assumption that the love potions worked.

In reality, Caesonia was remarkably well connected. Five of her six brothers were consuls, as were several of her mother's former husbands. Her uncle was great mates with Drusus II, son of Livia and brother of Tiberius. Entertainingly, her uncle committed suicide in 32CE when Tiberius got angry with him for allegedly implying that teenage Gaius was immoral. In the far future, Caesonia's niece would marry the emperor Domitian. Caesonia was of excellent stock. She just wasn't a 16-year-old virgin. Gaius adored her. He adored her even more when she had her fourth daughter and provided Gaius with an heir. Suetonius records that,

2. Barrett, 1989: 95

after marrying Caesonia, Gaius suddenly became monogamous – whatever that means in a Roman, slave-owning context – and that he thought she was so beautiful he paraded her naked in front of the troops to show her off. This little image, of course, has more to do with demonstrating that Caesonia was a shameless whore and thus Gaius was an effeminate, un-Roman ball of revolting for liking her than it has with any tangible reality, but it's useful to know that Gaius really, really liked her. He liked her so much, he did something that he'd not done for anyone but his sisters: he put her on some coins. This act came at the same time as he was performing obvious, public adoration of his tiny daughter, named after the late Drusilla.

This made the year 39CE a series of enormous red flags for Agrippina. For a brief moment, she had unparalleled access to the emperor, unparalleled influence and sanctity, the distinction of being the first and only of the siblings to have borne a next generation and her son would be the ideal choice for an heir to Gaius. Now, Gaius had taken a wife into his affections and she had the access and influence that even a sister couldn't rival. Caesonia had the influence that came with pillow talk and post-coital chat; she had the influence that comes with being the mother of a much longed-for heir and the potential to have many more. Caesonia, without a doubt, represented a threat to Agrippina's position and Nero. As soon as she had given Gaius a child, Nero stopped being the future of the Julio-Claudians and became a potential future rival instead. And this threat emerged at the exact same times as the laws that probably took down her mother and brother, and had certainly caused the deaths and downfalls of many others, were suddenly reinstated.

Agrippina, if she was the smart and aware woman I think she was, must have been concerned. Indeed, any person with power and influence should have been very worried indeed. Agrippina had another worry, too: her husband was probably quite ill. Domitius died in 40CE, with his cause of death being recorded as dropsy. Dropsy doesn't exist anymore; it's called oedema now and is the final symptom of various horrible long-term illnesses. It's a sign that death is imminent as the body retains fluids at an alarming rate and swells up. The stomach particularly becomes horribly swollen and quite awful to look at, so it was probably awful for Domitius to endure.[3] Whether or not Domitius had developed his dropsy yet isn't known, but he was certainly not a well man if dropsy was so close in his future. And the loss of a husband would open up a world of uncertainty for young Agrippina. Gaius would have been tasked with choosing a new husband for her, and father for her son, and he was not at this stage making brilliant decisions.

In September 39CE, things suddenly start moving very fast, in that way that simmering, long-standing tension which is invisible to the historian's eye can erupt into an avalanche of confused, disorientating action. The drama began with Gaius removing the consuls and smashing their *fasces* for reasons that are entirely unclear. At the same time, and for equally obscure reasons, Gaius fired and replaced the governor of Syria and the governor of Pannonia.[4] The Syrian governor was Lucius Vitellius, who will later be one of Agrippina's greatest political allies but in 39CE he had four legions who had enjoyed some great military successes under him. And no one knew better than Gaius how important the personal loyalty of legions was to anyone with an eye for power. Vitellius was merely fired, but Calvisius Sabinus in Pannonia got himself put on trial for allowing his wife to oversee the troops and committed suicide. Just prior to this, Gaius had recalled, tried and exiled the equestrian prefect of Egypt, Flaccus, also,

3. This kind of dropsy is now known to be the last stages of terrible renal failure or heart failure, but in the past it was thought to be a result of too much black bile (because the Romans adhered to the four humors theory of medicine where there are four types of coloured fluid that control the body and have to be kept in balance. It's quite adorable.) as a result of drinking too much water, drinking bad water, being too cold, haemorrhoids, liver problems and being bled too much. There were precisely three remedies for dropsy, as recorded by the medical writers Galen and Celsus, and one of them is bleeding the patient loads to get rid of the excess fluids. The others are pumping the patient full of diuretics in the hope that they'll piss out all the fluids, and covering them from head to toe in ox dung. I have no idea what the logic of the last one is.

4. Pannonia is the area that is now Hungary, Croatia, Austria, Slovakia, Slovenia and Bosnia-Herzegovina.

you'll be surprised to hear, for unclear reasons. During September, however, he decided that exile wasn't good enough and sent someone to kill Flaccus on his tiny island. Thus commenced a chase worthy of a Coen brothers' film in which soldiers pursued the hiding Flaccus around the little island, gradually cornering him and beating him to death. A bad omen for everyone.

All that happened during just a few weeks, and were dramatic decisions which put people on edge. At the end of September, Gaius quite suddenly took off in the direction of Germany with a ragtag band of unprepared escorts. The troop numbers in Germany were some of the largest in the empire, with eight legions being controlled at the time by two men: Gaetulicus in Upper Germany and Lucius Appronius in Lower Germany. In a deeply suspicious family connection, Gaetulicus was Appronius's son-in-law. In addition, it's likely that Gaetulicus took over command of Upper Germany from his own brother, meaning that the troops had inherited family loyalty. These are family ties enough that Gaius should have put a stop to it much earlier and everyone assumed he was going on some kind of visit to flex his power. On the way to Germany, though, Gaius stopped at Mevania (now Bevagna, in Umbria), at a family holiday home where Agrippina, Livilla and Lepidus (and presumably the rest of their families) were spending some time and, out of the blue, a message arrived at the Senate denouncing Agrippina, Livilla and Lepidus for immoral behaviour and stating that the three had been arrested. Gaius then, instead of returning to Rome with his now captive sisters, sped to Germany where Gaetulicus was also arrested and executed. On 27 October 39CE, sacrifices were made to celebrate the suppression of the 'wicked plots of Cn. Lentulus Gaetulicus against Gaius Germanicus' and were inscribed into the records of the Arval brethren.[5] The Senate, presumably confused, sent Claudius to Germany to congratulate his nephew. It is through this act that Suetonius came to record that Claudius

5. A college of priests in Rome based in a sacred grove. There were twelve priests. They are mostly known for their extremely detailed records relating to the emperors and their focus on praying for the imperial family.

congratulated Gaius for putting down the conspiracy of Lepidus and Gaetulicus in a completely unrelated biography. When Gaius returned to Rome, a hearing was held in which incriminating letters between Agrippina, Lepidus and Livilla were apparently read aloud. Lepidus was immediately executed, while the sisters were exiled. Agrippina was forced, in a bizarre parody of her mother and brother's more honourable pilgrimages, to carry Lepidus's ashes to her island. To commemorate the occasion, Gaius also dedicated three daggers to the temple of Mars the Victor.

What actually happened during those weeks, and whether Agrippina was genuinely involved in any plot, is entirely obscure. The one accusation that remains consistent across the source material, which manages to either avoid the subject of the plot altogether or be so confused as to be nonsensical, is that Agrippina was sleeping with Lepidus. Even Tacitus manages to slip this one in, when he lists the affair with Lepidus as the first of her sexual 'crimes'. He also states that this affair was specifically 'a means to power',[6] implying that he believed she had been involved in something political. If she was shagging Lepidus, and Lepidus was involved in some kind of convoluted conspiracy to take the throne with Gaetulicus's troops, then she must have known about it. Of course, all the sources (except Tacitus) claim that Lepidus was inexplicably maintaining some kind of three-way relationship with both Agrippina and Livilla, which is just a little too much like the exact same kind of masturbatory fantasy as Gaius fucking his sisters. It certainly makes no sense as a political tactic. Either the three of them had a very progressive polyamorous thing going on, which I wouldn't judge but also don't believe in, or the sex accusations are the kind of ridiculous filthy rumour that Romans liked to throw around whenever a man and a woman were seen standing too close together. Suetonius claims that the letters Gaius read aloud in the Senate proved that they were adulteresses who had combined sex and violence to plot against him,

6. Tacitus, Annals, 14.2. One (male) historian in the early 1980s took this opportunity to show how he saw Agrippina, stating that she was incapable of emotions but that pragmatism would entice her to shag Lepidus. Which is just disgusting.

and he had access to the imperial archives, but truthfully only three people know whose rude bits got bumped against whose, and they've all been dead for two millennia.[7] I do think, though, that there is evidence that Agrippina at least was bonking her former brother-in-law, and if she was bonking him then she probably was involved in some kind of plot. My best evidence is that Gaius made Agrippina carry Lepidus's ashes. This is a sharp bit of imagery on Gaius's part, contrasting the fallen Agrippina with her now glorious mother bringing Germanicus's ashes home and Gaius's own trip to repatriate their mother and brothers. The gesture is obviously meant to be an act of spite, which is fair; I can't say I'd be too kind to my sisters if I found out they were plotting to have me murdered. But the act of spite doesn't work if Agrippina isn't assumed to have had a relationship of some sort with Lepidus, and Livilla is not accorded the same punishment.

Let's assume, then, that Agrippina was having an affair with her brother-in-law while her husband was dying somewhere. Let's assume that Livilla was aware. And let's assume that the three of them were plotting, along with Gaetulicus in Upper Germany and Appronius in Lower Germany, to rise up against Gaius, who was their brother and best friend, and put someone else on the throne. It doesn't really matter who here. You can read another book for speculations about the inner workings of a conspiracy we know nothing about. What matters for us is that Agrippina thought she had a decent chance at a better life if her brother was dead, which is interesting. It might be that Caesonia was seen as a terrible threat to the influence and position that Agrippina and Livilla had. Even more likely, Caesonia and her fertile womb were a threat to Agrippina's son's future. There was every possibility that Agrippina's son would end up like Tiberius Gemellus rather than Tiberius if Caesonia kept having kids. The growing atmosphere of informants, distrust and uncertainty developing in Rome can't have helped. To be honest, in such a circumstance, had Agrippina not plotted and ended up accidentally brutally falling on someone else's sword because she sneezed on a coin with Gaius's face on, the historical record would write her off as an

7. Suetonius, Caligula, 24.

71

idiot for not seeing this as inevitable. Although it is perpetually interesting to me that modern sources on Agrippina have always portrayed her as plotting for her personal future, rather than trying to protect herself and her son from a potentially hostile atmosphere. I suppose women are only allowed proactive action if they are offenders rather than defenders. But Agrippina's way of going about protecting herself was her first act of true boldness and lack of concern for the conventions of Roman womanhood.

Until this point, our Agrippina had been the very model of a chaste, obedient and silent Roman daughter, wife, sister and mother. She hadn't said a word. She had been quietly married to a cousin, had a child, been glorified by her brother and has been entirely passive according to the historical record for the entire 24 years of her life. An empty female canvas, ready to have any number of ideals and images projected onto her by her brother. Until this moment, when she is revealed for a second as a real person who acted of her own accord. And she acted in the most dramatic way possible: banging her brother's best friend and trying to raise an army at the first sign of her brother going power mad. After she was sent off to her island, Gaius started firing even more people who were friends of the family, suggesting that Agrippina had also been sending out feelers among the political community. Seneca was the most prominent of these to go and his closeness with Agrippina was well known and long-lived. If Agrippina ever had any best friends, Seneca was one of them. But there weren't many executions or trials so the plot must have been in reasonably early stages when it was discovered. I imagine a horrifying scene in the Mevanian villa when it was revealed. A Poirot-esque showdown in the kind of grand and gorgeous villa you'd die to own. The emperor, surrounded by his guard, facing his sisters and best friend, brandishing letters. That moment of cold terror dripping down the spine as Agrippina realised that her gamble hadn't paid off. I imagine weeping, recriminations, a messy scene, on Gaius's part mostly. Because how could it not be. Gaius revered no one more than his sisters. He had made an entire empire, half the known world, swear allegiance to them. And they thought they might kill him.

The sisters were immediately stripped of everything and sent back to Rome to stand trial. As Gaius was present at the trial, we must assume that it happened after he came back from Germany so Agrippina must have sat in prison or house arrest for months, waiting to find out what her punishment would be. The trial was another humiliation. Like forcing her to carry Lepidus's ashes, Gaius reading Agrippina's personal (love?) letters aloud in the court was an act designed to publicly shame her as a slut. And it worked. The verdict of exile was only just better than death. Agrippina would be left on a tiny island with just a guard and some slaves for company, essentially erased from Rome and so erased from life. At the age of 24, Agrippina faced a long, long life of nothingness, separated from her son and waiting every day to find out if the emperor had changed his mind about her being alive.

The Exile

Agrippina's exile was carried out on the island of Pontia, now called Ponza, in the Tyrrhenian Sea. Ponza is about 70 miles off the coast of Naples, and where her brother Nero served out his exile. The island is tiny and volcanic, but Agrippina was not expected to live a life of total deprivation. The punishment was her being confined away from society; it was not to make her live in a cave. Archaeologists have found two villas on Ponza, both quite lovely. The biggest is almost ten acres in size, has a little theatre of its own, a solarium, glorious views and little grottoes full of fish carved into the rocks. She also had a significant staff of slaves and freed slaves to look after her: she wasn't expected to do her own hair. In short, she had the kind of life that many a quiet soul, or indeed writer, would long for. A private island off the coast of Italy. A luxurious home. Fish ponds. The sea to swim in and massive staff to wait on her and then bugger off when she was bored with them. A personal cinema. Given that we know Agrippina was a very strong swimmer (more on that later), I particularly like to imagine her taking a morning swim each day. Wading into the green-blue sea and swimming until her arms were tired and she could barely see the shore that was her prison anymore.

Which is, of course, what it was. Effortlessly comfortable Richard Branson fantasy though it is, a private island is only really fun when you choose to be there. When you can never leave, when your brother is occasionally sending you letters reminding you that he owns swords as well as islands, when you may never see your son ever again, and when you are a Roman woman, being on a private island – no matter how beautiful – is a torment. We know very, very little about what Roman exile was like, other than painful. We have just three reasonably well-documented exiles, in that they wrote while they were in exile and those writings survived. They are, obviously, all men: Cicero, Ovid and Seneca. Cicero experienced an older, less restrictive form of exile that allowed him to go wherever he wanted except Italy. He mostly hung out in Albania and Greece until he was allowed to come home and wrote letters to his friends and family in

Rome. His letters are dripping in pain, especially those to his wife, which are so tormented that you'd never know he abandoned her a few years later for a young girl in his guardianship, when he was almost 60. But on top of this, over and over, he also laments his humiliation. To be torn down from a position of power and strength, to be shown to be weak and to be thrown out of his own life. It was deeply, desperately humiliating. Even more than you can imagine because it was humiliation in a world where reputation was everything a person had. Agrippina was a proud member of a proud family. As we have seen, she was raised by a mother who understood that semi-divine blood flowed in their veins and that this blood entitled them to certain powers, powers that Agrippina almost had for just a minute. Powers that had been publicly ripped away from her as she was held up in front of the entire city as a traitor to her family and country. Her separation from her son would be unbearable, but her humiliation must have been equally as appalling to her.

Ovid and Seneca experienced the much harsher punishment that Agrippina received and were confined to specific places. Like Cicero, Ovid wrote letters from exile, but unlike Cicero he managed to come across as a massive complainer. Seneca on the other hand, being deeply stoic, refused to be sad about anything at all in writing, or indeed have any feelings. Instead – in a move that is either extremely patronising or admirable depending on your point of view – he wrote letters to his mum telling her to stop being sad because she was embarrassing him. Of course, Seneca got to go to Corsica which is lovely, but it is an unusual response to tell other people to stop being sad.

So how did Agrippina react to being exiled? To her humiliation and isolation? To her separation from her husband and son? Of course, we don't know. Undoubtedly she wrote letters. She probably wrote to Seneca given how friendly they were. Her husband Domitius was still around for a little while so she probably wrote to him but he died of his dropsy at some point in 40CE and their son was sent to live with her husband's sister Domitia Lepida so probably she wrote to her. Death would prevent letters getting to Domitius, though presumably someone wrote and told Agrippina that she was now a widow. I sort of assume that Gaius did. I feel that it would please him to break bad news. But did she write like Cicero, the broken-hearted family man, or Ovid, the grovelling urbanite, or Seneca, the Stoic? Of course, she wrote like none of them. She wrote like an imperial woman of a royal bloodline. And we have no idea what that might sound like.

In my heart, I am sure that she would never grovel to her brother. Especially not if she genuinely was plotting against him. She may have been broken-hearted about her separation from her husband and son, especially her child. She may have written letters like Cicero's full of tears and lamentation to her unofficially exiled husband and beloved son. I feel, though, that she would be closest to Seneca in her letters, no matter how she felt inside. She would be outwardly unaffected. Inside, the Agrippina in my heart would be deeply humiliated, but that humiliation would be felt as a burning white rage. When Agrippina returned from exile, she showed how she had been affected by this experience and we shall see how careful she was not to let this humiliation happen again, how carefully she controlled her surroundings. Certainly, Agrippina's letters would be full of pain, but, unlike the men whose letters survived, Agrippina's pain would be as painful for other people to touch as it was for her. This is one of the reasons why I am sure that she did not write her memoir while she was exiled, as some have suggested. Agrippina's memoir was a commentary of her life, her glorious life and the rise of her glorious family. Tacitus makes this much clear in his single sentence. It was the public statement of a public figure. It was not the complaining of an exiled woman.

Maybe, had Agrippina's exile lasted longer, things might have been different. I am sure that, after a couple of years, despair sets in for even the strongest of minds. Had Gaius lasted longer on the throne, Agrippina's fortunes would have been quite different. We'd barely even know her name. Luckily for her, and for us, on 24 January 41CE – a little over a year after Agrippina was exiled – a conspiracy led by the Praetorian Prefects Cassius Chaerea and Cornelius Sabinus successfully assassinated Gaius as he left the theatre, and then they murdered his wife and daughter. After two days of wrangling between the Senate and the Praetorian Guard – mediated by Herod Agrippa, who was the grandson of Herod the Great, aka Herod from the Bible who murdered all the babies, isn't that a fun fact? – the Praetorians finally defeated the Senate and Claudius was made emperor with everyone's full and in no way begrudging support. As with a great many emperors, Claudius's first acts were to reverse his predecessor's less popular ones and so Agrippina's uncle released her from exile. Agrippina was on her way back to Rome.

Chapter Three: Niece

The Return to Rome

The fact of her return must have been a huge relief for Agrippina as there were several days of chaos following Caligula's death and there were several ways that the situation could have ended in Agrippina being politely murdered on her island instead of being pardoned. This was what had happened to both her grandmother Julia the Elder and her Uncle Agrippa Posthumous when Tiberius took the throne, so there was precedent. But luckily for her, the world fell in the right order and she was recalled to Rome with her property reinstated and everyone was terribly sorry that she got exiled because of that plot thing and, as it turned out, they all agreed that her brother was a right bastard.

When Agrippina stepped back on Roman soil, she was about 25 years old and Nero was four. He had been living with his paternal aunt for a year, since his father's death, and hadn't seen his mother in maybe two years. Obviously, no source says a thing about reunion, but I hope it was lovely. Agrippina should have come back to Rome cowed and vulnerable, ready for a quiet life and perhaps chastened by her experience, but instead she came swaggering back like Liam Gallagher. She got off the boat from Pontia ready to swing for anyone who came near her. Her first act, in collaboration with her sister Livilla, was a massive middle finger to the Senate and to Claudius's palace. She exhumed the half-cremated, half-buried remains of Gaius from the gardens where he had been left, and held a proper full cremation and funeral for him which ended with his interment in the imperial Mausoleum of Augustus. This seems, to a lot of historians, to be a totally baffling move, partly because Gaius had literally just been brutally murdered and replaced for being a nightmare, which would suggest that people probably didn't want to think about him, and partly because Agrippina and Livilla had both been exiled by him. So why on earth were they making a big show of demonstrating their loyalty to an assassinated tyrant? Why were they antagonising Claudius like this? They could have just had a small, private funeral, or not done it at all. They could have interred Gaius in any other mausoleum or burial place that wasn't a huge monument in the centre of Rome. But they went as big and swaggering and public as possible. There is a selection of possible reasons for the sisters to make this their first action. My personal favourite is the idea that they did it to stop Gaius's ghost from haunting both the gardens where he was buried and the palace in which he was murdered.

This idea comes from a throwaway line in Suetonius, right at the end of his biography and in the same breath as the description of the murder of Gaius's wife and infant daughter, that Gaius's ghost haunted the gardens in which he was half-buried until his sisters completed the interment, and that 'something horrible appeared' in the palace in which he was murdered until it eventually burned down.[1] This is a useful glimpse at how enormously superstitious the Romans were. Ghosts and spirits of the dead creep through an awful lot of their religious practices, and Gaius wasn't even the only emperor ghost. Suetonius also has a good story about Augustus's ghost haunting his childhood nursery and beating up anyone who entered it without first being properly purified.[2] Which, to me, says an awful lot about dead Augustus's ego. But even at the more average level of society, there was a general cultural fear of evil spirits that needed to be pacified, and good spirits who should be commemorated in various religious festivals during the year. The idea of malevolent ghosts and spirits is not necessarily a left-field one for the Romans, and maybe the sisters were doing the Romans a favour by purging the angry spirit of Caligula.

There were also familial reasons why properly burying their murdered brother was a good move for Agrippina and Livilla: it was good *pietas*. *Pietas* was a uniquely Roman concept and is untranslatable into English. At its most base level, it meant duty to one's family and one's country. But this simple definition strips *pietas* of its depth and makes it sound a lot more optional than it was. *Pietas* also referred to various flavours of love, religious devotion, obligation, justice, gratitude, respect, compassion and friendship. *Pietas* also con-

---

1. Suetonius, Caligula, 59.
2. Suetonius, Augustus, 6.

tained a strong sense of natural law and natural justice, as in concepts which were perceived to be entirely fundamental to human behaviour. To act in a manner which undermined *pietas*, therefore, meant to act unnaturally. In this context, as the only living members of the family, Agrippina and Livilla had a strong obligation in both a religious, civic and familial sense (so far as those things could be separated) to lay their brother to rest properly with the correct rites and rituals. Failure to do this demonstrated not just a lack of familial duty and compassion for their brother but also a personal duty to Rome. It's quite possible that the idea of leaving their brother unburied was genuinely upsetting to Agrippina and Livilla, regardless of how they felt about his personality.

The other possibility, and the most likely one from a boringly rational perspective, is that it was good optics to bury Gaius because it's pretty clear from a bunch of sources that even though the Praetorian Guard and Senate absolutely loathed Gaius to his bones, the people and armies of Rome thought he was quite, quite wonderful. This is an underlying theme in almost all the surviving sources about Gaius's reign. Even Suetonius allows 20 paragraphs of his biography to record the good things that Gaius did and how popular he was among the plebeians. There is a slightly earlier source which covers the assassination of Gaius in enormous detail and that's Josephus's *Jewish Antiquities*.[3] Josephus describes Gaius showering the Roman people with gold and silver coins. And Gaius walking happily and comfortably among the people of Rome. And he also lets slip this little gem when describ-

---

3. Josephus was a Jewish scholar who was captured by the emperors Vespasian and Trajan when they broke the siege of Jerusalem and destroyed the Second Temple of the Jews. He was born Joseph ben Matityahu, but, like all great colonialists, the Romans didn't handle non-Latin names very well so they renamed him Titus Flavius Josephus. Now Josephus knew which side his bread was buttered and managed to save his own life when he was captured by telling Vespasian that the Messianic prophecies of the Torah (you know, the ones that predict the coming of a Messiah, the ones that form the fundamental foundation of Christianity) spoke of Vespasian himself coming from the east (Jerusalem) to conquer Rome and become emperor. Vespasian was apparently deeply susceptible to flattery and went for it, taking Josephus back to Rome with him. He became emperor and kept Josephus around forever. Josephus instituted himself as a semi-formal explainer of Judaism to the Romans and wrote a series of books about Jewish history for elite Roman readers. One of which was the Jewish Antiquities.

ing the assassination: 'it was no small danger they had occurred by killing an emperor who was honoured and loved by the madness of the people, especially when the soldiers were likely to make a bloody enquiry after his murderers.'[4] His narrative goes on to describe a private bodyguard and a citizenry who were appalled and incensed by the behaviour of a small group of senators. Josephus literally writes these people off as women, children, slaves and Germans (the worst barbarians), who were too stupid to know what was good for them. And so, the people and the soldiers formed a lynch mob and started hunting down and murdering people they thought were involved the assassination. A lot of people died. It took two days to sort everything out. All this happened just a few months before Agrippina and Livilla arrived back in Rome, and there was no way they were unaware of their brother's popularity with the army and people of Rome. Their decision to give Gaius a proper burial and inter him in the Mausoleum of Augustus alongside their glorious parents, their murdered brothers and their tragic sister can only be a reminder to Gaius's remaining fans that his family lived on. It was a reminder to the Roman world that they were still the children of Agrippina and Germanicus, still the great-grandchildren of Augustus and still the sisters of an emperor. It was a clear reinstatement of their power as Julians.

4. Josephus, Jewish Antiquities, 19.115.

The Situation in Rome

The political and cultural situation that Agrippina returned to was not a pretty one, which also potentially explains her powerful re-entry into the city. Rome had just experienced the first violent overthrow of a ruler for 80 years, since Julius Caesar had been stabbed at the foot of Pompey's statue in 44BCE. In 44BCE, however, the Senate was still officially the ruling body of the empire. By 41CE, this wasn't the case. Instead, there had been an extended period of tension, with no one officially ruling the state for two days while the Senate tried to put forward their own candidates for the Principate and Claudius gave each member of the Praetorian Guard 15,000 sesterces to support him.[1] Claudius and his heavily armed, well-paid supporters had obviously won, but almost no one was happy about it. The story still goes that Claudius was pulled out from hiding behind a curtain and forced to be emperor – and, if you believe that, I have a bridge in Brooklyn to sell you – but by taking the throne he had, effectively, enacted a violent coup of a legitimate ruler and somehow ended up with the backing of almost none of the most powerful families of Rome. He wasn't even connected to the Julian side of the Julio-Claudians except by the most tenuous of marital links. He made this worse by immediately executing most of the men who had put him on the throne and declaring – bizarrely – that the previous two days had not officially happened and were to be struck from the written record. I do wonder whether the Roman senators might have had more respect for him if he had just owned the military coup aspect of his reign. On top of the fact that he had stomped on the Senate with his private army, he also had almost no experience in the political world and a very tiny number of political allies. Until Gaius had taken the throne and made him consul at the age of 50, Claudius had never held a political position. He wasn't even a senator for much of his life. He was the fam-

---

1. That's 67.5 million sesterces in total. Not bad for a throne. It was, however, a significant jump from the 1,000 sesterces per soldier given by Gaius in 37CE as thanks for their support.

ily embarrassment. Suetonius preserves some cracking letters written by Augustus to Livia questioning whether Claudius was 'complete' or 'deficient in body and mind' and deciding to keep him hidden from the view of the Roman people in case they laughed at him.[2]

Claudius's major deficiencies seem to have been a stammer, a wobbly head, a limp and an inability to control his emotional responses so that he dribbled when he laughed and foamed at the mouth when he was cross.[3] Which makes him sound like one of those particularly drool-laden dogs and is why I will always imagine him as the charming but gross dog from the 1989 Tom Hanks comedy caper *Turner & Hooch*. One of the anecdotes told about his lack of emotional control concerns an early public performance to read aloud from his first book. As he was beginning, a very fat man entered the reading, sat down and broke the bench. Everyone laughed, the bench was replaced and the small commotion died down. Except Claudius didn't. He kept recalling the incident and laughing hysterically throughout the rest of his reading. Of all the anecdotes told about Claudius, getting the uncontrollable giggles during his first ever public performance is probably one of the most relatable, but it's told as if it were quite the scandal. And, if we're honest, if any of the minor British royals – Prince Andrew maybe – starting guffawing uncontrollably at the embarrassment of a fat person during a public appearance, we'd probably not take it too well either. Imagine the *Guardian* headlines. At another time, when he was emperor, Claudius was overseeing a Senate debate about butchers and wine sellers when he suddenly became overexcited by the thought of food and started telling pointless anecdotes about his favourite places to eat and drink when he was young. Again, relatable but unprofessional. The point of all this is that, like Gaius before him, Claudius had been kept far away from the Senate. Not because he was young, but because he was considered embarrassing. As a result, he hadn't spent any time in the Senate making deals, making friends, making compromises and establishing a base of support and experience in how the incredibly complicated, hypocritical

2. Suetonius, Claudius, 4.
3. Suetonius, Claudius, 30.

web of lies, counter-lies, obligations, deals and family entanglements that was how the Senate worked.

With almost no mates, Claudius retreated into his household as emperor and swiftly created the first proper Roman court, where literal employees of the emperor's personal household became incredibly politically important. Instead of power and access to the emperor coming through important political positions, like being Praetorian Prefect or consul, they now came through living in the emperor's house, being an ex-slave of the emperor's or being a member of the emperor's family. This was quite good news for Agrippina, because she was the emperor's niece, which meant she got to hang out in the emperor's house. But at the same time, and you'll remember this from every story you've ever heard about the court or any monarch, unofficial courts like this were unstable, and their constant fluctuations of power were obscure. People suddenly rose, and fell just as fast. Courts were dangerous. And the situation that Agrippina walked back into was particularly dangerous for her because she was the only member of the Julio-Claudian household who had a son, and Claudius had just had one of his own. In 41CE, Claudius was married to his third, disturbingly young, wife, the now notorious Messalina (we'll talk a lot more about her later) and Messalina had just given birth to their son Britannicus. Claudius had had a previous son by his first wife but he had died in his early teens after throwing a bit of pear in the air, catching it in his mouth and then choking to death on it. He also had a daughter by Urgulanilla, but he decided after accepting her that she was the product of infidelity and had her, aged five months, thrown naked on her mother's doorstep and disowned. He then had two further daughters, Antonia by his second wife Aelia Patina and Octavia by Messalina. But, as we know, daughters weren't worth much, so the birth of a son just 22 days into his reign was brilliant news for him and less brilliant news for Agrippina to come home to. Once again, just by existing, Nero was a threat.

Agrippina's situation was made even more unstable when, about 40 minutes after stepping back on Italian soil, and probably still with the soot from Gaius's funeral pyre in her hair, Livilla was exiled again. This time she was accused of adultery with Seneca.[4] No one can quite agree whose fault this is, whether Livilla really was knobbing Seneca or whether she was a genuine threat to the safety of the royal family. Messalina is always accused of sending her and Seneca away as annoyances because Seneca wasn't allowed to come home until Messalina was off the scene, but the situation was a little more complicated than that. Livilla was married to Marcus Vinicius, who was the Senate's pick in January of 41CE to be the new Princeps but lost out to Claudius and his swords and that does seem dangerous. It meant that Vinicius was known to have a significant power base and an imperial wife. And Seneca was almost certainly just a pain. But Livilla isn't our focus and it doesn't matter whether anyone slept with anyone. Our concern is Agrippina, who watched from the sidelines as she and her sister appeared to get back on safe, Italian ground only for it to be ripped away from Livilla immediately. Livilla was sent back to her island, where I like to imagine the staff were still packing up her furniture, and straight away Claudius sent a soldier to execute her.

This left Agrippina, at the end of 41CE, at 26 years old, as the only surviving member of her immediate family. She grew up with five siblings and they were now all dead. Four of those five died violent, bloody deaths on the orders of another family member. Agrippina and her son were the lone survivors of these blood-soaked decades. But they will not be alone for much longer.

---

4. You'll remember him from such letters as 'please stop having feelings in public, Mum, you're embarrassing me' which he wrote during this period of exile.

The Second Marriage

Upon her return to Rome, Agrippina is portrayed as getting straight on with the job of finding herself a new husband. She was married again by the end of the year 41CE. All our sources portray Agrippina herself as aggressively pursuing men to marry, which is an image I like because I am a product of my time and the image of a woman taking control of her own life and body pleases me. The Romans, however, and very much unlike me, reviled sexual aggression in women almost as much as they reviled murderers. Possibly more. You could make a knee-deep pile of all the poems Roman men wrote about women who dared to make the first move in a relationship and how extremely gross they were. From Ovid's command to 'hide it, don't look greedy at first sight' in his books of advice on the art of love,[1] to Juvenal's second-century CE sixth satire, a thrilling 661 lines bewailing how slutty and mean women are now (in the late first century CE), to Martial's epigrams from the fourth century CE that mock the idea of women who have an insatiable sexual appetite. The woman who approached a man, who had agency in her choice of husband or sexual partner, was a long-standing comedic stereotype for Roman men that was both hilarious, grotesque and terrifying. Much like the outrageous older woman in British comedy that is usually played by a man, or the Bridget Jones type of desperate lonely cat woman, this was a caricature of the kind of women that men are, basically, afraid of because they don't fancy them. Now I would perhaps be less likely to see the image of Agrippina pursuing men as part of this caricature if it weren't for a particularly theatrical and almost certainly invented scene that gets popped into her biography in Suetonius's life of Galba. Galba later became a terrible traitor, but got to be emperor for about 20 minutes for his traitorous efforts before being beheaded by Otho (he'll come up again later, too). Galba was enormously rich and famous and came from a highly distinguished family. There's a good story that he carried a copy of his family tree everywhere he went to show off his

---

1. Ovid, Ars Amatoria, 3.12.

credentials, which to me absolutely screams insecurity and was apparently considered to be weird enough for people to record it. As well as his own family connections, Galba had also been a favourite of Livia, so favourite in fact that she left him 50 million sesterces in her will. Don't you wish you had friends like Livia? He was also happily married. And yet the story goes that, upon her return to Rome, Agrippina homed in on Galba as a powerful, popular and extremely rich future husband, regarding his existing wife as but a minor obstacle. Suetonius claims that her sexy overtures to Galba were so public and obvious – despite Galba having no interest in her – that eventually Galba's mother-in-law stepped in, confronted Agrippina in front of a group of other women and warned her off with a slap. The idea of this happening in real life is both brilliant and ludicrous. First, because this is supposedly happening at the exact same time that Livilla was being exiled and murdered for improper sexual conduct, so if Agrippina was trying to marry the only other man who had been put up by the Senate to rival Claudius I'm not sure she'd have survived it. Secondly, the story is just too preposterous. We are supposed to believe that Agrippina stepped back into Rome and immediately, insatiably, began hunting Galba, this most upright and bluff of men, disrespecting the very institution of marriage to steal him away from his delightful wife. The image of the mother-in-law stepping in is just a little too on the nose. If you wanted to construct a story about a woman who everyone thought was a wicked slut and bad mother doing something that was wicked, slutty and upset mothers, this would be it. So as much as the image of Agrippina putting her foot in Galba's crotch at dinner parties and being slapped down by an old lady is very funny, I'm afraid I don't believe it for a second. It's much more likely that Claudius and his sidekicks identified Agrippina as a threat, and connection to her as a valuable asset, and so they married her to someone safe, trustworthy and unrelated to the imperial family.

The actual man who became Agrippina's second husband was a man with a name that would never fit on a modern form: Gaius Sallustius Crispus Passienus. He was only semi-related to her by marriage rather than blood, which was a serious step down from her first marriage.

He was her former brother-in-law, having been married to Domitius's sister Domitia Lepida. Passienus was very definitely a 'character', the kind that would either be really, really fun at parties or completely tiresome. He didn't come from a great birth family, but he'd done a bit of ambulance chasing and managed to get himself adopted by the incredibly rich but childless Gaius Sallustius Crispus in 20CE. He inherited a fortune, an ancient and famous name and all his adoptive father's clients and connections. He then went on through the reigns of Tiberius, Gaius and Claudius being very close to all three of them and surviving every regime change effortlessly. His primary skills were making hilarious bon mots, telling people how funny his own bon mots were, engaging in weird japes and being very unthreatening. He was everyone's sidekick. Passienus was famous for three things: marrying Agrippina, a couple of witty lines and being in love with a tree. The first witty line was made about Gaius, before he was emperor but as it was becoming clear that he would be next in line. Passienus remarked that the world would never know a better slave or a worse master! The second witty line came when Gaius was emperor, apparently having forgiven the former witty line. He and Passienus were out on a day trip and he asked Passienus if he had ever had sex with his own sister, as the emperor had tried out all of his. Passienus apparently had a quick mind and managed to wiggle his way out of either saying no, and potentially disapproving of the emperor's activities, or lying and outright saying something so terrible about his sister. His hilarious response was 'not yet!' If you take one thing away from this book, let it be that the Romans were absolutely tone deaf when it came to comedy. Yet more evidence for this truth comes from Pliny the Elder, one of Passienus's contemporaries, who records in a chapter titled 'Trees that Have Been Rendered Famous by Remarkable Events', that Passienus developed a fancy for a particularly nice tree in a particularly nice grove sacred to the goddess Diana, so much so that he spent time passionately kissing and embracing it and pouring wine over its roots.[2] One kind historian has described this as a manifestation of Passienus's 'lively sense of humour', though to me he sounds about as much fun as falling in a puddle.[3] Possibly, to other Romans,

2. Pliny the Elder, *Natural History*, 16.91

this was a very good joke indeed. Either way, his passion for the tree was enough to make the tree famous because Passienus was already famous enough.

Passienus had so far been a loyal companion and trustworthy ally of every emperor he had worked under. His aim in life seems to have been to be rich and famous enough to have a decent life, hang out near power and get statues erected with his face on, but not ever to look like he might want any kind of top job himself. He certainly spent a lot of time telling people that he was hilarious and brilliant but never sought political fame, only the social kind. Passienus would have been delighted by his hot new imperial wife. For him, marrying Agrippina was marrying up. Agrippina was a Julio-Claudian and was therefore much better than his previous, non-imperial wife. His marriage came at the same time as he got a nice couple of appointments which signalled that he was entering Claudius's inner circle. Plus, he eventually got a public funeral, which meant that Claudius really liked him. For Agrippina, however, this was a downgrade and I can't imagine her being anything other than furious with this choice. Of course, she was a woman, a valuable commodity, and who she married was not really up to her. As we saw with her mother, for example, members of the emperor's family could not just willy-nilly marry whoever they wanted whenever they wanted. They got married off. Agrippina was married off to a safe, boring lawyer with no imperial connections and a comparatively mediocre lineage. She was being given as a gift to an emperor's friend, and she was being tidied away. The marriage to Passienus wasn't insulting, but it was also not something to be particularly proud of. It was the kind of marriage that women who are not the daughter of Germanicus should have. Given that Agrippina and her sister had come blazing back into Rome like rock stars and started causing a stir, I don't necessarily judge Claudius for getting her out of the way with this marriage. Especially because, as soon as he was married to Agrippina, Passienus was sent off to be proconsul of Asia, with his new wife in tow.

Passienus was proconsul of Asia from 42 to 43CE, meaning that he was in charge of the administration of the province. As an assignment,

3. Barrett, 1996: 84.

Asia was a nice, careful balance for the new husband of the emperor's niece. In 27BCE, as part of his official consolidation of power, Augustus had divided the existing provinces into those controlled by the Senate and those controlled by the emperor himself. In essence, the emperor kept control of all the provinces that had dodgy borders, a large number of legions or a particularly important set of resources and only sent his closest friends to manage those ones. The senatorial provinces were those that were seen as safe, unthreatening and peaceful, and were mainly those that had a Mediterranean coastline.

Asia was a senatorial province and, despite having the same name as the continent, was actually pretty small. It took up the south-western third of modern Turkey and the associated Mediterranean islands, including Kos and Rhodes (and isn't the image of Agrippina in Faliraki a fantastic one?). It had no difficult borders, no hugely significant cities and, most importantly, no armies. So far, so boring. However, Asia was urban, rich and culturally lively, unlike quite a lot of other provinces. It had several good-sized and well-populated cities, including Ephesus, Pergamon, Miletus, Sardis and Aizanoi. As a place to live outside of Rome, it was fun in the good ways: all theatre and proper baths and good food. This urban culture made it the second best of the senatorial provinces, pipped only by Africa because in Africa the proconsul got a legion and to lord it over Carthage.[4] As a runner-up prize, Asia was okay, though. No one ever made their name in Asia, but it was a good, solid position to have and was a strong suggestion that the Senate liked you and the emperor didn't think you were a total dick. The evidence that Agrippina (and presumably Nero) went with Passienus and spent the year outside of Rome is primarily in the form of a statue erected in a temple on the Greek island of Kos. The statue recognises Passienus as the proconsul, and honours Agrippina as his wife. It was probably safer for Claudius to have Agrippina out of Rome in Asia where she couldn't cause too much trouble. And she didn't. She was so good and quiet that, if we didn't have that single inscription, we'd not know that she was there at all.

As the wife of the governor in Asia, her role was essentially dec-

---

4. The province of Africa was also much smaller than it sounds. It covered modern Tunisia and the topmost sliver of Libya.

orative and we are forced to assume that she stuck to this. Not that there was an awful lot for her to do in Asia that would cause trouble. Other women had been previously prosecuted for overseeing the troops or being involved in army duties that were seen as wildly, and slightly disgustingly, inappropriate, but Agrippina had no troops to parade or order about. Tacitus records a debate that occurred in the Senate under Tiberius in which a particularly pompous man named Caecina tried to institute a law banning governors from taking their wives out to their provinces with them, claiming that 'women are not only weak and easily tired: give them scope and they become hard, ambitious and scheming'.[5] In speech reminiscent (to me) of the *Brass Eye* sketch about gay men in the navy, Caecina claimed that women in the provinces attracted bad people, did bad business, got involved with malicious schemes and generally made the Romans look bad. His was not a majority opinion, as he was essentially asking the Senate to vote themselves into going abroad without their families for years at a time, but it is a tiny insight into the kind of thing that conservative Romans thought women were doing out in the provinces: hanging out with bad sorts, getting involved in schemes and corrupting their husbands. Agrippina, for everything else that was flung at her, got away without being accused of anything nefarious in Asia so we must assume that she did her duty as the wife of Passienus and the representation of the imperial family in the east, and that she was generally appreciated for it as they commemorated her. It is impossible to know whether this was a good year for Agrippina, or whether she longed for Rome. Were it me, I would be glad to be out of the city that was still working out its transition to Claudius's leadership and getting over the collective trauma of an imperial assassination.

Indeed, it turned out to be lucky for Agrippina that she had been dragged away from Rome because 42CE was the year in which there was an outright attempt to overthrow Claudius. One of Gaius's murderers, who somehow survived, teamed up with the general in Dalmatia and gathered quite a gang of senators and equestrians to support

5. Tacitus, *Annals*, 3.33.

him as he had a bash at taking the throne for himself. The revolt lasted five days, sort of collapsed in on itself, and then everyone who was in Rome and looked a little suspicious was put to death. Because we all know that killing your enemies is the best way to make sure that you don't have any enemies and definitely makes you a very popular leader indeed. Had she been in Rome, as a prominent member of the imperial family, Agrippina may well have come under the kind of blood-tinged scrutiny that no one wanted. But instead, she was safe and sound in Ephesus, once again watching the chaos from afar.

At some point in 43CE, Agrippina returned to Rome. There's no way of knowing when or what she did during that year. The law dictated that Passienus had to leave his former province within 30 days of his successor arriving, so, assuming that happened at the start of 43CE, there is a year or so missing from Agrippina's biography. Pure extrapolation suggests that they returned to Rome, based on two things. First, in January 44CE Passienus was given his second consulship, a particularly special honour that suggests he was back in Rome with Claudius. Secondly, during this year Passienus made Agrippina the primary heir to his fortune, a process that sort of required him to be in Rome. The reason that I have dated Passienus making his will to before 44CE is that he died. The exact date of his death is, as you're probably now bored with hearing, unclear. Historians have placed it anywhere between 43CE and 49CE, but I'm putting it here in early 44CE because of the slightly weird way in which his name is recorded in the consular *Fasti* for that year. The *Fasti* were lists of consuls that were used for dating in the Roman system. As we in the west date years as X years from the birth of Christ, Romans dated years by saying 'in the consulship of X and Y', and the *Fasti* existed as official records of who was consul when. Now normally in the *Fasti*, if one of the consuls in a given year had been a consul before, in recognition of that honour, his name would come first — he would be the X in the X and Y. As 44CE was Passienus's second consulship, we would expect therefore that year would be recorded as 'the year of the consulship of C. (Sallustius) Passienus Crispus and T. Statilius Taurus'. Except, completely uniquely, in the *Fasti* for 44CE Passienus is listed second. And a second inscription from May 44CE lists the consuls as T. Statilius Taurus and P. Pomponius Secundus. And the best explanation for these two things is that Passienus died very early in 44CE.

This left Agrippina widowed again, just three years after her first widowhood. She was a 28-year-old double widow, which was not hugely unusual for a Julio-Claudian woman. This time, however, she was suspected of killing her husband. With the benefit of hindsight, it definitely looks a tiny bit suspicious that Passienus made Agrippina the heir to his enormous fortune and then dropped dead of something. However, it doesn't seem that anyone at the time was particularly suspicious of her. Only one source explicitly states that 'Passienus was slain by the treachery of Agrippina' and that is a confused marginal note on a much later manuscript of Juvenal's fourth satire. This satire mentions a Quintus Crispus, and, at some point in the fourth or fifth century, a scholar attempted to add a helpful note to the margin of his manuscript explaining who Quintus Crispus was. Unfortunately, the scholar got a little muddled with his Crispuses and accidentally wrote a 115-word mini-biography of Passienus Crispus instead. While unhelpful for anyone writing about Quintus Crispus, this little note is the only source that mentions how Passienus died. It's worth mentioning that the note was written several centuries after Agrippina lived and died, and that it therefore saw her second marriage through the lens of her third. But still, the accusation lingers.

At the time of his death, Passienus was given an elaborate public funeral, a move that Claudius would have had to have signed off on and which gives a significant hint as to Passienus's high standing in Roman society. At a public funeral, Agrippina was once again on display to the whole city as a mourning wife. She walked with Nero behind the corpse of her husband through the streets of Rome from their home to the Forum. Her hair was uncovered and loose, while Nero's head was covered. In front of the corpse were actors wearing wax masks of the faces of Passienus's ancestors, those from his adopted family presumably. Behind the family were Passienus's slaves and freed slaves. In the Forum, someone stood at the Rostra and gave a eulogy for the deceased. We don't know who gave Passienus's eulogy, but they probably didn't mention the tree thing. They probably did mention Agrippina, though, as she was the most glorious thing that ever happened to him. After the eulogy, the procession took the body out of the city walls and down the Appian Way to where Passienus's tomb had been already built. There he was cremated on a pyre.

It is disappointing that we have no way of knowing how Agrippina might have reacted to the death of Passienus, how she might have felt watching the flames rise and consume him. We don't know whether her marriage was happy, or whether she loved him or even liked him, or whether she mourned him. We don't know if she was indifferent to him or hated his guts and was glad to watch him burn. Maybe the anonymous late antique scholar is right and she manipulated him into making her his heir and then poisoned him and all she felt as the fire rose was satisfaction at an Agatha Christie-esque murder gone right. Whatever she felt, the consequences were financially fantastic for her, and the funeral was public so she didn't even have to pay for it. As Passienus had no children, other than any legacies he might have left to friends and clients Agrippina inherited his entire massive fortune and several very nice estates, including one by the Tiber. Because this money was her money, she could spend at will, unlike the money Nero inherited from Domitius, which she controlled but couldn't legally do anything with because she had to hold it intact for Nero when he came of age. That basically meant that she could live in the houses, but she couldn't spend any of the money on nice dresses or bribes. The money from Passienus, on the other hand, could go entirely on dresses, jewels, stuffed quails and honeyed wine if she felt like it. Agrippina never really had a taste for extravagance, though. Possibly because she grew up as part of a royal family, her prestige and status came not from money but from the blood of Augustus and her name. Instead, for Agrippina, money meant power. But again, of course, that's speculation because as soon as Passienus dies and Agrippina is no longer attached to a man, she vanishes from the record completely. For five years.

The Emperor's Niece

It was during these years that Claudius did some interesting things. His first act, and probably the most significant of his reign (for those of us who are English anyway), was to invade and conquer the island of Britannia, or at least some of the bits that are now called England. The invasion took place in 43CE and was the most significant military action since Augustus had closed the doors of the temple of Janus in 29BCE and announced that the *Pax Romana* was now in force. It is an invasion that Suetonius dismisses, with excellent scorn, as a 'campaign of little importance',[1] while strongly suggesting that the main reason that no leader had bothered with Britain since Julius Caesar was not because of all the civil wars and then Augustus's prohibition on expanding the empire's borders, but because it was a cesspit. It's a point that the Romans would return to about Britain. Repeatedly. On his return to Rome in 44CE, Claudius was extremely impressed with his own success and threw himself a triumph to celebrate his excellence as a military leader and his brilliant conquest. We know that Claudius sat in his triumphal chariot, and that Messalina followed behind him in a carriage, probably with Octavia and Antonia and the about-to-be-renamed Britannicus. Agrippina would have been there, part of the wider imperial family, in a seat of honour watching the parade, probably rolling her eyes. The triumph was held in the early months of 44CE but perhaps Passienus was already dead and so Agrippina wore dark clothing, a dark mantle covering her head. Perhaps she sat by Vitellius, the senator who would become her most loyal ally, with six-year-old Nero between them in his child's tunic.

Wouldn't it be wonderful to know what she thought at that moment, a widow for the second time, watching weird Uncle Claudius be paraded as a military hero? Whether she felt hilarity at the sheer ridiculousness of a man primarily famous for his dribbling and limp to be given the highest military honour of the empire, or disgust at that image. Like her mother, Agrippina had a strong sense of the

---

1. Suetonius, Claudius, 17.

power of the blood that ran in her veins, and I wonder if she felt that blood pulse a little stronger as Claudius ascended the steps of the Capitol on his knees in a show of extreme traditionalism that conveniently covered his limp. He was supported by his sons-in-law: Gnaeus Pompeius Magnus and Gaius Silanus. The former was the great-grandson of Pompey the Great, the latter shared with Nero the honour of being the great-great-grandchild of Augustus. The honour they were given as the future husbands of Claudius's daughters (who were both still children), and as integral, visible parts of Claudius's triumph while Nero sat at the sidelines must have burned at least a little. Everything visible was a message, and this message told the Roman viewers what the next generation of emperors would look like if Claudius had his way. And Agrippina would not be part of it.

If Agrippina schemed, in that moment, to find a way to wrestle that throne from those men whose fingertips were brushing it now, she did it very quietly indeed. She made absolutely no move for five years. Her complete disappearance from the sources at this time is perhaps in itself a tiny hint as to what she was doing, because the emperor's wife at the time was Messalina, and Messalina is generally presented as spending the early years of Claudius's reign as waging a war against every other woman and child who might have posed a threat to her and her son, no matter how slight. And Agrippina was by far her greatest rival. Agrippina had a better claim to the throne through her relationship to Augustus than either Messalina or Claudius, and she had the enormous reflected popularity that came with being the daughter of Germanicus. Her son had a better claim to the throne than anyone else alive, except perhaps Gaius Silanus who was safely betrothed to Messalina's daughter. So why didn't Messalina attack Agrippina as she did essentially everyone else? Even though Tacitus tells us that Messalina always loathed and feared Agrippina? The best possible answer to that question is that Agrippina wasn't in Rome. She had several houses and estates in Italy that she could happily and safely live in, and things that happened outside of Rome literally never got written down unless they were a battle or Tiberius's sex grottos. And why would she be laying low in Padua or Tusculum? Because of Messalina.

In the evolution of Roman empresses, Messalina laid a lot of the groundwork for Agrippina and is herself remembered as a spectacular transgressor of social and cultural norms. By the reign of Domitian at the end of the first century CE, Messalina was remembered in Juvenal's horrible misogyny-fest of a sixth satire as a literal prostitute who secretly worked in a brothel and would only return to the palace when forced to: 'her taut sex still burning, inflamed with lust/Then she'd leave, exhausted by man, but not yet sated'.[2] Nice. Messalina loomed large over the first years of Claudius's reign, and it was the manner of her downfall that paved the way for Agrippina to step in and take the reins, so I'm going to take a brief detour here and have a look at her.

Valeria Messalina was Claudius's third wife (the other two I mentioned earlier) and as usual she was a member of the family. Her mother was Lepida, the sister of Domitius Ahenobarbus and therefore Agrippina's sister-in-law. Her maternal grandmother was the elder Antonia, her maternal great-grandfather was Mark Antony and her maternal great-grandmother was Augustus's sister Octavia I. Messalina's father was Marcus Valerius Messalla Barbatus, whose grandmother was also Octavia I. Octavia I had two husbands. Her first was Marcellus, with whom she had three children. The youngest daughter of Octavia I and Marcellus was Messalla's mother. Octavia I's second husband was Mark Antony, with whom she had two daughters, Antonia the Elder and Antonia the Younger. Antonia the Elder was Lepida's mother. So, Messalina had the same great-grandmother on both sides, Octavia I, but different maternal and paternal great-grandfathers. Antonia the Younger was Claudius's mother and Messalina's great-great-aunt, and so husband and wife were first cousins once removed. This should tell you something about the age gap between them. Confused? I'm sorry. They're a terrible family. At the beginning of this book, I called them a horrible clusterfuck and this is why. Please go and look at the family tree because it will help. For Agrippina, Messalina was her niece by marriage, and Nero was Messalina's

2. Juvenal, Satire VI, 129–30.

first cousin. I am consistently amazed that there weren't more birth defects in these kids to be honest. The gene pool for this family was tiny.

The year of Messalina's birth is unknown; it was perhaps somewhere between 17 and 20CE, meaning that when she married Claudius in 39 or 40CE, she was aged between 18 and 21; Claudius was in his early fifties and just finishing his first ever stint as consul. Being married to Messalina was a good sign for Claudius, whose previous wives had been decent women from outside the family. Not embarrassing matches, but not exactly marriages that promised great things. Claudius and Messalina's marriage would have been approved, if not arranged, by Gaius and was a sign that Claudius was on the up and up in the imperial esteem because he was being tied more securely to the Julian side of the family. It's quite possible that Claudius divorced poor Aelia Patina because he had been offered a better wife. Messalina was the more prestigious wife than Aelia Patina because there was no family with higher status than his own, so marrying a cousin was the best possible marital achievement for both Messalina and Claudius. This was inner circle stuff. This was probably Messalina's first marriage, as (contrary to popular belief) late teens was an average age of marriage for women.[3] I do wonder how she might have felt confronted with her limping middle-aged cousin on her wedding day, but I assume that at least a part of her felt grateful to have a match of decent status. Claudius wasted no time with his young, hot wife and Messalina was knocked up within a few months of their marriage. Her daughter was born just about a year after the wedding and was named Octavia II as a nice, extremely unsubtle, nod to Messalina's Julian heritage and blood relationship to Augustus – a relationship that Claudius himself lacked and often felt the lack of. Another year later, a son was born and he, being more important, was given a good solid Claudian name: Tiberius Claudius Caesar Germanicus. No one remembers this, though, as two years later Claudius conquered Britannia and renamed his kid Britannicus. One of the few upsides of being a girl in the imperial family was that your

3. Princesses like Agrippina and her mother are a deviation from the norm because of their role as peacemakers and useful connections for the emperor.

name wasn't changed every ten minutes to make a propaganda point. It's a small one but as women we take what we can get sometimes.

Britannicus was born three weeks after Claudius became emperor, when Messalina was between 21 and 23 years old. Messalina remained Claudius's wife for the rest of her life, until she was executed in 48CE aged between 28 and 31. She was so terribly young for Claudius's entire reign, and that is very much worth remembering. Until Messalina there had been no proper emperor's wife since Augustus's death in 14CE pushed Livia into the mother role. Livia had always acted as a proper Roman gentlewoman in her time as the emperor's wife and mother. She remained publicly invisible as much as possible and carefully maintained her influence through charitable work, the financial sponsorship of certain individuals and gentle, demure advice given to her husband behind the scenes. Livia was always the woman behind the emperor, and never the woman next to him. She lived in quite a different time to Messalina. An entire generation had passed since Livia and Augustus, the Principate had evolved, become embedded and developed its own norms, and there had been no imperial women in-between to carve a path through changing times. Tiberius had no wife for his entire reign, and Gaius changed wives more quickly than he changed shoes. Caesonia might have been the first, but her horrible murder cut things short. Messalina, then, was suddenly and unwittingly thrust into a role that essentially did not exist before her and for which there were no rules. It's with this in mind that we should look at Messalina, though almost no author has had a jot of empathy for the poor girl who went from being a carefree teenager to being a mother of two and the most powerful woman in the world within 24 months.

In the popular narrative of Claudius and Messalina, Claudius is portrayed as a bumbling fool, distracted by pointless tasks, the pointless invasion of Britain and pointlessly adding letters to the alphabet, while Messalina is a violent sex-mad whirlwind, a failure of appropriate womanliness, who regularly had people killed just because they wouldn't shag her or because she wanted things they had, like their gardens. While Messalina used the power of the state to pursue her passions for sex and killing, and Claudius was pissing about in libraries and on grim, rainy islands, the actual empire was being run by ex-slaves. Worse, Greek ex-slaves. Specifically, Claudius's three best mates who he used to own as property, the freedmen Pallas, Narcissus and Callistus. These men were, respectively, in charge of the imperial treasury, the emperor's correspondence and the justice system and are portrayed as the true power behind the throne. Rather like Sir Humphrey in *Yes Minister* but with even more job security.

However, it is Messalina who is at the centre of Tacitus's narrative about the first years of Claudius's reign. At least, we assume so, because the first six years of it are completely lost. We get to pick up Tacitus's story in 47CE, bang in the middle of a story about Messalina prosecuting a guy because he had previously slept with a woman who was trying to seduce an actor that Messalina wanted to sleep with. So, Messalina accused both the man and woman of adultery and got them out of the way so she could make a move on the actor without any competition. This weird personal drama made public policy serves as a warm-up for the affair that led to Messalina's execution, where Messalina allegedly married her boyfriend Gaius Silius and thereby technically divorced Claudius without telling him. This was perceived to be an attempt by Messalina and Silius to overthrow Claudius somehow and so both were put to death without trial. Tacitus's telling of the story is both highly theatrical and implausible, but is a great read. It switches back and forth between Messalina partying at her illegal wedding reception and Claudius learning about the wedding, then hiding in the praetorian camp.

The main actors in the drama are the three freedmen, one of whom made the official decision to execute Messalina, while both Messalina and Claudius are portrayed as stupid, pathetic and passive. Claudius's only response upon being told that his wife had married someone else was to beg that his freedmen assure him that he was still emperor. Messalina for her part was described a classic weak woman. As soon as her mates heard that Claudius knew about the marriage, they abandoned her and she was left with just her mother in some gardens trying, and failing, to kill herself. She is shown being too morally weak to even stab herself effectively as a good Roman would do. Instead she was murdered by a soldier on the orders of a freedman. This story as

Tacitus tells it is not a truthful account of events, but a moral lesson about Claudius being a weak and pathetic emperor, incapable of controlling his own household let alone the state and empire. Messalina is collateral damage in this narrative, painted as a teenage nymphomaniac in order to make her husband look bad.

This brings us back to what we said at the start of this book: women don't exist in political narratives unless they are telling us something about the men they represent. Messalina doesn't really exist anymore in her own right as I exist or you exist. She exists exclusively as a part of Claudius: a representation of certain aspects of his masculinity and leadership. In the same way, the freedmen don't really exist as individuals in their own right; they were not citizens of Rome; they used to be the literal property of the imperial household and they remained wholly dependent on Claudius for their livelihoods. Like Messalina, they are in the sources as mere extensions of Claudius and demonstrations of his failures and weaknesses.

As emperor, Claudius was the head of the Julio-Claudian family, its *paterfamilias*. The job of a *paterfamilias* was to be responsible for the behaviour of everyone in his power. Claudius sucked at that. And so, what we get from our sources are these incredible (quite literally incredible, unless you are really quite gullible) stories about Messalina's time in power that include Juvenal's tale of the empress working as a prostitute. And his second story about Messalina in which he claims that she threatened to kill Gaius Silius if he didn't marry her. Or the stories from Tacitus that Messalina had Appius Silanus murdered based on a dream that she made up,[4] and poisoned Marcus Vinicius because he wouldn't shag her. Or Pliny the Elder's throwaway remark, in a chapter of his *Natural History* about how different human sexual behaviours are from the animals, that Messalina once competed with a well-known prostitute to see who could shag the most men before tapping out. Messalina won with 25 'embraces'; the prostitute's score is not recorded.[5] Pliny the Elder is the only other source to admit to reading Agrippina's memoir and so a little part of

4. Appius Silanus was another of Domitia Lepida's husbands. She had really bad luck with them.

5. Pliny the Elder, Natural History, 10.83.

me likes to imagine that this story came from Agrippina. I enjoy the image of Agrippina writing petty, spiteful little vignettes about her rival being a literal prostitute even when I know it's unlikely. My personal favourite story about Messalina comes from Cassius Dio, writing 150 years after Messalina's death, in which he states that Messalina tried to seduce the actor Mnester (the same actor she had a woman killed for in Tacitus) and he turned her down. So, Messalina went to her husband to complain that she was not being obeyed and persuaded Claudius to have a little chat with Mnester. Claudius did as he was told, unaware of the true nature of the command Mnester had refused, and summoned the actor. Claudius solemnly ordered the actor to obey Messalina and, thus, Claudius was tricked by his wicked wife into commanding another man to fuck her.

In modern writing about Messalina, the sort that isn't really bad porn or trashy historical novels, she now tends to be portrayed as a ruthless woman determined to ensure her son's place on the throne after Claudius. Most biographies of Claudius take this line, painting Messalina as a woman willing to use sex to smooth her son's passage to power. That argument means you don't have to ignore any of the good stories you see, and means that you get to fetishise female sexual behaviour and maintain patriarchal ownership of it by claiming that she didn't do it because she liked it; she did it because all she had that was of value was a hole to fuck. This is the exact same story that is told about Agrippina, and all women who brushed power, from the Romans to the Tudors, because it maintains the narrative that women are powerless in everything, including sex. And so it was that Messalina died in ignominy and the people responsible for her legacy were the people who killed her, while her children were never in a position to save her reputation and would only have painted her as a virgin anyway. Being a woman near power is lose-lose most of the time.

Regardless of whether she was a little sex maniac with a bloodlust, or a flint-eyed mother protecting her son's future, or a woman terrified of being murdered in her home like Caesonia, Messalina made the atmosphere at Rome extremely uncomfortable for members of the imperial family. One potential insight into how odd and uncomfortable Rome was during the early years of Claudius's reign is seen in Suetonius's life of Vitellius, who was emperor for eight months in 69CE before being overthrown by Vespasian. Suetonius tells us that Vitellius's father Lucius, in order to curry favour with the imperial family, begged Messalina to give him one of her shoes. He then proceeded to carry it around under his toga, occasionally taking it out to kiss it. Not that Claudius is off the hook either. To Claudius, Lucius Vitellius would cover his head and prostrate himself on the floor when they met, as if the emperor were a living god. Unlike Tiberius and Gaius, who were revolted by such behaviour, Claudius seemed to rather enjoy this. The fact that these acts were recorded perhaps shows that they were unusually extreme but no one seems to have stopped Lucius from enacting his foot fetish, and he became a close friend of Claudius. So, Agrippina probably laid low, stayed out of the city and protected herself and Nero. She watched the murder of her brother from her island, she saw the Dalmatian revolt go down from Asia, she noted the purges after each and the anger and the vigilance and the trials and the consuls lying prostrate in front of her unpredictable uncle and his scared wife, and realised that Rome was not safe for the daughter of Germanicus. If we assume, for the sake of simple argument, that both Agrippina and Messalina were two women with the same overall plan for their children, we can understand why one had to die. In the small Roman court, they are basically Harry Potter and Voldemort.

Messalina and Agrippina

The surviving manuscripts of Tacitus's narrative kick in again for 47CE, which coincides conveniently with Agrippina's return to Rome. The occasion for her return was the celebration of the Secular Games, and the appearance of her and Nero in public caused almost as much of a stir as the games themselves. The Secular Games were only supposed to be held once every *saeculum* as a celebration of Rome's founding. A *saeculum* was the perceived longest possible lifespan of an individual person and was either 100 or 110 years long, depending on who you asked. The purpose of the Secular Games was to celebrate Rome lasting past the end of one whole generation of human life and into another. They were, quite literally, a once in a lifetime event. Except that the calculation of a *saeculum* was open to interpretation and the idea of linking oneself to the foundation of Rome was a bit too attractive for too many emperors so the games ended up being held pretty randomly, whenever an emperor felt insecure. Augustus had held them in 17BCE, and Domitian held them again in 88CE, which is 64 years before and 41 years after Claudius respectively. Both Claudius and Domitian had to torment some numbers a bit to come up with a good reason to hold the games. Entertainingly, Tacitus admits that he was personally responsible for the recalculation of dates that allowed Domitian to hold the games in 88CE, so his open scorn for Claudius's tormented calculations is especially funny. Claudius at least tortured the numbers in such a way that they eventually made sense (he used the 753BCE date for the foundation of Rome, but, where Augustus had used 110-year *saeculi*, Claudius used 100-year lengths, and so he was able to claim that 47CE was the 800th anniversary of the city). Tacitus helped Domitian out by reverting back to Augustus's 110-year lengths, and then declaring that it was fine to hold the games six years early even by that calculation. It's confusing and ridiculous. Don't worry about it.

What you need to know is that, despite this ridiculousness, the Secular Games were still a very big deal. They held a lot of symbolic importance for the Romans and so Agrippina attended. Probably she returned to Rome because Nero had been invited to take part in the big opening ceremony in which the young sons of all of Rome's greatest, oldest and most prestigious families performed a re-enactment of the battle of Troy. Nero, aged ten, and Britannicus, aged six, were the stars of the show. Except Nero stole the limelight from his cousin, and Agrippina stole the heart of the Roman public from Messalina. Their appearance delighted the public, who cheered and waved and made their adoration of Germanicus's sole remaining daughter and grandson clear. Crowds went wild for Nero and openly expressed their sympathy for Agrippina's difficult life: her entire family dead, her two husbands dead, her retirement from imperial life because of Messalina's attacks. She appeared as Rome's tragic princess. Adorable, fatherless Nero only added to the pathos. Rome's hearts broke for them both. Suetonius claims at this point that Messalina was so jealous of Nero's popularity over Britannicus that she attempted to kill him while he slept. However, as the assassins approached Nero's bed, a snake darted out from under Nero's pillow, frightening them away. Agrippina was so delighted with this proof of her son's divine protection that she had the snake skin encased in a gold bracelet that Nero wore as a permanent reminder of his destiny. When that open attempt to kill Nero had failed, Messalina set her allies up to plague Agrippina with endless, vexatious legal cases, each designed to exhaust and frighten her until one got her successfully executed or exiled. Agrippina, though, wasn't tired or financially depleted. She took the blows stoically and accepted Messalina's hatred. She had survived Tiberius and Gaius and she wasn't that afraid of Messalina yet. She waited the empress out.

Agrippina managed to shake off the accusations, what Tacitus calls her persecution, in part because of her enormous popularity with the people of Rome, the armies and the Senate as a result of her father's reputation, which meant that no accusations were taken seriously, and because Messalina fucked up really badly just at the same moment that she should have been gunning hard for Agrippina. In a genuinely baffling and extraordinary move, Messalina waited until Claudius went out of town for a night and then bigamously married her boyfriend, Gaius Silius. More than any other crisis of Agrippina's life, the pseudo-marriage of Messalina and Silius is a headscratcher. Even Tacitus seems confused by it. He absolutely cannot understand how the couple managed to hold a wedding, an extremely public event, an event that includes a parade, in a city where people literally pooed next to each other. It's so baffling to him, and he assumes to his readers, that he feels compelled to address it. I know this sounds preposterous, he says, I know it seems impossible that anyone would think that they could keep a wedding a secret in Rome, but it happened: 'I have added no touch of the marvellous,' he reassures his readers.[1] Tacitus's suggestion is that Messalina had basically lost her mind because she got bored with normal adultery. A kind of marital extreme sports. Juvenal, bless him, suggests that Messalina was driven by lust, while Silius was just a victim of his own extreme handsomeness, forced into a marriage he never wanted. Modern scholars are oddly unwilling to accept that Messalina and Silius maybe just really liked each other – I think a lot of them don't really believe that the imperial family had feelings. Instead, they have tied themselves into knots trying to work out what Messalina's great plan was. The general consensus is that the pair planned to kill Claudius, have Silius adopt Britannicus and smoothly take the throne. Quite why Messalina thought this would give her more power is unclear. Truthfully, the incident is baffling and my best conclusion is that possibly Messalina just wasn't very clever. Not in a bad way, just in a total inability to plan more than one step ahead way. She had never had a plan stronger or more long term than 'identify threat, eliminate threat' and, whatever she was thinking when she married Silius, she didn't have a contingency plan.

Obviously, Claudius heard that his wife had married someone else within hours of it happening – because of course he did – and he sped back to Rome where he proceeded straight to the praetorian camp to hide behind his private army. Claudius was about as useful as a brick in a political crisis, and his Praetorian Prefects were so afraid that they both legged it and pretended that they'd not got any messages. So Claudius's freedmen stepped up and took the opportunity to get rid

1. Tacitus, Annals, 11.27.

of a woman who had turned out to be a total liability. In particular, Narcissus handled things, took charge of the Praetorian Guard, told a consul off for defending Messalina, and gave the order to kill her before Claudius remembered that he fancied her and let her off. In the bustling praetorian camp, while Claudius rocked and moaned in a corner, the Greek ex-slave handled things efficiently, shut down any attempts to question Claudius's reign and maintained the status quo. Messalina died, weeping on her knees in a garden as her mother, Lepida, held her. Like so many of her extended family, it was the pointy bit of a praetorian sword that ended her life. And Claudius almost instantly forgot her. Or at least showed no outward signs of mourning, even in the face of his weeping children; a reaction that would have been lauded as perfectly stoic in anyone but Claudius. He did not weep, but he did rage, taking out his fear and shame on men. He put to death a collection of equestrians, praetorians, senators and poor Mnester the actor. Anyone who was at the wedding party or who knew about it was removed. He became, reasonably, even more swivel-eyed in his terror of plots.

Although Messalina had been schtupping Silius for months, the collapse of her power and her death took less than a day, and it created a vacuum in Claudius's life, a vacuum that Agrippina ended up filling. We have no idea what Agrippina was doing while the wedding and crisis meetings were taking place, though I like to imagine her reclining in her nicest house with her pals – maybe even Silius's first wife, Julia Silana, who we know was a cousin of hers – as messengers ran in and out delivering updates. The day would have been a particularly exciting and tense one for Agrippina; one that could have extremely grave consequences if it went wrong. If somehow Messalina and Silius had managed to kill Claudius and wrestle control of the Praetorian Guard and the Senate into their hands, Agrippina and Nero would have been first on the list of people to be purged in the aftermath. There would have been no accusations or sneak attacks if this happened; just a soldier with a sword kicking in the door. The freedmen Narcissus, Pallas and Callistus knew that they would receive the exact same treatment and at least one of them was already Team Agrippina. This was Pallas, who would turn out to be a great ally of Agrippina's, and he may well have been communicating with her about what was going on. So there would be a great deal of fear in Agrippina. But at the same time, if Messalina failed, if Narcissus and Claudius won, virtually every threat to Agrippina's life and happiness would be eliminated. Without Messalina, there was no one who could truly rival her in the imperial family. She was, therefore, a player in the double-or-nothing gamble that Messalina started. She would win or lose everything. I wonder sometimes if she was afraid. This was the third time in her 32 years that a crisis had threatened her life, where she had to wait to see if she would live through the night or not, whether her son would see another day. Did she cling more tightly to life now? Did she hold Nero close and pray to a god, to her ancestors, to protect them? Or was she more arrogant than that? Maybe she sneered at Messalina's bizarre attempt at a coup, maybe she drank and laughed and ate sweet treats as she watched the woman who hated her collapse. Whatever the answer, I'm willing to bet that she sent Lepida a deeply unconsoling letter of condolence when it was all over.

The Aftermath

The immediate aftermath of that day was chaotic and horrible. Messalina and eight men were executed without trial and the Senate declared a *damnatio memoriae* — the official erasure of her memory. This is what had happened to Agrippina the Elder previously and it meant that Messalina's name and image were scrubbed from statues, inscriptions and even coins. She was erased from the official narrative of Claudius's reign as if she had never existed and her children just sprang from nowhere. Tacitus intones on all this, with characteristic gloom, that the reaction was just, but the consequences were grim.

The consequences Tacitus is referring to here are Agrippina and Nero. From this point on, Tacitus tells a story in which Nero's reign and its eventual collapse were inevitable, with Agrippina at the centre of that story. Now this is good news for us because it means that, between now and her death, there's not much we don't know about what Agrippina was supposedly up to. The bad news, of course, is that the Agrippina in the texts is not a real woman. She is a representation of the kind of general moral decline that allows women to become public figures. But we cling onto what we have and try to make the best of it.

The first step in this story is Agrippina marrying Claudius. Claudius's desperation to marry again makes Agrippina's remarriage after her exile look positively sloth-like: he managed to get the law changed and marry his niece within three months of Messalina's death. There are various reasons offered for this. Tacitus, with pleasant naiveté, suggests that Claudius was unable to stomach celibacy; as if he hadn't spent the previous chapter reeling off the names of Claudius's favourite concubines.[1] Claudius was the emperor of the Western world; he had many problems but getting his dick wet wasn't one of them. Tacitus's other suggestion is that he just couldn't live without

---

1. Calpurnia and Cleopatra, in case you were interested.

being under a wife's thumb, which is just a strange thing to say. I'm pretty sure any woman could dominate him if that's what he liked. Certainly, his freedmen did. The terribly serious scholars of the world have taken more of a *post hoc, ergo propter hoc* approach to the whole thing and decided that because he ended up marrying Agrippina, he must have been looking for a wife with Agrippina's useful qualities. Such an approach chooses to assume that these qualities were the only logical ones: she's part of the Julian family, she's got good lineage, she helps legitimise his reign and he can connect himself even more strongly to the popularity of Germanicus. All very convincing, and allows everyone to nod and think about how sensible and pragmatic and excellent Claudius actually was. Except that everyone agrees that Claudius entertained the possibility of making two other women his fourth wife: the extremely rich and beautiful Lollia Paulina, who had previously been married for a fortnight to Gaius, and his own second wife Aelia Patina. Neither of these women offer any use in terms of popularity, dynasty or legitimacy. They were both just hot.

Tacitus is, as always, the cause of all this as he includes a long scene in which each of Claudius's freedman best friends/employees/former property picked a woman to advance as a candidate for marriage, with the hope that the future empress would therefore be indebted to the successful freedman, and they all held a round table discussion with Claudius and tried to persuade him to pick their woman. Narcissus forwarded Aelia Patina, declaring that she probably wouldn't hate Messalina's children (unclear why) and everyone knew where they stood with a woman Claudius had already been married to. For all Narcissus's alleged brilliance, this was a piss-weak argument and if Narcissus had forwarded such points in a debate he should have been immediately fired for being bad at his job as a ruthless palace manipulator. Callistus took the side of Lollia Paulina. Lollia Paulina was generally considered to be one of the most beautiful women in Rome and was extraordinarily rich. She also sounds insufferable. There's a cracking story about her turning up at a party absolutely dripping in pearls and emeralds. Pliny the Elder, who was at the party, says they were 'upon her head, in her hair, in her wreaths, in her ears, upon her neck, in her bracelets, and on her fingers'.[2] The effect was very much ruined, however, by the fact that she wouldn't stop telling people that it all cost 40,000 sesterces, and, apparently worried that people might not believe her, she carried the receipt around with her when she wore it and liked to show people.[3] Sometimes I wake up in the night from nightmares that I ended up at a dinner party with her and her receipts, Galba waving his family tree and Lucius Vitellius licking Messalina's shoes. Too horrible to countenance. Anyway, she was hot and rich enough for a bad personality to be only a minor impediment to being an emperor's wife for a second time so she was in the running. Callistus's pragmatic point in her favour was that she was infertile so she wouldn't threaten or be threatened by Britannicus and Octavia, which was just harsh. The debate then came to Pallas. He offered Agrippina and said that, in short, she deserved the job because she was Germanicus's daughter, and had a proven womb so she might even give him more babies. I can imagine him winking here, which is awful.

All this is told by Tacitus as if people regularly held sensible debates in the style of philosophical dialogues. Maybe Claudius was boring enough that his mates really did discuss matters of palace life as if they were abstract concepts, but, given how many dead bodies there are littered around the palace at this point, it seems unlikely. Notably Tacitus's version also pretends that Claudius has little to no say in whether he married or who he married, which is just silly. Thankfully, Suetonius is a bit kinder to Claudius. Only a bit, mind, but he does allow Claudius the dignity of being a bit involved in picking his own wife. At least every source respects Agrippina at this moment in history, and, by respect, I mean recoils in misogynistic horror at her alleged actions. Everyone agrees that Agrippina saw Claudius's bachelorhood as an opportunity for self-advancement, and that she managed to both identify and use her best assets: familial access to Claudius that other women didn't have and sex appeal. And so, there are plenty of salacious and titillating stories, in which Agrippina is rather presented as a young girl despite being a 32-year-old woman, of Agrippina hanging around Claudius an awful lot, seducing him with hello

2. Pliny the Elder, *Natural History*, 9.58.

3. For context: an average salary in Rome was around seven sesterces a day.

kisses that perhaps just lingered a little too long and fluttering her eyelashes until he was entirely captivated by her and forgot all about those other women. Historians have tended to try to match up all these confused stories into a coherent narrative in which Pallas and Agrippina worked together to persuade Claudius to marry her for their own nefarious purposes, while Claudius simultaneously decided to marry her for perfectly logical and excellent dynastic reasons.

I have a sneaky suspicion that historians are keen to latch onto the idea of Claudius going into the marriage for sensible reasons because they are unconsciously revolted by the idea of a 59-year-old dribbly man getting boners over his biological niece. His own brother's eldest daughter. A niece who he apparently repeatedly referred to as being like his own daughter, who he held as an infant. I am not unsympathetic to this perspective because the very idea is grotesque. It's much more pleasant and palatable to believe that it was a passionless marriage of convenience for them both, which involved no bodily fluids. The ancient authors, on the other hand, found it easier to shift all the blame for this horrible set of images onto Agrippina herself. It's just easier to believe that the woman made all the moves for us too, isn't it? A young woman taking control of her sexuality and using it to gain power is just a 1990s 'strong sexy woman' trope from all the films. It's easier to think of that than an uncle sliding up to his niece and trying to put his hand up her tunic. Or just telling her that he was marrying her because she had no legal rights as an individual and actually couldn't say no.

This is why the general consensus is that Agrippina was an active participant in her own marriage. Part of the reasoning behind this consensus is that Agrippina doesn't come off in the sources as someone who would let men boss her around. But that reasoning conveniently forgets that Agrippina appears in the sources only when she is doing something that the men think she shouldn't be doing. Those five years when she was being quiet and good? Silence. Her entire first and second marriages? Silence. In a while, we shall see that she vanishes again. It is only when she is overstepping the invisible boundaries of female behaviour that she gets noticed. So, our sources show us an interpretation of one single facet of Agrippina as a real, living human being. The other infinite fragments of Agrippina's personality are lost forever. Certainly, any form of vulnerability is subsumed beneath a narrative about her as a ruthless, cold woman with a single-minded determination to rule the world. I don't deny that this is a pretty great story, but it's just a story. No one is just one story. The truth, such as truth can be found, is confusingly, desperately complicated and contradictory. I think we can all agree that it's a challenge to imagine any woman in her thirties being really excited by the prospect of snogging her dad's older brother. But equally, just because I – a woman in my thirties – would rather cut off my own tongue than put it in my uncle's mouth, doesn't mean that Agrippina felt the same. It may well have been a small enough price to pay to secure her life and that of Nero's. It might have been a small enough price in the face of all the power she would gain, power that she definitely believed that she had a right to. Maybe she did the only thing she felt she could do.

This moment in Agrippina's life is always tinged by memories of her mother's furious confrontation with Tiberius in which Agrippina the Elder informed him that it was she, not his statues, who was the incarnation of Augustus's divine blood. Tiberius's response was that not being empress was not an attack. I can't help but feel that at least a little of her mother's arrogance and belief in her divine right to the throne would have rubbed off on Agrippina. A little of them both believed that not being an empress was indeed an attack. Her entire identity was constructed around the core tenet that she was the descendant of Augustus and the daughter of Germanicus. When Pallas was presenting his argument in favour of Agrippina to Claudius, he stated that she brought with her 'the grandson of Germanicus, who fully deserved an imperial position'.[4] So it may well be that Agrippina saw this marriage to her uncle as her best and most pragmatic route to get her family back the throne they had the right to, and a little hand-holding would be okay in the long run.

While I am, on balance, open to the story that Agrippina saw the

---

4. Tacitus, Annals, 12.2.

marriage as a good thing and was even complicit in planning it with Pallas and Claudius, I confess I am entirely sceptical of the stories of her sticking her tongue in Claudius's ear and sexually seducing him. Tacitus later tells us that Claudius and Agrippina were engaging in pre-marital incestuous bonking and that everyone knew about it, which sounds like they were spending time together. Quite possibly they were spending time together because they were planning ways to break Claudius's daughter's engagement to Lucius Silanus so that Octavia would be free to betroth to Nero, as this happened at the exact same time as rumours of their plans to marry emerged. Silanus had been betrothed to Octavia when she was still a baby because he was the great-great-grandchild of Augustus.[5] At the time of the betrothal, he had been the best way to tie Claudius's side of the family to the Julian side and absorb any potential threats. Mere minutes after the death of Messalina, however, Silanus was expelled from the Senate and from his job as a praetor by the censor Vitellius on the basis of the accusation that Silanus had been conducting an incestuous affair with his sister Junia Calvina.[6]

Although the census of the senators had been ongoing for about a year already, the timing of Silanus's expulsion, the tediously familiar nature of the incest accusation (at this point it would almost be more unusual to have not been accused of incest), and the ridiculousness of a man who was about to marry his own niece accusing anyone else of incest all come together to make Silanus's fate look highly suspicious indeed. Each of our three surviving sources gives a separate account of who was to blame for this event, and which one you choose to believe will depend on where you would like to see the story of Agrippina going. First, Tacitus claims that the censor Lucius Vitellius (who had presumably flung Messalina's shoe into the Tiber by this time) came up with the accusation all by himself in order to suck up to Agrippina and essentially gift her a free bride for her son. Suetonius, who doesn't really believe in nefarious double dealing, straight up says that

5. He was the son of Julia the Younger's eldest daughter Amelia Lepida, who had herself been betrothed to Claudius in her time.

6. A censor is an official but sporadically filled position in the Roman world and his job was to examine the background of every senator and equestrian and make sure that they met the financial and moral requirements of their class.

Claudius did it and that the main problem was that Silanus didn't get a trial. Suetonius is not much use if you like complex political plots, to be honest. Finally, Dio obliquely says that Claudius initiated it at Agrippina's behest. So, was Agrippina a woman on the rise who suddenly has men throwing others under the bus to grab her favour, an innocent or a scheming mother manipulating her husband? The general consensus among historians has usually been that Agrippina engineered the whole thing but, again, that is part of a narrative which sees Agrippina as a single-minded schemer rather than a complex human being.

Here's my theory on Agrippina's position in the last few weeks of 48CE. After her return to Rome had caused such a stir, she had been threatened and in a dangerous position. This danger only passed because Messalina was very silly and got herself killed in a plan so stupid it almost looks like an elaborate suicide. The greatest threat to Agrippina's life, the one she and Nero had been avoiding for five years, had gone, and Rome was reeling. Agrippina took the initiative to get closer to Claudius and his household, understanding that any other wife would see Agrippina as even more of a threat than Messalina did – they wouldn't even have Messalina's Julian blood. Given that uncle–niece marriage was illegal and gross, I cannot believe that marriage was her initial plan. That would be an enormous leap to make. I think the original plan, perhaps made with Vitellius was to get Nero engaged to Octavia and protect themselves that way. Perhaps she floated it to Claudius in one of their cosy chats: 'what if Octavia married my son? That would be good for you… shame about Silanus…' The idea was good for both of them. Nero would be safe and Claudius would take some of Nero's reflected popularity. It was tough – Claudius did so like Silanus – but ruling an empire was all about tough decisions. He didn't want him exiled or executed, though. Just a little disgraced. Vitellius understood and Vitellius had noticed that Silanus and his sister were sometimes a little unguarded in their public displays of familial affection. Not so much as to warrant an execution, but maybe just enough to disbar him from being the emperor's son-in-law. So Vitellius brings the prosecution. Silanus was expelled with much fanfare and the betrothal was broken. But everyone hated that this had happened. The Senate somehow seemed to hate Claudius even more, almost as much as they feared him. No one felt safe. Moreover, that was three members of the Julian side of the family that Claudius had killed or ruined in a couple of months (including Silanus's sister Junia Calvina). This was beginning to look like a Claudian coup, and the Claudians were not the divine side of the family. Claudius now needed two bits of good news to announce (one to cancel out the bad news, and then some good news). And there were the freedmen with their sage advice, suggesting he find a new wife as quickly as possible. And there was Pallas with the best idea: what could be better than a wedding? A wedding to a Julian woman, of course. And so, Agrippina's plan to get Nero engaged to Octavia ended up with her getting engaged instead.

Quite how the agreement was made that Claudius would have the law changed so he could marry Agrippina, I can't guess. I do not have a good enough imagination for that. But the agreement was made, and Vitellius had now proved himself loyal to the comfortably ingratiated Agrippina and dispelled any lingering concerns that he might have been loyal to Messalina and her children. The rest of the Senate now needed to be persuaded to allow Claudius to change the law. This is one of those moments that really highlights the strange, hypocritical web of pretence upon which the Roman Principate lay. Claudius could happily and without consequence kill, destroy, torture and exile anyone from his bed and for any reason, under the thinnest and most pathetic guise of legality. He could introduce and reintroduce laws and his own letters of the alphabet and it was all fine. But marrying his niece was so weird and likely repulsive to the Roman people, he had to go through a pretence of persuading them to agree with him so it looked legitimate and so they wouldn't rise up and kill him like they did his nephew. But at the same time, they had to go along with what he was proposing lest he decide to kill, destroy, torture or exile them for some imaginary charge of *maiestas* or incest very soon. It was a fine balance of bullshit; a sort of Mutually Assured Destruction. The careful balance led to preposterous situations like the one we now see, in which Claudius couldn't ask the Senate directly to let him marry his niece because that would make him look like a creep begging to be allowed to do something extremely disgusting that no one had ever done before.

Instead, he let Vitellius do the asking, and Vitellius carefully worded it so that Agrippina looked like a gift being presented as a lovely surprise to a reluctant Claudius by the Senate and people of Rome as a reward for being so great at being emperor. Indeed, the direction of Vitellius's speech to the Senate was that they should force Claudius to take Agrippina as his wife, even if he protested, because it was such a brilliant idea. Those poor children have no mother, he said, and they deserve only the most noble, pure and loving mother. He described Claudius as having no conjugal comforts, no one to care for him after a long day of worrying about the empire and working so very hard. The emperor was now widowed in the most dramatic circumstances, and Vitellius knew (I imagine him looking pointedly around the room here) that other senators knew what it felt like to have their wife taken in violent circumstances by the cruel whim of an emperor. Didn't Claudius deserve a wife, Vitellius asked; didn't he deserve only the most honourable, most distinguished wife? And what family was more distinguished that Claudius's own.

At this point, we can probably assume that at least three senators had been sick in their mouths, because he then started talking about how incestuous marriages were normal in other countries, to which my mother would certainly reply that he wouldn't be jumping off cliffs if other countries were, but that's why my mother would make a terrible Roman senator (that and her XX chromosomes). The senators who had managed to keep their composure for the whole speech were those who had worked out what was being demanded of them and they all leapt up and rushed out of the Senate house to find Claudius, who was nonchalantly walking around the Forum, just hanging around outside the Senate house for no reason, as emperors do, and insist there and then that he marry Agrippina. I'm sure you can imagine the look of entirely convincing surprise on his face as he immediately took them back into the Senate house and got them to officially make uncle–niece weddings legal before they had time to reflect on the matter. The whole situation was a marvellous piece of acting on all sides. Everyone knew what was really happening, everyone knew that everyone else knew what was really happening, and yet this script was played out without anyone forgetting their lines. And so it was that Agrippina was officially betrothed to her uncle and, within three months, was swept from being afraid for her life to being a hair's breadth from the throne.

The wedding was formally held on New Year's Day 49CE. Agrippina would have been led once again from her home to Claudius's imperial palace on the Palatine hill, with the veil over her eyes for the third time. As she anointed the walls with oil and stepped carefully into the palace, she was finally entering the very centre of power. As she stepped across the threshold, she became the most powerful woman in the Western world. If I imagine Agrippina becoming steely and determined, I imagine that it happened at this moment. As she made her ritual careful step, supported on each side, through the door and into the atrium, I imagine that she felt she was finally where she belonged. Perhaps she had not allowed herself to feel safe and secure until this step. Maybe she remembered those dark, lonely days on Pontia, or the moment Gaius confronted her and Livilla at Mevania, or how exposed and alone she had felt when she heard that Livilla had been killed, all those times that her life had seemed to be at an end, or even just the long years of a quiet undistinguished life of boredom that seemed to last forever. Maybe all those memories crowded in as she stepped carefully over the threshold and into her new life. And maybe she decided in that moment that neither she nor Nero would let this slip away: they were going to take all that they were owed.

Chapter Four: Wife

A Masculine Tyranny

'From that moment the country was transformed. Complete obedience was accorded to a woman...'[1]

Agrippina and Claudius married on New Year's Day 49CE and Tacitus depicts this day as though an earthquake had struck Rome. Tacitus describes Agrippina as the most horrifying thing he can imagine a woman being: masculine. The Romans fundamentally believed that women were incapable of controlling their behaviour. Women were, medically, perceived to be failed men and a part of their failure was that they were entirely subject to their emotions, passions and desires. That's why they weren't allowed to control their own affairs or make their own decisions: they just weren't logical or controlled enough not to accidentally spend all their money on shoes or something. They could not control themselves, so they needed to be controlled. For their own good and everyone else's. Messalina is perhaps the ultimate vision of what Roman men thought happened when women were released from control: their knickers came off, their hair came down and they got real violent. There is no higher purpose to any portrayal of Messalina in the ancient sources – any attempt to make her alleged actions logical is purely modern speculation – because she is a construction of pure Roman femininity. She didn't plan, she didn't plot, she just wanted to get laid and get rich. Agrippina is positioned as the precise opposite of this and Tacitus's words are guaranteed to send a shiver down any Roman man's spine. At the moment of her marriage, Tacitus tells us that Agrippina was austere, rigorous and masculine. To really hammer home this message, he tells us that she was unmoved by sex or money: she only fucked and saved to access power. Tacitus's Agrippina was not feminine in any way; she was not subject to her desires. She had a plan and she would subjugate anyone to achieve it.

1. Tacitus, Annals, 12.7.3.

127

Tacitus places four events as occurring at the same time as the marriage and demonstrating three important things about the rest of Claudius's reign. First, Silanus committed suicide on the day of the wedding. He clearly did this to make a point and ensure that there was a tinge of horror to what was supposed to be a happy day. To be so cross about someone that you literally kill yourself to make your point is a fantastically Roman thing to do and I'm almost impressed by it as an act of defiance. The second event was Agrippina immediately demanded that Seneca be recalled from exile and installed as Nero's tutor. This is now the second time that Agrippina has saved Seneca and he was expected to remember that.

The third event was the exile of Lollia Paulina. Lollia Paulina's exile, and then assisted suicide, happened at some point in 49CE, so within months of Agrippina's marriage to Claudius. Lollia was also, if you remember, in the running for imperial wife and apparently knew about that. The official charge laid against her was consorting with magicians and asking an oracle for a prediction on the future of Agrippina and Claudius's marriage. Pretty harmless in the modern view of things, but the Roman perspective on such things was more severe. Asking an oracle about the emperor was itself considered to be treasonous as it was believed to suggest that the asker wanted something bad to happen to the emperor. In Roman eyes wishing ill upon the emperor was only a hair away from coming at him with a sword. Speculating that the emperor's marriage might end and consorting with magicians is no different from Lollia planning something nefarious against Agrippina with a view to being the fifth Mrs Claudius. Perhaps her short time as Gaius's wife had given her a particular appetite for imperial marriage. She was caught, given a public trial (though she wasn't allowed to speak at it) and then exiled by Claudius. But that is not how our sources tell it.

Their take on Lollia's exile is that Agrippina, driven by a terrible jealousy of a woman she believed to be a rival for Claudius's affections, personally accused and prosecuted Lollia. Dio being Dio, takes the story the furthest and adds some gruesome detail, claiming that Agrippina sent soldiers to Lollia's place of exile with instructions to bring back her head. When the soldiers appeared with Lollia's now presumably revolting head in a bag, Agrippina couldn't recognise her face (because of the decomposition? Who knows.) so she opened the mouth and inspected the teeth to make the identification. This story has everything you need for a classic 'Roman woman in power' anecdote: she was driven by feminine jealousy and rage, she particularly persecuted women for personal reasons and she was unnecessarily violent and cruel in her heartless desecration of the dead. It bears more than a little resemblance to one of Agrippina's closest literary parallels: Mark Antony's third wife Fulvia. We'll come back to Fulvia in more detail later, but for now you just need to know that she despised Cicero because Cicero gave a series of excoriating anti-Mark Antony speeches and Fulvia adored her husband. Cicero was murdered by Augustus, Antony and their ally Lepidus as part of the second triumvirate's purges of their enemies. A classic story goes that Fulvia had Cicero's head and hands removed, put one of her hairpins through the tongue that had spoken against her husband and then nailed the hands that wrote his speeches to the door of the Senate house.

These stories of silly women expressing their uncontrolled and uncontrollable emotions through extreme cruelty are common in Roman literature and work to demonstrate to the male audience exactly why women shouldn't be allowed power. The story of Agrippina poking about in the half-decomposed mouth of her ex-sister-in-law is obviously preposterous. Although, I have seen at least one historian suggest that it is 'plausible' because Agrippina herself had double canines and might have 'taken a special interest in the teeth of others', which is almost as preposterous and offensive a suggestion as the original story.[2] The fact that Lollia was given a public trial and there was a clear, actual crime that she had committed, however ridiculous that crime seems to us, gives away how different from the pre-Agrippina years this prosecution actually was. In the earlier years of his reign, in fact just months before this, Claudius was holding secret pseudo trials of prominent senators for ridiculous sexual crimes in his bedroom in the presence of his wife based on a dream she had. The prosecution of Lollia was obviously just public business as usual

2. Barrett, 1996: 108.

given a nefarious but fictional Agrippina twist in order to make a political point about women in general. Isn't Roman history fun?

The final event in Tacitus's narrative of 49CE was Nero and Octavia finally being formally betrothed to one another. You'll remember that was mentioned before Claudius and Agrippina married, but it didn't officially occur until after the wedding. Obviously, the imperial couple couldn't suggest such a thing themselves and so a willing volunteer got up and proposed that Nero would be the best – the only – possible option as a husband for the emperor's daughter. Ten-year-old princesses require husbands who are equal to them in rank and honour and the only person left who fit that bill was Nero. The motion was carried with much nodding and voting of prayers, and Nero became Claudius's future son-in-law mere months after becoming his stepson. This was a noteworthy step. In Roman culture, stepsons were essentially meaningless. In very broad strokes, they still belonged to their biological father's family and their stepfathers had no obligations to do a thing for them. A son-in-law, however, was being – symbolically – brought into the wife's family circle as well as their own. This is why Augustus's sister and daughter were repeatedly married off to his friends and frenemies. Sons-in-laws were just a step away from sons.

So, with these events, Agrippina tied herself and her son even more closely to the throne and to the real power. Her son would be married to Claudius's daughter, and his guardian would be Seneca, a trusted philosopher and friend who was now tied exclusively to her in terms of gratitude and obligation. Her only potential rivals had been eliminated. Within a matter of months, everything had fallen into line neatly for Agrippina.

The increasing closeness between Nero and Claudius, however, was not universally popular. The sources writing after Nero's reign in particular saw this as the first step in Agrippina's carefully laid plans to disinherit Britannicus for the purely selfish purpose of advancing Nero through, essentially, force. Now, that's not entirely unlikely. Given the stark choice, Agrippina would certainly have placed Nero on the throne before Britannicus. But she was not the only one who would have made that choice. There was at least one very obvious motivation for many others to promote Nero and try to get him into a position to inherit power from Claudius instead of Britannicus, and it is purely selfish: the freedmen and the Senate wanted to avoid the possibility of Britannicus avenging his mother. Regardless of Messalina's real or imagined crimes, her death was ignoble and the *damnatio memoriae* that followed was a deliberate insult. Britannicus may only have been a small child in 49CE, but he was unlikely to forget the circumstances in which his mother was taken from him. There was a very real possibility that he would harbour resentments and grudges that would result in some nasty deaths when Claudius eventually passed on. Even Tacitus lets slip that many feared Britannicus's future vengeance. Such a fear was a pretty good motivation for factions within the Senate to use Nero to save themselves without Agrippina ever even being a consideration. Regardless of Tacitus's heavy handed doom-mongering (and the Roman's penchant for fortune telling), no one could see the future and no one could have known at that moment how much of Claudius's power Agrippina would end up sharing. The elevation of Nero from stepson to son-in-law may well have been a genuine combination of sycophancy, Julian self-interest and senatorial pre-emptive skin-saving.

That alignment of interests allowed Agrippina to open up an even stronger relationship with the men who became her best allies and public representatives: the freedman Pallas and the consul, censor and sycophantic shoe sniffer Lucius Vitellius. Both were instrumental in the death and subsequent destruction of Messalina and would both be top of a list of men to fall on swords held by soldiers if Britannicus ever came to power. At the same time, both were canny sycophants who were able to see that Agrippina's power and influence were not going to be limited to the private sphere of female jealousies and hot actors. For Agrippina's part, she needed men to do her public work for her. Her gender would always be a legal and physical barrier. She could not enter the Senate or speak in public: only men could do that. She could not actively engage with the apparatus of the state or give orders to the Praetorian Guard or sign documents in her own name. She could only negotiate with men who held official or unofficial power so that they would do the official bits for her, and she gave them the privileges, access and influence that she had as the emperor's wife in return. When Vitellius was being accused of treason by an anonymous rival, for example, Agrippina interceded and ensured that the accusations went nowhere and that the accuser was safely exiled. The relationship was a win-win for everyone.

Except, of course, Agrippina in the historical long run, because Agrippina is a woman and so these relationships are characterised as being sexual by all our sources. Rather than being remembered or written about as a canny politician, Agrippina is remembered as a woman who used her tits to get ahead and sex to control weak men. Before becoming empress, Agrippina had been accused of sleeping with Lepidus, her own brother, her uncle (pre-maritally) and a guy called Tigellinus in the first year of Gaius's reign. Within minutes of becoming empress, she was accused of shagging everyone. The notion that she was involved in a long affair with Pallas was particularly common as Pallas was her greatest ally and advocate in the palace and it appears that Roman men could not even imagine a scenario in which a man and a woman have similar aims and a platonic relationship. The accusations that Agrippina and Pallas were banging come early, as Agrippina swiftly got stuck into the permanent power struggle that was a domestic royal court and made an enemy of Narcissus. Narcissus liked to tell everyone that Agrippina had prostituted herself to a freedman for the throne, valuing 'her dignity, her modesty, her body, her all, cheaper than the throne!'[3] Narcissus had an excellent flair for the dramatic. Tacitus makes the same accusation in a much later passage set during Nero's reign, in which he invokes her prostituting herself to Pallas as being a marker of how degraded and debased Agrippina was from the start. Dio, just to be a bit different, flips the degradation. Instead of Agrippina being degraded by her adultery with a freedman, Dio claims that Pallas was degraded by his 'association' with Agrippina.[4] We shall see that, as time went on, Agrippina was to be accused of shagging Seneca, Tiberius's great-grandson Rubellius Plautus, two entirely random dudes called Faenius Rufus and Aulus Plautius, and her own son. By the time she died, she

3. Tacitus, Annals, 12.65.
4. Dio, Roman History, 61.3.

had been accused of having sex with her brother, her uncle, her son and two cousins. The only reason that she wasn't accused of shagging her dad is that he died when she was so young. Had the Romans not practised cremations, I'm pretty sure that someone would have claimed that she dug up her dad's body just to fuck it for some reason. But, of course, none of this matters. Who she fucked and why she fucked them is none of our business and it was none of Tacitus's. No one ever worried about how many women Claudius or Nero or Augustus fucked because it isn't important. It is nothing more than misogyny that I won't pander to, because Agrippina was about to show the world what she was born for. She was going to take some of the limelight for herself.

Agrippina Augusta

In 49CE, Agrippina got stuff done. She consolidated her place. But the things she got done were all essentially private, small-scale acts. Things to do with the family or her friends. None were particularly outside of the realms of expectation for an imperial woman. There's some evidence, though, that she was working hard behind the scenes, and, for all her reputation as the wickedest woman in history, Agrippina seems mostly to have been an amazing diplomat and negotiator. One of the best ways to see this is to compare the 'pre-Agrippina years' of Claudius's reign against the 'Agrippina years'. The latter are by far the more stable, prosperous and pleasant for the whole of Rome. Let's look at executions, for example. We know that over the 13 years of Claudius's reign he executed 35 named senators and between two and three hundred equestrians, and yet only about four of those executions can be dated to the Agrippina years after 49CE. This is despite the fact that our best and most detailed source has a big hole where almost all the pre-Agrippina years should be, so restoration of that source could only increase the number of known pre-Agrippina executions. Another metric is revolts. In the early years of Claudius's reign, the Senate first tried to prevent his becoming emperor and then factions initiated two large-scale attempts to overthrow him. The Agrippina years, in contrast, are characterised by a complete lack of political agitation, no significant coup attempts and a good, strong, productive relationship between Claudius and the Senate. The only thing that changed was Agrippina. The first year of her marriage to Claudius, in my mind, was spent building the bridges and relationships that would make Claudius a stable ruler and Rome a stable empire. What that meant was that Claudius's power and stability rested on Agrippina's diplomacy. And that was power in itself. So she took that power as it came to her and then, mostly, used it to ensure that Rome was a stable state with a strong emperor, a peaceful empire and that everyone was generally pretty happy.

By 50CE, Agrippina had, in public, spent the previous year standing behind Claudius as his good wife and building her base of support.

Now she felt confident enough to step out of the shadows and stand beside him as his partner. She appointed herself the partner in his labours and started smashing expectations.

The first major act was Claudius's adoption of Nero. This was actually the moment where Nero was given the name Nero, losing his original name of Lucius Domitius Ahenobarbus pretty much forever. The adoption of a son who doesn't have a living father is not an easy process in Rome, despite how frequently it happened with emperors. Like Tiberius, Claudius had a biological son and had not yet reached the age considered to be too old to have more sons, so his adoption of a stepson was extremely not okay. Indeed, Suetonius calls it reprehensible; he also says that Britannicus is an adult when he is under ten so he's not entirely on the ball, but the sentiment is pretty clear. All the sources believe that the adoption was an act forced by Agrippina for her personal gain and later regretted by Claudius. At the time, though, the adoption was passed as smoothly as Augustus's mass adoption and marriage plan but without Claudius having any of Augustus's charm or political savvy, and not that long after a couple of serious attempts on Claudius's life. Now, either Claudius learned a very important lesson from those coup attempts and had some charm and diplomacy lessons, or Agrippina got on the case. Could be a little of both, of course. I do quite like to imagine Agrippina kicking Claudius under the dinner table as he said something particularly embarrassing about farts, but of course the Roman elite didn't have dinner tables. The ease with which the Senate and people's council agreed to allow Nero to be adopted is probably a testament to the strength of Agrippina and Nero's popularity and the general goodwill felt towards them. Remember that Nero's right to an imperial position was raised by our resident consul and foot fetishist Vitellius as a reason why Claudius should be allowed to marry Agrippina. Given Nero's Julian, Augustan, semi-divine blood, it's likely that there was a decent contingent of people who thought he absolutely deserved to be Claudius's heir over Britannicus, the small child who was just a rubbish Claudian anyway.

The adoption of Nero had a pretty obvious benefit for Claudius: it neutralised an enemy with a better claim to the throne by basically promising him it one day in the future. It also neutralised anyone who was still worried about Britannicus coming to power and getting revenge for his mother's death. Claudius didn't need worried people in his Senate. However, it did upset tradition. The whole point of having the people and the Senate and the priests get involved in an adoption and having a long, complicated, high-level procedure for adoption was to protect any biological sons, like Britannicus, from losing their rightful inheritance. Even potential future sons were protected by the ban on men who were still considered young enough to get laid from adopting sons. Poor little Britannicus being prevented from inheriting anything good just made people a little uncomfortable. But, then, so did the idea of women climbing into bed with their dad's middle-aged brother and that stopped nobody from approving this marriage. Claudius also introduced three new letters into the Roman alphabet, quite interesting ones, too, so, for all his perceived academic stuffiness, he was actually pretty open to innovation in the realm of literacy and family relationships.[1] Really his reign was a period of remarkable creativity where his own whims were concerned. And so he steamrollered ahead, and Agrippina negotiated, and Claudius was the head priest of Rome anyway, and they got their way. Nero was formally adopted. Claudius liked to stress that Nero was the first ever person to be adopted into the Claudian family in the 700 years of the family's history. This isn't technically true, but it obviously made Claudius happy to desperately reassert the importance, age and status of his bloodline over the Julian one. It might well be a subtle dig at the Julian side of the family for the sheer number of adoptions that had had to take place for the line to continue properly. A little bit of snobbery: 'Well of course we've never had to adopt any sons. Producing males has *never* been a problem for the Claudians' etc., etc.

The adoption formally took place on 25 February 49CE and meant that Agrippina was the wife of the emperor and very likely to be the mother of the next emperor. At about the same time, Agrippina received an astonishing honour, one that probably silenced wine bars when it became known: she was given the title Augusta. She was

1. The anti-sigma Ɔ, the digamma inversum ꟼ, and the sonus medius Ⱶ, in case you are interested.

only the third woman in history to receive this title and the first wife of a living emperor to receive it. Livia was always denied it while Augustus was alive for fear that it might dilute the thunderous symbolic power of Augustus's own designation. Once you give a title to a second person, it sort of loses its unique cool factor. After Augustus's death, however, and the application of Augustus to essentially mean 'emperor' in symbolic terms, Tiberius allowed Livia to take the title and associated honours. As his elderly mother, she was no threat to his power and it only enhanced his own majesty to have an Augusta for a mother and a god for an (adoptive) father. After Livia's death, Gaius gave the Augusta title to Antonia, his grandmother, who was 73 at the time and dead within the year. This was one of his early celebrating the family acts along with elevating his sisters and was basically, as with Livia, a nice symbolic act that meant nothing in practical terms. Granting the title to Agrippina was something very different indeed. Agrippina was 35, vibrant, full of semi-divine blood and the wife of a living emperor. Making her an Augusta gave her official status, if not an official role, in the Roman state and made her the most powerful woman the Western world had ever seen.

It is really impossible to overstate how massively significant the granting of the title of Augusta was for Agrippina, and for the entire institution of the Principate. Under Augustus, the fiction that everyone agreed to go along with was that he was just the 'first man' of the Senate, who just so happened to be deserving of holding an inordinate number of separate powers at the same time and have the backing of a private army who just crushed literally every potential rival. So he was given the very special title of Augustus to show how uniquely special he was. By the time we get to Claudius, however, the reality of the Principate as a military backed, somewhat hereditary dictatorship had taken hold. The way that Claudius wrestled power away from the Senate while hiding out in the praetorian camp really hammered that home. When Claudius was given the title Augustus, it was exactly the same as a king being upgraded from a prince. The granting of Augusta to Agrippina, on the other hand, was a massive shift. It said that the king had a queen who was of equal standing. We do that with our royals, too. We understand that the queen's husband has to go out and shake hands with plebs and cut ribbons and nod at people's bloody awful stories. But until Agrippina, the Romans didn't have that at all. The emperor was just a man doing a job. A job he had inherited from a relative, but still it was a public job like consul or being the aedile in charge of the sewers. He could give his male relatives other public jobs and that was basically the same as any client–patron, father–son relationship of obligation. Female relatives were still private citizens, staying at home and spreading their influence through pillow talk and charitable donations. Until the moment that Agrippina was granted the title of Augusta, the Principate was just a heightened version of what was already done in Roman politics and culture. Agrippina becoming Agrippina Augusta while her husband was still alive, while she was the mother of the emperor's son, meant that she was being given a public honour. She was stepping out of the shadows of private life, the only life considered to be appropriate for women for the entirety of Roman history, and standing right next to her husband, giving the finger to the Senate.

Her first actions as a public figure were to start receiving clients in a public role. Some historians think that she was included in Claudius's daily *salutatio*, which was the morning ritual by which each client visited their patron and said good morning. It was a fundamental part of how Roman society functioned, and how a lot of people made their living. The *salutatio* was also one of the ways in which the hierarchy of the city was continually reinforced and how people knew where in the hierarchy they stood. The clients would turn up at their patron's house very early in the morning, every day, and wait around in the entry hall until they were called into the atrium, say hi and maybe receive a gift of food or money. If you were low down in the hierarchy, you might wait ages or be called in as part of a group, or, worst of all, just get a brief hello in the atrium and not even get to go inside properly. If you were high up, you could be invited to hang out with your patron all day as part of his retinue, for his walk around the Forum, for example, or visiting friends. It was through these daily rituals that stuff got done in Rome, and how everyone knew where they stood and where everyone else stood on a day-to-day basis. This was very much public business, though, and it was the realm of men.

But now, Claudius's clients – who were certainly numerous – came to find Agrippina sitting by his side in the palace atrium, receiving the same deference in a masculine realm. Every single morning, the men who technically did all the administration of the state came and offered their allegiance, friendship and obligation to a woman as the emperor's equal. This isn't just symbolic. If Agrippina was there then she was being presented to Roman society not as a wife, but as an empress; an active public woman who could get stuff done.

The degree to which Agrippina inserted herself into the public life of the Roman Empire is shown by what is perhaps the crowning glory of Agrippina's achievements in the year 50CE, when she founded her own city in the place of her birth. The city was originally called *Colonia Claudia Ara Agrippinensium*, but quickly became known as Colonia Agrippinensis – the Colony of the Agrippinians – and sat on the banks of the Rhine. It was founded as a military colony, which meant that army veterans who had finally completed their term of service were taken to the new colony and settled there as a reward for their decades of hard army work. That makes it sound a bit awful and coerced, but it was mostly a good thing. Essentially, soldiers were promised, as part of their contract, an amount of land to settle on as payment for a lifetime's military service by the Roman Senate. Originally this had been Italian land but at this time there were far more soldiers than there was Italian land going spare, and plenty of soldiers were not of Italian origin anyway, so settlements in new territories became a win-win for everyone. And these veterans weren't being dumped in the middle of nowhere. Colonia Agrippinensis was built on top of an existing town which was the home of the Ubii Germans, who were Roman allies and many of whom were in the Roman army. This was, from the Roman perspective, barely a liveable place as it lacked proper Roman conveniences, culture and togas, but it was a town good enough to house the local altar to the imperial cult. So whenever it was necessary or useful to pray for the emperor, everyone in the area would roll up at what was then called the Ara Ubiorum (the altar of the Ubians) and do their sacrificing and the like. Becoming a colony was a significant upgrade for the Ubii. They went from being allied barbarians to full Roman citizens living in a city patronised by the empress herself. Colonia Agrippinensis was the only colony of the period to have originated as the pet project of a member of the imperial household, and the only space to be founded at the location of an empress's (or emperor's) birth. And that was extra prestige on top of an already decent amount of prestige.

The point of a colony was to be the pinnacle of Roman culture in a region, to be the show town effectively so everyone in the surrounding area knew how great being Roman was. And being a Roman, in comparison to being anyone else in the west, was pretty damn great. So Colonia Agrippinensis got a temple to the gods known as the Capitoline Trio – Jupiter, Juno and Minerva – as well as the altar to the imperial cult. They got Agrippina as a patron, which meant that the empress herself was advocating for them to receive nice useful things like money and new buildings and tax breaks and the like. They also got the Roman way of life – the bath houses where they could socialise and rub themselves in oil, and forums where they could work; Roman law now applied which was considerably more consistent and offered more protection than random custom and unwritten rules. I'm about two seconds from reciting that speech in *The Life of Brian* because it is essentially accurate. If you've not seen it, you obviously should, but, to be brief, in *The Life of Brian*, Reg (reluctantly) recites the good things that the Romans brought to Judea: sanitation in the form of sewers, education, wine, public order, irrigation, medicine, the fresh water system, public health. All these were things you got if you lived in a Roman colony: they loved civil engineering projects. But two things stand out from Reg's list above all these because they changed the very landscape and nature of a place: roads and peace.

Roads meant roads that were straight and traversable in all weathers (i.e. not mud pits for a third of the year). Peace meant the elimination of most threats to life during travelling or going about one's day-to-day business and the placement of a standing army to protect you from external threats like angry Germans. Both those things meant that everyone could get more done. Men didn't have to go off to war on a regular basis to kill other Germans. People could travel from one city to another without the fear that they would fall in a pit or be killed by bandits or get stuck. In practice, these two come together to mean more industry and more trade. In Colonia Agrippinensis, specifically, the people very swiftly found a niche making and exporting glass in huge quantities, both artisanal glass and mass-market stuff. For centuries, even after it was taken by the Franks in the fourth century, Colonia Agrippinensis remained one of the centres of glass manufacture and artistry in the west. It was a hub of trade and art and culture from its beginning, and it was all done in Agrippina's name.

The people of the new colony, both the settlers and the Ubii who were already there, were thrilled by their new position and by their patron. Very quickly, and for a long time after, they referred to themselves simply as the Agrippinenes – the Agrippinians. The city itself, however, gradually became known as The Colony. Much like Constantinople over the centuries became just The Town,[2] so Colonia Agrippinensis became Colonia, which blurred into its modern name: Cologne (Köln). Back in 50CE, Agrippina could not know that in 1,950 years' time her city would still exist and still be important. Just a handful of colonists were settling into the landscape and beginning to build the temples, the walls and the theatre (which still hasn't been found by archaeologists). They hadn't yet started to call themselves the Agrippinians. At that moment, for Agrippina, the foundation of the colony was her demonstration to the people of Rome, of the Senate and the court, that she had genuine power.

Unlike any Roman woman before her she held true power, not influence. Tacitus tells us this in his horrified introduction of her reign when he uses a word that is never used in conjunction with a woman. He says she had *potestas*. *Potestas* stood in opposition to influence, which is what women usually had. Influence means that she had to persuade a man to carry out her wishes, or encourage him towards a certain path. Influence was transitory and fundamentally quite useless. The first quote I wrote down when I began this book was one from Tacitus. He wrote, 'influence is rarely lasting, such is its fate'.[3] It relies on someone else doing the thing itself. This is why Agrippina wanted *potestas*. *Potestas* was the ability to act. It was the power to do things

2. Istanbul derives the word for The Town in Greek.
3. Tacitus, Annals, 1.30.

in public. In Latin, it holds connotations of domination over subjects. The father in Roman law, for example, held a legal right called *patria potestas* (the father's power) which gave him the right to control everyone under his power. Slaves, wives and children all lived under the *patria potestas* of the head of their family. This *potestas* included the ability to kill anyone under it, if the reason was good enough, without any form of legal or social repercussions. In practice, of course, this was extremely complicated, but this was the implication of the word *potestas*. It was not a passive influence, it was an active power. And Agrippina was the first woman in Roman history to hold it. Sort of.

As with everything, both Tacitus and Agrippina were misrepresenting the situation a little. Agrippina literally, within the structures of Roman law and politics, could not hold true *potestas*. She could not turn up to the Senate house and command the Senate to do her bidding. She could not sit in judgement in a court and decide the fates of her subjects, she could not raise and command an army, although I have no doubt that she dreamed of such things in quiet moments. Instead, the pinnacle of her power was this strange liminal space between public and private, between power and influence, between active masculinity and passive femininity. As Augusta, the empress, sitting next to her husband and founding cities, she was infiltrating spaces never before allowed to a woman, but the door remained half-closed to her. Like the contestants on *The Crystal Maze* trying to guide a colleague confronted with nine foam blocks and a toy car, she could only shout her instructions through a crack in the Senate house door and hope that the men holding true *potestas* would do as they were told. Thankfully for her, it seems that they mostly did exactly as she instructed them to and did it happily. Unlike the earlier years of Claudius's reign, there's no evidence of serious attempts at rebellion or political unrest. In part this seems to be because people liked Agrippina and liked the things she did. The foundation of a city in one's own name sounds a bit like the behaviour of a leader gone mad with power; it tends to be associated with tyrannical dictators, which, of course, the Roman emperors were, but in reality the settlement of colonies was pretty popular. It was the spread of good Roman culture to poor barbarians who hadn't yet embraced the freedom and luxury of a good toga after an olive oil rub. It was a demonstration of Roman power and dominance on the very edge of the empire, and the beginnings of a full encroachment into what would later become the official province of Germania Inferior.

In the eyes of the Roman upper classes it was a perfectly normal display of Roman civilisation, in line with Claudius's previous efforts in this area but done much better, albeit in a manner that honoured the empress. It helped that Claudius had fucked up his most recent colonisation effort in Britain by founding a colony where hostile peoples already lived, taking away the original inhabitant's land, not giving them anything in return and killing a lot of people in the process. So in comparison to Claudius's solo efforts on the imperial civilising project, Agrippina's input was peaceful, connected to the glorious legacies of Agrippa and Germanicus and glorious in itself. Agrippina had a natural talent for finding things that were good for her, and good for everyone else and this was the key to her glory years.

The final touch for Agrippina, the cherry on top of the 50CE cake, was her representation on coins across the empire as Claudius's equal. You'll remember from her brief period as the emperor's beloved sister that Agrippina had the shared honour of being the first living woman to be named on a coin. Since then a few women had been on coins – even poor Messalina got on some – but Agrippina had come to reclaim her crown as the most significant woman of the period in every realm, including numismatics. The traditional format for imperial coinage was usually (not always, but usually) much like our own. As British coins mostly have the queen on one side and some pattern or image on the other, imperial Roman coins would have the emperor's face on one side and then an image on the other, usually something they wanted to celebrate or commemorate or a virtue they wanted to associate themselves with. On Agrippina's first trailblazing coin, the sisters had appeared as three goddesses representing harmony, security and good fortune on the back of a coin which had Gaius's face on the front. Gaius was still the main event. Agrippina's innovation was to appear alongside her husband on the front of the coin, as his equal. She was no longer a generic cypher for divine virtues, or used to reflect well on a man, she was a real woman in her own right, an empress. Moreover, there are loads of surviving coins of this type, plenty in beautiful condition, too, which suggests that there were huge quantities of them produced at the time. Enough that no one in the area could miss it. I say in the area because these were not coins produced in Rome; that would have caused an apoplectic meltdown among the senators which would compare to the sad rage of men who've just found out that the Ghostbusters are women now. They were produced in huge quantities in Ephesus, which you'll recall is the city where Agrippina spent a year with Passienus at the start of Claudius's reign and where they appeared to adore her.

But still Agrippina hadn't finished showing off her power and exceptional position. She also had several coins and statues produced of her wearing a crown, specifically a diadem, which is halfway in size between a big gold hat-type crown and a dinky tiara. Exactly as with the title Augusta, no woman had been represented wearing a diadem while they were still alive in the entirety of Roman history. This is because, exactly as with the title, the diadem confers an air of royalty and divinity. And yet, diademed statues of Agrippina are now scattered across Europe but mostly seem to originate from Rome. From the same time, we see a statue from Aphrodisias (don't giggle) carved into the side of the temple of Augustus showing Claudius, who is nude and looking suspiciously young and ripped, being crowned by a man who has sadly lost his head and is therefore unidentifiable, while clasping right hands with Agrippina. The holding of hands was a very common image in Roman art and what it primarily represented was equality and alliance. Claudius wears the crown in Aphrodisias, but Agrippina is the partner in his rule.

Empress of Rome

As 51CE dawned, Agrippina was having the time of her life. Somehow, despite being queen of the Western world, her star kept rising. Between 51 and 54CE, Agrippina ruled the empire alongside Claudius without shame or any attempt to disguise her role. I'm going to cover these years together as there was almost nothing that challenged her power or Claudius's reign. Instead she worked diligently and carefully to ensure that the empire ran smoothly, that there were no disturbances and that Nero would be the next in line to the throne.

The year opened with Claudius taking his fifth consulship in order to celebrate ten years since Gaius was murdered and Claudius used the army to subdue the Senate. He tended to call it his ascension to the throne but, hey, everything is open to interpretation. Right at the start of the year, there were some significant public ceremonies that placed Agrippina and Nero at the very centre of the imperial family. According to Tacitus, Claudius's first act was to grant Nero his *toga virilis*. This was just about the earliest that Nero could receive the toga and be eligible for the rights and obligations of citizenship. And that was a very big deal, both personally for Nero, for the state of Rome and for Agrippina.

We met the *toga virilis* rite earlier with Gaius. Nero received it at a normal age and in a big showy display. The ceremonies began with the removal of the *bulla* and its dedication to the household gods. This was the imperial household, though, which had divinities in it, so probably Nero dedicated his *bulla* not just to the generic *lares*, but to great-grandfather Divine Augustus, and great-great-grandfather Divine Julius. This was the intimate, private part of the transition to adulthood. The removal of the *bulla*, something that had been a permanent part of him since birth, and the personal communion with the family gods would be extremely important. Leaving the dependency and protection of childhood behind to officially enter the world of adulthood was a big step, one they had no control over. Like any big ceremonial occasion – imagine your wedding day, your first communion, the day you lost your virginity, your bar mitzvah, the moment you felt yourself stepping into adulthood – it was fraught with excitement and fear.

The next step was the formal change of clothing. Male children wore a tiny toga marked with a purple stripe, just in case anyone missed the big pendant around their neck and mistook them for an adult, while adult men wore a plain white toga. Nero then fully shed his childhood clothing and stepped into the completely new identity that came with the new wardrobe. When he walked outside the house, which was the next step, he was seen completely differently. He was as clearly marked as an adult as he had previously been as a child. Once he was dressed, presumably the household cooed over him in his new grown-up toga, much as families coo over children on their first day at big school now, in their new uniforms looking so grown up. I like to imagine Agrippina here, waiting in the atrium of the palace for his big reveal in his toga, her scrawny 13-year-old son, maybe just emerging into puberty. I like to imagine her bursting with pride and maybe relief as he comes out, finally a man. After the years spent separated from him in exile, followed by the years avoiding Rome and living in fear of Messalina's ambitions for Britannicus. After the flicker of terror she must have felt when Nero was cheered so much more than Britannicus at the Secular Games and she had known that Messalina would not stand for it, and the rising tension in the weeks that followed. After all that she had experienced as the sister of Gaius and the daughter of Germanicus, she had secured safety for herself and for Nero. And then, she had made herself empress and her son would be her heir. Because the public significance of the *toga virilis* ceremony was to make the continuation of the family line clear, to shout 'this is my son and he will follow in my footsteps'. For Marcus Bloggs from Capua, that was a statement heard by few, but for the emperor it was heard across the world, and so was its implication: the next emperor had been named.

To make this statement out loud, Nero and Claudius, led by a large number of lictors and presumably followed by a small army of clients and flunkies, walked from the palace to the Forum of Augustus and undertook a formal ceremony there, surrounded by the imagery of

Roman glory and filial duty that Augustus designed. The Forum of Augustus was completed in 2BCE and was an overwhelming monument to Augustus's abilities as a propagandist. At the end stood the temple of Mars Ultor, dedicated after Augustus defeated Brutus and Cassius at Philippi and took his revenge for the murder of Julius Caesar. At the bottom of the temple steps stood arches dedicated to Tiberius's son Drusus and Nero's grandfather Germanicus. Circling the Forum were statues of Aeneas and Romulus, the two founders of Rome, the former another divine ancestor of the Julian family, along with many famous heroes of the Julian line, including Augustus himself as the Father of Rome. For any boy, this first entrance to such a huge, monumental space would be overwhelming. For Nero, it would be a glorious, and possibly terrifying, celebration of his family and his obligation to continue the extraordinary achievements of his ancestors. On the steps of the temple of Mars Ultor, an official ceremony of transition took place. This was solemn and in the presence of the Senate and people of Rome. Afterwards, Nero was officially an adult, a citizen and, unofficially, the designated heir to the Roman Empire.

Once the ceremony was done, much like after a wedding, there was a party. The whole Senate, plus clients and family and friends were invited. Claudius was renowned for throwing a decent dinner party, and he is rumoured to have had up to 600 guests, plus all the trappings of a good Roman shindig. This party would be a blowout. Nero's super sweet 16, quinceañera, bar mitzvah and debutante ball all at once. It was a huge celebration of his entry to adulthood, the end of his protected, dependent childhood and the start of his life proper. And at the head of it was Agrippina, sitting next to Nero so there would be no doubt whose true son he was and to whom he owed this spectacular party and his future. Agrippina and Nero were, in the art of the time, inseparable. When a statue of young Nero, before he became emperor, was erected, his Julian descent was emphasised over his adoption into the Claudian line, and either his mother or maternal grandfather are mentioned. In Asia, a statue went so far to identify him as Nero, the natural son of the divine Agrippina, with no reference to his adoptive father and actual emperor of Rome at all.[1]

This happened in Rome, too. At some point over the next year or so, Nero fell ill but recovered and official thanks were given for his recovery in the Senate. We know this because the thanks were recorded in the Arval records of Senate business and Nero was described as the offspring of Agrippina and the son of Claudius. Even in the official records, Agrippina is intertwined with Nero, taking precedence over her husband, which is a staggering thing to say in a world that considered women to be walking, untrustworthy uteruses and when her husband was the emperor. Through Nero, Agrippina was able to transcend even her position as the emperor's partner, and become, in some ways, his superior.

Over the next days, the imperial trio of Nero, Agrippina and Claudius made sure that there was no one left in the empire who didn't know Nero's name. He donated gifts to the people of Rome and handed out cash to the soldiers, this being the best way to get people to like and remember you, of course. He then took the Praetorian Guard on a drill, leading them through their manoeuvres which was actually just a run around some monuments on the Campus Martius in full armour. Having Nero out there, carrying a little shield and in armour, leading the big tough private army on a run, was an impressive visual and not one that people forgot. Of course, the big praetorians were certainly trotting along behind this tubby little child at a quarter-pace, desperately trying to make it look like they were really trying while also absolutely not overtaking their future emperor, and I'm sure that was a miserable morning for them. But they got paid and not killed and the optics really were very good.

These three years are the years of Nero being dragged into the limelight, but he was not alone. He was next to his mother. Agrippina's next great moment occurred at the arrival of Caratacus in Rome. Caratacus was a prominent British rebel who had been leading the British resistance against Roman colonisation. He was the son of the king of the Catuvellauni, one of the biggest tribes of southern England, taking up chunks of Hertfordshire, Bedfordshire, Cam-

1. Inscriptiones Graecae ad res Romanas Pertinentes 4.280, 330, 560. The Greek east of the empire were keen on calling the emperor a divinity well before they died or were formally deified in the west. That they call Agrippina a divinity is emblematic of her status as an empress.

bridgeshire, Buckinghamshire and Northamptonshire. While the Catuvellauni themselves didn't seem to have a big problem with the Romans – what is now St Albans (then Verulamium) was built under them and became a decent city – Caratacus took the invasion both personally and poorly and teamed up with the Iceni and a bunch of other tribes to cause them trouble and make the settlement of Britain even more miserable than it already was for the Romans. After years chasing and being chased by the Romans, Caratacus was finally defeated in a brutal showdown in Wales and ended up taking shelter with Cartimandua, queen of the Brigantes in Yorkshire, who loved the Romans. She handed him straight over to the governor who, in absolute delight, packed him off to Rome as a prisoner of war to be paraded before the Roman people and humiliated before Claudius.

Tacitus absolutely loves Caratacus, because he absolutely loves the stereotype of the noble savage. Another of Tacitus's books is called the *Germania* and it's the Roman version of the staggeringly racist books about Africans written by the British as they trampled all over that continent, in that it is patronising, racist and considers the Germans to be twee, barely human paragons of virtue because they were too poor and stupid to be otherwise. It is noble savage territory. In Tacitus's telling, Caratacus, our noble savage, was brought to Rome. His reputation in Rome was so fierce as a result of his decade of pissing off the Roman army that Claudius decided to hold a sort of mini-triumph to celebrate his capture and let everyone in Rome see him. Caratacus, his wife and children and allies and all the loot that came with them were paraded through the city in front of crowds of gawping Romans desperate to see a real-life British barbarian. The parade ended in front of Claudius, sitting in a throne upon a dais raised above his subjects, with the Praetorian Guard displaying their standards behind him. But next to him, on a separate dais, in front of the Roman standards, sat Agrippina. To quote Tacitus's astonished words, 'it was an advertisement of her claim to a partnership in the empire that her ancestors had created'.[2] As a sight, this was unique. No woman had ever sat in state before to receive a foreigner in any official capacity, or would again for a very long time. No woman had ever dared. It was a statement of

2. Tacitus, Annals, 12.38.

Agrippina's power at this time that she was able to do this. To have the dais and throne prepared and placed next to her husband's, and then to walk out of her home alongside Claudius, to approach and mount the dais and sit in front of the crowds, the Senate, the army. No doubt every eye in the city was on her in that moment, and she was conscious of her every move. But though I have no doubt that everyone whispered and jaws dropped and senators trembled with horror, no one dared stop her. Her dais and throne were ready and she stepped up and sat beside the emperor. To truly hammer home her equality and her power, Caratacus himself then did something extraordinary. He gave a speech, written by Tacitus to be excellently noble, which charmed Claudius so much that he pardoned Caratacus and his family and freed them. The Britons gave thanks and presumably sycophantic praise to Claudius, which was traditional, but they then turned to Agrippina and repeated their praise and thanks to her as Claudius's partner. How could they not, as she was sitting there beside him, regal and stern. The first, true empress of Rome.

Mother and Stepmother

'Let the people see the one in the insignia of imperial command, the other in his puerile garb, and anticipate the destinies of each.' [1]

Being empress of the Roman world, however, was not all sitting on thrones and riding in litters. It was only really 25 per cent that. The rest of the time it was hard graft. The emperor (and empress) was not merely a ceremonial position, like being Queen Victoria, Empress of India. It was a proper full-time job that involved an awful lot of admin, listening to people droning on about things and reading and dictating letters. We have some insight into the workings of the job from Pliny the Younger's ten volumes of letters, of which one entire book is just letters to his emperor Trajan, sent while Pliny was proconsul of Bithynia (Turkey). [2] The letters are unbearable. They're boring and sycophantic. As undergraduates, my friend Helen and I used to refer to them as the P.S. (Trajan) I Love You letters. Admittedly, Pliny was sent to deal with a troubled province, but the level of detail in his questions shows just how involved in the day-to-day lives of people across the empire the emperor could be. They're all about tedious stuff like whether the local people should be allowed to start a fire brigade (nope), whether he should cover a smelly sewer (yes), about debts, whether he should kill Christians (yep) and Christian apostates (nope), whether his wife is allowed to use an imperial courier (yep) and on and on and on. There was almost nothing Trajan didn't know about the goings-on in Bithynia and Trajan spent his entire reign conquering people. Claudius spent a week just about conquering the British and spent the rest of his 13-year reign answering letters. The amount of information flooding in daily from officials and armies and individuals across the empire was enormous. And it was

---

1. Tacitus, Annals, 12.41.
2. Pliny the Younger was the nephew of Pliny the Elder and a dedicated politician.

the emperor's job to deal with all of it. No wonder he let Agrippina get involved; she probably broke up the tedium.

Before Agrippina, there were the freedmen. You'll remember them from such debacles as 'the assassination of Messalina' and 'the unconvincing round table debate about wives'. This is the reason that the three freedmen were so powerful: they controlled the flow of information to the emperor and the implementation of the emperor's demands. For Claudius, it was Narcissus who controlled the correspondence. He received it, read it to the emperor, took down the response and gave the necessary orders. He used this position to ingratiate himself so well with Claudius as his friend and, I really must emphasise this, former property who was still extremely loyal, that he was packed off in 43CE to deal with a rebellion among troops and was instrumental in guiding the whole Messalina business while Claudius was hiding, crying and eating. During his lifetime in this role, Narcissus managed to amass a fortune of 400 million sesterces, which is enough to feed a Roman for 57,154,857 days, or 156,555 years. It's too much, to be honest. But it's representative of the kind of money that was rolling around the Roman upper classes that we're talking about here. These aren't average Romans. These are the Warren Buffets and Saudi kings of the world. The 1 per cent of the 1 per cent. Narcissus was also given the trappings of the quaestors, which was the lowest position in the Senate but was far higher than a freedman, who again used to be a slave and was legally forbidden from acting in public business states as much as women were, should ever have been allowed. This upset people.

But, after the death of Messalina and Agrippina's entry into the imperial household, Narcissus was nothing in comparison to Pallas. Pallas was in charge of the imperial finances, basically funding the entire empire, and managed to get enormously rich. Rich enough to make other rich Romans feel bad. Richer than Narcissus, he also bested him in the fancy clothing and status racket as he was granted the trappings of the praetorians: a military honour which was even better than a praetor. He was granted thanks in the Senate for an excellent proposal concerning the status of free women who marry slaves and those thanks are recorded by Pliny the Younger who was actively repulsed by the idea of a freedman having access to the Senate. Pliny the Younger wrote two long letters annotating the speech of thanks given and the text of the monument that was erected in Pallas's honour on the main road out of Rome, the Appian Way, and you can practically hear him vomiting into a bin as he writes. His repulsion is genuinely palpable. He also tells us that Pallas was granted the right to wear a golden ring. This seems like a trifle perhaps. I am wearing a golden ring as I type this. But in Rome the golden ring was a right called the *jus annulorum*, or *jus annuli aurei*, and was a right granted only to senators and magistrates. Everyone else was stuck with iron rings. A freedman walking about wearing a gold ring was like a woman wearing a toga, or a donkey talking: just laughably incorrect. But Pallas did it and Agrippina got the Senate to grant him that right. He would never actually be able to be a senator or cast a vote or lead an army, but to the casual onlooker he could never be differentiated from those men who could.

Agrippina immediately became intimately involved in the matter of running the empire, which meant she had to work with Pallas and Narcissus a lot. Working with Pallas was grand; they were best friends who had each other's backs. Agrippina made sure that Pallas got showered with honours and cash and looked out for his family, and Pallas in return made sure that Agrippina got what she needed and the money to do it. Narcissus, on the other hand, was apparently a more difficult colleague. Narcissus was chagrined that his absolutely terrible (but, at least, not incestuous) suggestion in the great wife debate of 49CE had been turned down. He had also become the public face of the Messalina disaster, as he had taken charge and ordered the execution. The summary execution of Messalina had been pretty unpopular, people just didn't like the idea of imperial women being murdered in gardens by ex-slaves, and Narcissus had attracted a good deal of the bad feeling. Not that this bothered Claudius, but apparently it bothered Narcissus. When Agrippina came on board as empress with Pallas behind her, it signalled an obvious enhancement of Pallas's status, which Narcissus didn't like either, for fairly obvious reasons. The fact that Agrippina then went on to very quickly eclipse any of Claudius's previous wives and be an almost legitimate public partner for Claudius incensed Narcissus. Under Claudius's previous three wives, Narcissus had been the closest thing Claudius had to a partner in life, both public and private. Narcissus did all his troubleshooting and fixed his fuck-ups and made decisions when Claudius couldn't. And then this woman appeared, this young, beautiful, formerly disgraced woman, and took his special powers away from him. The fact that it was a woman – a woman! – was even more galling. Remember Narcissus had been Claudius's mother Antonia's slave, and Antonia was terrifyingly traditional. Antonia's reputation is so scary that she is rumoured to have starved her own daughter to death as punishment for adultery. Just locked her in a room in her house and listened to her scream for food for days. It doesn't matter if it happened like that or not; she was scary enough that people believed that of her. Antonia would have eaten her own foot before she would act as a public figure. She'd have torn Claudius's throat out with her teeth if she'd ever known that her son had allowed it. Agrippina was to Antonia what girls in the 1960s wearing miniskirts and demanding access to safe abortion were to their Victorian grandmothers. Agrippina was spitting in the eye of traditional female roles and Narcissus loathed it. I can sometimes imagine him clutching a portrait of Antonia and weeping.

The primary narrative of Tacitus, and therefore pretty much every modern historian, is that Agrippina was single-mindedly focused on making sure that Nero would succeed Claudius for the entirety of her time as Claudius's wife and that this was the centre of her poor relationship with Narcissus. In Tacitus and Dio's version of events, Narcissus was a big fan of Claudius's biological son and wanted him to be emperor. As a result, the historians construct a feud between Narcissus and Agrippina that makes Agrippina nothing more than a power-grabbing whore using her own child for personal gain while destroying an innocent little boy and his rights. Narcissus doesn't exactly come off as heroic, because he's a Greek freedman and is therefore about equal to a woman in terms of being disgusting in the eyes of a Roman senator, but he is seen to be on the side of immutable Rightness. He was defending Britannicus's natural right to be emperor (a weird thing for Tacitus to be promoting, you may think, but do remember how much he hates Agrippina) and was the only one to recognise Agrippina's extremely nefarious plan to sideline poor innocent Britannicus and replace him with Nero.

Such a narrative is obviously ridiculous. For one thing, Narcissus personally gave the order to murder Britannicus's mother. If there was anyone Britannicus probably didn't want on his team, it was Narcissus. If there was one person who was going to accidentally brutally cut his own throat while combing his hair when Britannicus became supreme ruler of the Western world, it was Narcissus. The idea that Britannicus, a boy who was eight when Agrippina married his dad and nine when Nero was adopted, was a viable proposition for ruling anything at all is laughable. The idea that Narcissus would start fighting for the rights of a nine-year-old out of the goodness of his heart and strong desire for biological justice is even funnier. Finally, from the day Nero got his *toga virilis* – a ceremony that, remember, Claudius enthusiastically participated in – it was painfully obvious that Nero was a man and a citizen while Britannicus was a boy. Nero was dressed in the plain toga of an adult while Britannicus was dressed in a tunic or striped toga, with his massive *bulla*. A lot tends to get made of this distinction, as if the fact that Nero was a teenager and was presumably going through puberty and growth spurts while Britannicus was still a small child wasn't a factor. But still, in terms of optics, it was fairly effective. But, fairly effective is never enough when it comes to the highly difficult subject of succession, so Nero was also made the consul designate, which meant he got to wear consular robes. So this wasn't just a 13-year-old standing next to a nine-year-old, or a man standing next to a child, it was a magistrate standing next to a child. A nine-year-old standing next to the vice president. Just in case that still wasn't enough, they threw Nero some games and rode the imperial family past the crowds for them to cheer, as was traditional. Britannicus went past in the Roman version of school shorts, but Nero was dressed as if he were receiving a military triumph. Tacitus says that the aim was to 'let the people see the one in the insignia of imperial command, the other in his puerile garb, and anticipate the destinies of each' because he's very good on optics.[3] And the point is undeniable: Nero was very obviously being displayed as Claudius's successor.

3. Tacitus, Annals, 12.41.

To really, really emphasise this, Nero was also granted the title of *princeps iuventutis*, which is usually translated as the Prince of Youths or Leader of Youths. It's a title that was made up by Augustus for his grandchildren (and Agrippina's uncles) Gaius and Lucius Caesar, in much the same way that he made up Augustus and Princeps for himself. Before Tiberius – long before Tiberius – Gaius and Lucius were marked as Augustus's first choices to be his successors. They were his biological grandchildren, the sons of Julia and his best mate Agrippa, and he was so delighted with them that he adopted them in 17BCE, when Lucius was only months old and Gaius was three. When they received their togas of manliness in 2BCE they were also granted the *princeps iuventutis* title. It was a way of acknowledging that they were too young to be officially powerful or have any real offices, but they were special, better than anyone else and if anyone touched them there would be some serious trouble. The whole Prince of Youths thing was Augustus being as clever as he ever was about making sure that he wasn't a one-off monarch, but that the system of government he spent decades building continued smoothly and that there would be no more descent into the horror of the civil wars. Unfortunately for Augustus, Lucius died of fever in 2CE and was followed 18 months later by Gaius dying of a different illness. Augustus had to adopt Tiberius, with palpable reluctance, and the rest is history. And that was the last time that Prince of Youths had been used properly.[4] Claudius giving Nero this title was a direct copy of Augustus granting it to Gaius and Lucius and everyone knew it. As much as Claudius was giving Nero and Agrippina an honour and painting himself as a new Augustus, he was also someone who was thinking about the future.

He also copied Augustus by making Nero a consul designate, which Augustus did for Gaius and Lucius. This was a promise for the far future, saying that when Nero turned 19 he would be the consul. But it gave Nero status above other youths his age, and above other senators who were not on the list, and it gave Nero proconsular powers outside of Rome. This meant he could take lictors outside of Rome

---

4. For pedants, Tiberius Gemellus was given the name by Gaius but then he was killed weeks later so it barely counts.

and boss people about. All this sounds like a lot of responsibility for a child of 13, and it definitely was, which was a bad idea as it turned out, but it was important to demonstrate very, very clearly that Nero was a man with his own power and authority and that he would carry on the smooth running of the city when Claudius died.

Within two years, when Nero was 15 in our counting, he started to take on official roles within the running of the state. He was allowed to preside over courts in 53CE and judge cases, which sounds extremely stressful. I can't imagine how humiliating and infuriating it must have been for citizens to bring their problems, their contract disputes and crimes that were hurting their family, to wait and wait and then find that a 15-year-old boy was going to be making the final judgement. Of course, they weren't likely to be much better off if they got a Claudius day because he would occasionally get bored in the middle of listening and only hear one side of a case or, according to a fun little satire called the *Apocolocyntosis* (pumpkinification) of Claudius, just not bother to listen to either side and make his judgement based on his imagination. But still, at least he was a grown-up. A teenager was equally unlikely to enjoy listening to people whinge on about their problems all day, and have to make decisions and manage a jury at the same time. I have long suspected that this experience is one of the reasons he got so bored with being emperor in his twenties. But we'll get to that.

As if that wasn't enough, he was also made prefect of the city of Rome at the same time. This wasn't a job with a lot of responsibility; it merely sounded good and reminded people of how important Nero was. It's a job with only one task, which was to be technically responsible for the care of the city when the consuls were out of town for the Latin festival, but this was mostly ceremonial. Suetonius tells us that it was traditional for famous lawyers to compete against one another to bring their silliest cases before the prefect at this time, because that was funny to a Roman, I guess. For Nero, though, the lawyers all tried to bring their most important cases, although Suetonius offers no explanation for how we are supposed to react to that news, which is absolutely typical of Suetonius. Nero also got to plead cases in front of his new dad almost immediately. He presented the cases of Bononia (Bologna), Rhodes and Ilium, which means he tried to get them exempted from a tax burden. Ilium is a town in Turkey, now called Hisarlik, but which was once known as Troy. Troy, of course, is where Aeneas fled from when the Greeks stormed it, beginning his years of adventures which culminated in him founding the city that would become Rome. You can read Virgil's *Aeneid* for more on Aeneas's frolics, though I don't recommend it. Having Nero stand up in front of the Senate and give a speech advocating for Ilium was a pretty clear reminder that Nero was descended from ancient gods and heroes as well as modern ones, and had a near divine right to be emperor. As a bonus, it was a descent he claimed exclusively through Agrippina and so it was also an unsubtle reminder that Agrippina had divine blood and a birthright. It's at this point in Suetonius's life of Nero that he brings up the story about baby Nero being protected by a snake, which also has divine connotations: it alludes to the myth of Hercules who killed two snakes that were sent to kill him while he was an infant.

This was how Roman imperial succession was built by Augustus and then by Claudius and Agrippina: it wasn't a single crown that could be gifted in one go or legitimately bequeathed in a will; it was layers upon layers upon layers of prestige and honour and legal powers taken from here and there and impressive visuals. It was necessary to make the idea of the chosen successor inevitable, so that they seemed inescapable. And there were a lot of legal and imaginary layers of inevitability being built here. But Claudius's reign had not been stable; there was now precedent for just murdering the emperor and successfully installing a new chap and Britannicus existed and would always be a threat, so what had been done so far was not enough. Nero was not yet inevitable. Over the next couple of years, between 51 and 53CE, it was necessary for Nero to become inevitable and for Britannicus to be a rank outsider. And the legitimacy of Claudius's succession plan rested entirely on Agrippina being his wife. She was the key to the success of the Julio-Claudian dynasty.

The process of making Nero the inevitable next emperor is a contentious one because it is very easy, with the benefit of hindsight, to see this period as being characterised by Agrippina relentlessly pursuing this single goal for her own purposes, not for the good of the family and the empire, and that leads to a strange and mono-faceted version of Agrippina. It means we get stories like the one told by Dio that Agrippina somehow incited a riot over bread prices in 53CE so that Claudius could calm it down and then issue a proclamation that Nero would also be capable of dealing with such problems. Apparently Agrippina's reputation was so poor by Dio's time, almost 200 years after she died, that he believes her capable of either raising bread prices in Rome for personal gain or coordinating with the Roman plebeians to get them to riot. But then Nero wouldn't actually have ever dealt with it, because he wasn't emperor, so she just made Claudius tell everyone that Nero totally *could* have handled it if he had needed to and that was her plan. It is an obviously untrue story, and a totally baffling one that seems to exist just to demonise Agrippina as much as possible, regardless of things like narrative or logical sense. Not that this has stopped historians taking it seriously and claiming that the letter demonstrated that Agrippina was uneasy when Claudius fell ill with some unknown sickness and that she demanded he make the proclamation just in case he died, making this imaginary proclamation an official announcement that Nero would succeed the throne. Such a proclamation would be a drastic break from Claudius's long-term emulation of Augustus's succession plan, which is to officially pretend that there's no such thing as a succession plan and also he really thinks this child should be given more leadership opportunities, and instead blurt out all his succession plans in a public document. I suppose this might have happened if Agrippina really thought that Claudius was dying and seriously panicked, but it seems unlikely. Especially as the best way that historians have been able to make this letter theory work is to take it away from the riot at the start of the sentence, place the riot two years earlier, and move the proclamation to a different point in time, which is the kind of jiggery-pokery with sources for which I have little time. A better argument is that it just didn't happen.

Claudius's illness in 53CE is well covered in the sources, though, or at least as well covered as such things get in that we know that Claudius was ill and that the illness lasted long enough that Nero and

Agrippina were able to put on some games for Claudius's health. Suetonius says that the games included beast-baiting, and Dio says they
included races, so take your pick. Either way they took some organi-
sation and were a nice way for Nero and Agrippina to appear in public without Claudius attached. Dio claims that by this time Agrippina
was regularly appearing in public, sitting on a separate but equal dais
next to Claudius, receiving ambassadors or visitors or transacting the
tedious daily business of the empire, so she would be used to being
treated as his equal in public but only by his side. This was a chance
for Agrippina to be on display without her husband and oversee some
games in her own right. More importantly, it was a reminder that the
empire endured and everything continued as normal when Claudius
was not around. Just in case anyone was worried.

At about the same time, 53CE, the final touch to Nero's position as
successor was completed and he was officially married to Claudius's
biological daughter, his adoptive sister, Octavia as she was finally
old enough to legally marry. You may remember that Octavia's first
fiancé had been accused of incest with his sister and removed from the
engagement before killing himself on Claudius and Agrippina's wedding day and so she had been formally betrothed to Nero a couple
of years back. There had been one minor hurdle to overcome before
the marriage could happen: in Roman law, marrying an adoptive sibling was considered to be incest. However, marrying a close blood
relative hadn't been a problem for Claudius and Agrippina so there's
no way they were letting something as ridiculous as the law stand in
the way of this brilliant plan either. At the same time, though, their
definitely incestuous marriage had raised more eyebrows than were
ideal, so they needed to deal with the situation carefully. Their solu-
tion was to have Octavia adopted out of the family so she was no
longer technically Claudius's daughter and then immediately marry
her back in, which was complicated and time-consuming and an utter
farce of a situation but worked. Two years after the engagement was
announced, Nero was now Claudius's son, his son-in-law, the Prince
of Youths, the consul designate and able to act as a magistrate; he held
imperium (military power) both inside and outside the walls of Rome,
and got to march about in consular robes all the time and in triumphal

robes on special occasions. The deed was done. According to Dio, the gods warned the Romans of the coming terrors. On their wedding night, he tells us, the sky appeared to burst into flames.

However, the pushy stage mum isn't the only narrative that Agrippina gets during these years. She also gets a classic wicked stepmother story. The wicked stepmother is a tale as old as humans and it's a favourite of the Romans. In this story, Agrippina is the wicked stepmother abusing poor Britannicus, who is our Cinderella: the adorable innocent, cruelly abused. There is no doubt that Britannicus was sidelined in the imperial family. As the youngest child, he was sort of the most useless, but he was also the most potentially dangerous as Messalina's son and a rival for the throne. Thankfully he was tiny, so he couldn't get involved in public life properly unless Claudius granted him his *toga virilis* at a preposterously young age. Although the idea of a nine-year-old senator is very funny and quite adorable, funny isn't really what Claudius and Agrippina were ever going for. There was, however, an incident in 51CE, shortly after Nero was adopted by Claudius and got his new name, when Britannicus called him by his old name, Domitius. Remember that Britannicus was about nine here so it was probably an accident. The story goes that Agrippina heard about this, because there were no secrets in the palace, and was incensed. She marched to her husband with this news and accused Britannicus of deliberately using Nero's old name because he did not respect the adoption, stating that he was dishonouring Nero, dishonouring his father and dishonouring the Senate and people of Rome. You can imagine her tall and indignant and full of 'I demand to speak to the manager' pseudo-righteous fury at this moment. According to Tacitus, she was kind enough not to blame the child himself, but blamed his tutors and teachers for inciting hostility. Again, in full get-me-the-manager flow, she demanded that Claudius get rid of the malign influences and replace them with better ones just in case this whole situation escalated and riots broke out. Which is an argument that would work on Claudius who was still notable for his understandable terror of unrest. The sources all portray Agrippina as being a manipulator who leapt upon a chance remark and turned it to her advantage, but it's not that unlikely that nefarious elements would coalesce around Britannicus, recognising him as a potential pathway to power.

If we accept the possibility that there might be undesirable elements lurking around little Britannicus making their own little schemes to grasp some imperial power for their own, because who wouldn't want to be the regent for a child emperor, then we also accept the likelihood that the palace wasn't that stable. The adoption of Nero in 50CE marked an obvious move by Agrippina on the three-dimensional chessboard that is court politics. Anyone who had been hanging around Britannicus expecting him to be the new emperor would be put in a defensive position. Whether or not they actually made a move (by somehow convincing a kid to piss off his new, older adoptive brother? Who knows), Agrippina was not silly enough to let people who could create too many ties of friendship or loyalty or stir up hostile thoughts in the boy spend too much time with him. It's much more sensible to prevent alliances around the kid from forming. So let's assume that Agrippina took this as an opportunity to clean house, not necessarily to sideline Britannicus per se, but to eliminate potential threats to Claudius, herself and her son. That may not seem like much difference, but it makes Britannicus collateral damage rather than the primary target of Agrippina's actions. The same can be said for the accusation by Tacitus that Agrippina removed officers in the Praetorian Guard who she thought were sympathetic of Britannicus's claim to the throne. In a classic Tacitus move, he claims that she did this by promoting them to the natural next step in an officer's career. Dear God, the cruelty. In a different book Tacitus complains about how badly the emperor Domitian treated Tacitus's beloved father-in-law Agricola, and his primary evidence of harm is the fact that Agricola was given the governorship of Britain, was allowed to lead a series of military campaigns and was granted triumphal decoration. Again, the depths of his torment are unimaginable. His quiet, rich retirement after a distinguished career must have been almost as horrific as the elevated careers of the Praetorian officers who became centurions. Really, sometimes Tacitus comes across as a paranoid fantasist, but we persist with him because persist we must.

Some perfectly reasonable promotions aside, Agrippina and

Claudius did replace the two Praetorian Prefects, who were the leaders of the Praetorian Guard. They had an enormous amount of power and access to the emperor. You'll remember that it was the Praetorian Prefect Chaerea who murdered Gaius. The current prefects were Lucius Geta and Rufrius Crispinus, who had been appointed in 47CE, when Messalina was still alive. During the crisis in which Messalina was killed, Crispinus had scarpered and couldn't be found to do his job, while Geta sort of stood around uselessly agreeing with everyone but failing to do anything. They both sound like absolute cowards and, in my imagination, Agrippina hates them for this reason. Certainly, it was clear that neither could be trusted to protect the emperor in a crisis. Both got packed off to new jobs where they could do less harm in 51CE. They were replaced by a single man, which was a fun innovation: Sextus Afranius Burrus. He was a military man from Gaul with an injured hand, a take-no-prisoners attitude and an unshakable loyalty to Germanicus's daughter.

As always, everyone claims that Agrippina was personally and solely responsible for this appointment. Dio tells us that Geta and Crispinus were replaced because they would not obey her. Tacitus tells us that she suspected they were loyal to Messalina and wanted someone who owed their loyalty to her and Nero. Both fair arguments. It's not much use to the empress if the leaders of the Praetorian Guard are insubordinate and untrustworthy. They may have resented her being empress, either because she was a woman who was apparently exerting a new power to boss them around, or because she wasn't Messalina, but it doesn't really matter. Neither emperors nor empresses could keep people around who resented and obstructed them. Both prefects got a decent promotion to a nice procurator position somewhere and no one got hurt. This replacement of hostile prefects and removal of potential problems from within the Praetorian Guard through peaceful means where everyone gets something good out of it was, if it was indeed part of a plan, a completely brilliant one. The other option was to accuse them of *maiestas* or incest or something and have them exiled or killed, but we've seen from Claudius's early years and the reigns of Tiberius and Gaius where murdering everyone got an emperor. Using Agrippina's method, there were no resentments, no grieving widows or parents or children looking for revenge, no festering fear or show trials. Just a loyal guard, who now owed their position to Agrippina, and potential enemies who had been put safely out of the way but not aggravated into trying anything. As Claudius seemed to quite enjoy murdering people who scared him before Agrippina came along, I don't think that ascribing this peaceful and conciliatory approach to her is a huge leap. And it was an extremely careful, diplomatic and clever strategy for maintaining power. It suggests that Agrippina had spent her years under her great-uncle, her brother and her now husband uncle watching and learning, noting the consequences of tyrannical actions and learning what not to do. It also suggests that she had the charm and diplomacy, and straight-up power, to get these deals done without anyone getting upset.

The subtlety and diplomacy of these little deals with the Senate and the freedmen and Claudius undermine the charges laid by Tacitus and Dio that Agrippina was nothing more than a cruel and pitiless stepmother to Britannicus. Such behaviour would be too dramatic, would draw too much attention. Not that this stops the sources. Dio also says that she kept him under house arrest and prevented him from appearing in public or seeing his father. Tacitus goes even further and claims that Agrippina wouldn't even let him have slaves. How was a prince supposed to live without slaves? Was he supposed to strigel his own back? These are more serious charges of cruelty and rather impossible to prove or disprove. The implications in these accusations are twofold: first, that allowing Claudius to see Britannicus would arouse Claudius's natural paternal sympathies and he would realise how cruel he was being to the little boy by not making him the next emperor and Agrippina's plans would be lost, and secondly that Agrippina had the power in the imperial household to prevent the emperor and his son from seeing one another. Claudius is a nonentity in this story; it's not about him. You can decide for yourself what he was supposed to be doing while his only biological son was kept away from him for three years: weeping into his cups over his beloved son? Idly trying to remember if he ever had a son? Completely oblivious? It's impossible to know. Of course, it doesn't really matter whether this actually happened or not, or even whether it is plausible; what matters is that the story emphasises the fact that Agrippina was a wicked stepmother taking away Britannicus's natural right to inherit the throne which aims to make the reader feel pity for little Britannicus. The pity makes Agrippina seem all the more villainous, like all wicked stepmothers should be. And Agrippina is absolutely being forced into that trope.

She is moulded so hard into the wicked stepmother role that it's quite easy to forget that she had two stepdaughters, too, Antonia and Octavia. Antonia was 20 when Nero was adopted and married to her second husband, Faustus Cornelius Sulla Felix, so she was probably out of the household and spent her time being a good Roman wife. She certainly didn't do anything that a good Roman wife wouldn't do or else we'd know about it. Octavia was younger, just ten or so when Nero was adopted, and being raised in the imperial palace. She was 14 when she married the 16-year-old Nero and he hated her as much as she hated him. Eventually, he murdered her. Because she was empress for a little while as Nero's wife and was, like her name-sake, seen as such a deeply tragic, ideal woman, she was the subject of a tragedy written by an anonymous playwright that tells the story of her sad life.[5] Agrippina is in it as a ghost, which is quite fun. The story focuses entirely on the cruel persecution of Britannicus and then Octavia's terrible treatment at the hands of Nero. Agrippina appears to talk about Nero and his second wife Poppea but not Octavia. The relationship between Agrippina and her stepdaughter, who then became her daughter-in-law, is completely obscure. Stepdaughters are no threat to the stepmother so they just don't matter. Stepdaughters are also entirely irrelevant to the wider story that Tacitus and Dio are telling, which is that Agrippina's power marked a period of extreme dysfunction for the Roman state. She is little more than a symbol of every possible kind of disorder and destruction.

5. The Octavia used to be ascribed to Seneca, but that has been debunked and the author is generally called Pseudo-Seneca.

Ruling the Empire

The sources we have for the three years that Agrippina spent being Augusta to Claudius's Augustus are heavily focused on what she was supposedly doing in her private life, but are fairly quiet on what she was doing on a daily basis as an empress. Claudius's day-to-day activities are assumed to be obvious to the reader, who is expected to be a Roman senator himself, but only a few of Agrippina's more extraordinary activities are recorded.

We know, for example, that in about 51CE there was a coded move against her in the Senate, when a guy named Junius Lupus (this time it is lupus) accused her best friend in the Senate and notorious shoe fan Vitellius of having designs on the empire for himself. The accusation itself is bizarre: Vitellius was extremely old and doing very well for himself. He was very close with Claudius and Agrippina and had got a lot out of that closeness, mainly by being unbearably sycophantic. The idea that this was all some kind of years' long ruse so that he could rise up from within, as an elderly man, and take the throne is very silly. More likely it was an attempt, in response to Agrippina's now enormous power and Nero's obvious position as successor, to resist her by taking on her closest public ally in one of the only ways possible. It was an act that had no hope of success, and Junius Lupus must have known this, so it was an act of quite remarkable bravery. He stood up and made a pointless case to resist what he saw as tyranny. Admittedly, his idea of tyranny was shaped by his misogyny and revulsion at being ruled by a woman, as his move against Vitellius came at the point when Agrippina was implementing her most obvious changes to the structure of the Praetorian Guard and the imperial family with the elevation of both Burrus and Nero. In return, Junius Lupus was exiled. Tacitus says that Claudius would have believed him and he may have taken down Vitellius had Agrippina not stepped in and saved him, but that seems unlikely as Vitellius was as close to Claudius as to Agrippina and the accusation was an attack on the pair, not just the wife. Not that this fact stopped conspiracy theories from springing up that Claudius engineered the accusation, using Lupus as a proxy, in order to curb Agrippina's power and warn her that her proxies and allies were not untouchable. The point of this conspiracy theory is obvious: it is to make the argument that Agrippina was working alone and against Claudius to gain individual power, and that Claudius was too weak and pathetic to put a proper stop to her plans. For the conspiracy theory to work, though, Vitellius had to be an enemy of Claudius's, and that's simply not true. If the charges against Vitellius were a warning from anyone, they were a warning from a group of senators and both Agrippina and Claudius were its targets.

The case against Vitellius was easily put down, though apparently the stress was a bit much for Vitellius himself and he died from a stroke shortly afterwards. This left Agrippina and Claudius without their main senatorial champion, which was an issue as the standard procedure for passing legislation such as 'men can now marry their nieces' and 'let's build a golden statue of the emperor' was to get some senator to suggest it and then pretend that the emperor was being forced to go along with it. Unconvincing, time-consuming and tedious though this procedure may have been, it was expected and deviation from it got an emperor stabbed up, as Gaius showed. The most popular emperors were always those who let the Senate pretend that they had come up with everything all by themselves and dragged the emperor behind them. Claudius only had three friends, and only one of them was a senator, so it was a bit awkward that the same senator kept suggesting beneficial things for the emperor every time. Had Vitellius died when Messalina was still around, there might have been a problem with the Senate and palace as Claudius would have had to make new close allies. Thankfully for Agrippina, it occurred under her watch and she had no trouble keeping the pipeline between the Senate and the imperial palace open.

There were two more disturbing prosecutions in Rome a couple of years later, in 53CE. The first was against Titus Statilius Taurus, who was consul alongside poor, doomed Passienus in 44CE and the other was Nero's paternal aunt Lepida, who we shall discuss in a minute. Taurus was one of those men who, during their time, was enormously famous, influential and rich, and famous for being rich in

Rome, which meant he was very rich indeed, but then slipped out of view as soon as he died to be forever forgotten. He just dropped into the pit of darkness that is most of history, except this one moment. He was accused by a subordinate after his stint as proconsul of Africa (the absolute best province to be proconsul of) of both corruption and being addicted to 'magical superstitions'. What these superstitions consisted of is not stated as superstition is a very nebulous concept. Christianity counted as a superstition at this time. Consulting astrologers was a superstition that Claudius banned. People who were too religious were superstitious. People who practised any kind of religion that was foreign were superstitious. There's no way of knowing what he was actually accused of. One historian thinks that Taurus was consulting astrologers, another thinks it was a made-up charge by a poverty stricken underling. We're all making it up based on our guts, though, because literally all Tacitus says is 'addicted to magical superstitions' so you can think what you like.[1] Go ahead, make up your own version. Tacitus himself says that the accusation was somehow Agrippina's fault, presumably that she somehow forced the underling to accuse his boss, because she wanted his money and his gardens. This might seem oddly familiar, as it is the exact same accusation made by Tacitus against Messalina way back when. Some have argued that Agrippina actually did do this, that she falsely accused a famously rich and favoured man of superstition so she could have his stuff, but that this was good because his money would finance some key public building projects so this was actually sound financial management. It is, in fairness, the exact kind of financial management that Augustus did during the civil wars. When he initiated the second triumvirate with Lepidus and Mark Antony in 43BCE, they had nearly 2,000 people executed and their property stolen to pay for the war. Cicero was one of those victims. That was very much wartime economics, though, and not the kind of thing that heads of state considered during peacetime. Even Augustus didn't do it once he'd won the war. Suddenly starting up a new economic scheme that involves murdering people would also be quite the change of approach for Agrippina who, until this point, had been both frugal and politically savvy.

1. Tacitus, Annals, 12.59. Barrett, 1996: 135; Levick, 1990: 211.

Indeed, Tacitus himself calls her austere and notes that she didn't go in for luxury like most women did. Instead she saved money as a power base for herself, aware that money was the strongest form of power in peacetime. Getting all murdery over a garden just seems out of character, no matter how nice the garden was.

In the end, it didn't work out for anyone. Taurus killed himself and the accuser was chucked out of the Senate. Apparently the removal of the accuser, Tarquitius, annoyed Agrippina and she tried to stop it but the Senate did it anyway. This, to me, is the more interesting part of the story. What we have here is a rare glimpse of Agrippina trying to guide the Senate's behaviour and them refusing. This was what the day-to-day ruling of the empire looked like. It was a constant ongoing negotiation between the Senate and the palace. The Senate was essentially a massive, complex maze of obligations, ties, alliances and grudges. It was made up of individuals, all of whom had their own family names to protect or make, their own webs of clients, patrons and obligations, their own decade-long feuds and resentments, their own ambitions. Everyone wanted to be on Claudius's team, which meant being on Agrippina's team, because everyone wanted to be consul one day, and get a cool proconsular position so that their sons would be known as the son of a consul and their granddaughters would be married to consuls because of their grandfather's position. They wanted to match the achievements of their parents or great-grandparents, or be the first in their family to scramble to the top of the ladder. Everyone's sisters and brothers and sons and daughters and niblings and cousins and aunts were married to one another, which created big blocks of men who were tied together through family relationships and owed each other loyalty.

Here's how it worked when it was successful. Agrippina had a senatorial client whose career she had supported, and she mentioned what she wanted from the Senate. Her client was married to the sister of an ex-consul, and had a praetor as a client of his so he gave them the message and they were obligated to join in. They passed it along to those who owed them; perhaps the ex-consul had two sons-in-law and three new men as clients, who had ties of their own through their parents, their wives and so on and so on. The ties of obligation spread out until everyone knew what Agrippina needed doing. And in return, Agrippina would do a little favour for her client, who would do a favour for his brother-in-law who would help find an appropriate wife for someone else and… you get the picture. This worked very similarly to Chinese *guanxi* in that families were tied together, not individuals, and that these were obligations not choices. But for every obligation there was another individual with a counter-obligation, working in the interests of another family who loathed Agrippina or, presumably in this case, supported poor Taurus's family. So Agrippina explained her desire that Tarquitius be kept in the Senate and not punished for his role in Taurus's suicide for whatever reason, but Taurus's family or other interested parties made it equally known among their supporters that they required Tarquitius to be punished for what he had done. There were a lot of talks in reception rooms during the *salutatio*, and in the Forum as men walked with one another to see and be seen, and over dinner each night as people passed from group to group and negotiated, debated and came to little agreements. Eventually, more groups decided that Tarquitius did not deserve his place in the Senate anymore and decided to defy Agrippina when the time came for the issue to be raised in the Senate house. But the next day the negotiations would begin again over something else and this was what political life was and what Agrippina should not have been doing. The only difference between Agrippina and every other powerful figure in Rome at this time is that she could not actually stand up in the Senate on the day and make her final case, and everyone else was a man. So it was incredibly impressive that she was able to build such a strong network of support and that her network was so strong that her wishes being denied was worthy of comment. It suggests, as we know, that she was diplomatic and charismatic enough to make and maintain connections with friends and clients, and powerful enough to have something tangible to offer her connections, but that she was unscary enough that people defied her.

Another time we see how Agrippina's power actually worked in practice was when trouble kicked off in Jerusalem in 52CE. Jerusalem was in the Roman territory of Judea within the wider province of

Syria. It had been absorbed into the empire by Augustus and sort of left to its own devices under the usurper king Herod (the famous one) until 6CE when Augustus got fed up with Herod being a dick and took it under Roman control, although he let Herod and Herod's sons rule it mostly. There were two major problems in Judea as far as the Romans were concerned. First, there were several religious and ethnic groups living in the territory and they all hated one another. Secondly, the Jewish population of Judea utterly despised living under any non-Jewish rule, which included Herod who was not hugely observant. Thirdly, the Jewish population especially loathed the dispassionate ignorance of Roman rule that was a result of the Romans seeing Judea as an insignificant place that caused problems. The Romans most made their presence felt in Judea when they were meting out violent oppression and punishment. Thus, the Jews saw the Romans as foreign colonisers and oppressors, while the Romans saw the Jews as bizarre religious zealots who liked a fight. The Romans could never understand why the Jews wouldn't just accept being ruled and taxed, and the Jews couldn't understand why the Romans kept failing to understand their unique religion and culture and were continually fucking about with the Temple. There was absolutely no trust on either side.

Claudius had installed the famous Herod's grandson Herod Agrippa I as the ruler of Judea in 41CE as a reward for his role in Claudius winning the throne. The Herod family were Babylonian Jews but were not particularly observant of Judaism as a way of life. Herod Agrippa's first act before he left Rome to take over Judea, for example, was to make a sacrifice at the Capitoline temple to Jupiter, which observant Jews did not like one bit. In Judea he did his best to compromise between the Jews, who were theoretically his people, and the Romans he owed everything to, by pouring money into the Second Temple, but letting the Romans pop a massive eagle over its door, which mainly just upset the Jews more than the renovations pleased them.

The incident in 52CE was the middle of escalating tensions and violence that would end with the great Jewish revolt in 66CE, which itself ended in 70CE with Titus sacking Jerusalem and destroying the Second Temple leaving just the western wall (now known as the Wailing

Wall) standing. These tensions began at Passover 51CE when thousands of Jews were feasting at the Temple, watched over by Roman troops who insisted on keeping an armed eye on every gathering of more than about six people. This time, a particularly stupid Roman soldier, fuelled by whatever dickheadery fuels these things, lifted his tunic, dropped his Roman knickers and mooned the celebrating Jews in the Temple. And then farted. The ensuing riots killed hundreds and were brutally put down. This came very shortly after a small dispute over an imperial messenger being robbed had turned into a massive dispute because a Roman soldier burned a copy of the Torah in retaliation. Just months later, a Jewish pilgrim was attacked and beaten by Samaritans on the lash and the Roman procurator appeared to favour the Samaritans so the Jews took matters into their own hands.[2] They raised what was basically a militia, marched north and started destroying Samaritan towns. The situation had got out of control. The Samaritans appealed to the procurator Ventidius Cumanus, who called the governor of Syria for help, who tried to fix the situation by executing people from both sides, then tried to calm the Samaritans by beheading 18 extra Jews, and when that didn't work (I know, I'm surprised, too) called in the big guns: the emperor. He packed Cumanus and representatives of both sides off to Rome.

In Rome, the situation stopped being about people's lives and livelihoods, because no one in Rome gave a damn about either the Jews or the Samaritans. It became instead about palace politics. On the one side were a group described by Dio as 'the freedmen', which presumably means Narcissus, and on the other was Agrippina. Agrippina supported the Jewish cause and was allied with Herod Agrippa, who was doing his best to protect the people of Judea. Narcissus supported the Samaritans. Claudius, however, had the official final say in how this would pan out, so both sides worked on him in private and separately from the delegations of actual Jews and Samaritans. Josephus claims that Claudius wouldn't have even bothered to hear the Jewish side if Agrippina hadn't intervened and insisted. It amuses me to imagine her telling him off like a naughty puppy when she discovered his plan ('bad Claudius, naughty Claudius') but it was probably more

2. Samaritans being people from the neighbouring territory of Samaria.

of a rational discussion than that. In the end, Agrippina's arguments won: Claudius heard both sides, Herod Agrippa represented the Jews, Claudius decided that the Samaritans were to blame for the whole situation and executed a few for good measure. Cumanus was fired for being very bad at his job and some random soldier, maybe the one who farted on the Temple or the one who burned the laws, was publicly tortured and beheaded in Jerusalem in some attempt to rebuild relations. The public humiliation and execution of a Roman soldier as a kind of conciliatory action was quite extraordinary. Like any massively arrogant colonial power, the Romans tended to assume that any problems were the fault of someone else. A little of me wonders if this action was Agrippina's idea. Cumanus's replacement was, in an innovative move, Pallas's brother Felix, who was also an ex-slave. Given Pallas and Agrippina's close working relationship, we can assume that Agrippina definitely had a say in this appointment. Also, Felix's first act was to start minting coins in Judea with Agrippina's face on them. The notion that Agrippina would have ideas about how to calm down the Judean situation, and that Felix would listen, is not unlikely. We know from Pliny the Younger that letters between provincial officials and the palace on even the most trivial matters were not unusual. Felix stayed in charge of Judea until 60CE and oversaw a whole lot of controversies without anything disastrous happening, marrying first the daughter of Antony and Cleopatra, and then Herod Agrippa's daughter. He was eventually recalled for unspecified misdeeds, which he suddenly started engaging in just months after Agrippina died. I could make a case that Agrippina was advising his rule in Judea and that her death meant he had to start handling things on his own and fucked up. I couldn't prove it beyond this most circumstantial evidence, but I could make it.

So that's how the empire was ruled and what Agrippina's day to day was: friends of Agrippina and Claudius were rewarded for being good pals with positions as proconsuls and procurators and governors of imperial provinces and, when things got really bad, they got kicked up the chain until they become yet another issue in the perpetual court politics of the imperial palace where people picked a side in every debate to enhance their own position. The ongoing niggles of court intrigue and power struggles get shown up in the disaster that was the Fucine Lake project in 52CE. The project was started almost immediately after Claudius became emperor and was an attempt to drain the Fucine Lake in central Italy completely because it kept flooding. The drainage would stop the floods and free up some more farmland, which was always needed in Italy. In a display of the sheer bloody-minded ambition, it involved not only the destruction of a bloody great lake, but also the digging of a five-kilometre tunnel through the centre of a mountain. By hand. The project had been overseen by Narcissus from the beginning, had taken over a decade and employed 30,000 men. In 52CE, Narcissus declared the project complete: the tunnel had been dug, gates had been put in place and the Roman state now controlled the level of the Fucine Lake and could drain it as it pleased.

The final goodbye party for the lake was planned and it was enormous. Staggeringly so. More enormous than you're imagining. Narcissus put on a giant mock naval battle (the Romans loved mock battles) on the lake, starring almost 20,000 slaves and gladiators fighting on proper boats. The hills surrounding the lake were packed with thousands and thousands of Romans ready for the spectacle of a lifetime. In the centre were Claudius, Agrippina and Nero who were glittering. Claudius and Nero were dressed in their military finest, in red and gold and bronze that reflected the sun. Agrippina showed them both up. She wore a cloak made of gold thread that glittered and shone and dazzled. Pliny the Elder travelled from Rome to see the show and commented on Agrippina's cloak, which was a form called a *chlamys*. It was a Greek short cloak, if you imagine taking a blanket and wrapping it around your shoulders so that the joining corners meet at your right shoulder rather than at the front; so your right arm is free, but your whole left side is covered. That's what a *chlamys* looked like. It fell to about knee or mid-calf length and was, and I cannot emphasise this enough, a man's cloak. A Greek man's cloak. Made of gold. It represented both military bearing and royal status: both things that Agrippina wasn't really allowed but was doing anyway.

Can you imagine her appearance there? Her back straight and her cloak falling across her shoulders. Can you hear the gasps and the ripples of conversation that became a hum when thousands were whispering all at once? All those eyes directly on Agrippina. Do you think she smiled and waved and said hi to her pals in the good seats? Or did she sit cold and regal and intimidating, radiating majesty? I think the latter. I think she sat cool and calm and unsmiling, grandeur leaking out of her every pore. As imperial as a mint. Like Jadis in *The Magician's Nephew*, she gave no one a second to doubt her place on the throne.

Agrippina's cloak alone was a decent attempt to upstage Narcissus on his big day. Despite being one of the richest men in the Western world, he still didn't get to wear sparkly gold cloaks. His day got worse, though. The show was supposed to end with the tunnel opening and all the water rushing out, leaving an empty lake and an awed population. What happened instead was the gates were opened and the lake stayed still. The awkward silence in the moments that followed the realisation that the water levels weren't dropping must have been excruciating for everyone, but especially Narcissus. The horror that must have filled Narcissus at that moment, and the embarrassment. He failed so spectacularly in front of half the country. Unbearable. Everyone was sent off home, shuffling awkwardly as the day ended with the dampest of squibs and the lake remained full. Investigators quickly established that the tunnel was not even close to deep enough for the water to be forced out. Men were sent out again to do it properly and, an unspecified amount of time later, another grand opening was held. They couldn't do the same thing twice, obviously, so this time they set up gladiatorial battles on pontoons. Instead of boats banging into each other and people going ooh at the rowing prowess, this time they had small groups of infantry having hand-to-hand battles while trying not to tip themselves into the water. It sounds like a particularly deadly episode of *Total Wipeout* but they had spunked all their best ideas on the first grand opening.

Still, thousands showed up because there wasn't much else to do but watch people die in Italy, and this time Claudius and Agrippina set up a banquet situation by the tunnel entrance so they could dine and enjoy a close-up of the tunnel (civil engineering was very exciting, apparently). The show had the same ending planned: the gates open, the waters drain, everyone applauds. There was slightly more success this time, in that the waters started rushing out, leading to cheers that quickly turned to screams as it became clear that the tunnel was now too deep and was being overwhelmed by the torrent of water rushing into it. The torrent overflowed and the flood swept everything in its way into near oblivion. Which included Claudius and Agrippina and their dining companions, who were almost drowned. At least there was no awkward silence this time, but the trip back to the palace with Narcissus must have been, once again, uncomfortable.

Agrippina saw the whole spectacular disaster as an opportunity to undermine her rival. She openly accused Narcissus of deliberately mismanaging the project, skimming money off the top for himself and hiring incompetent contractors. Narcissus effectively retorted with the inevitable response of defensive men and he called her a whore and a bitch. Again, the empire's business became part of the personal squabbling of the emperor's court.

Or at least that's what the sources would like us to think, because the sources want, and indeed expect, us as the reader to be as appalled as they are that a woman and a man who was once property would dare even have a peek at the plans for such a project, let alone run one. They think that Narcissus calling Agrippina a bitch and a whore is the reasonable bit, because they think that Agrippina is in fact a bitch (an 'imperious woman') and a whore ('an unchaste woman') and that this is a lot worse than just messing up a great engineering project. Another reading of the situation is that Agrippina was genuinely concerned about the massive waste of resources and lives and the size of the embarrassment for their regime and reputation. Claudius was already thought of as a bumbling incompetent: the Fucine Lake disaster did not help him. It is a testament, though, to Narcissus's popularity with Claudius, and Agrippina letting the thing go, that all that happened to him is a slightly damaged reputation. Others had died for much, much less.

This representation of Agrippina as being a shrill, angry manipulator, rather than a woman with legitimate concerns about a seriously botched project, is exactly what Tacitus is going for. You might remember that Tacitus claims Agrippina's first act was to have Lollia Paulina killed for being too pretty; that story comes immediately after pages and pages of detailed description of a complicated dispute in Armenia with the Parthian Empire and several battles in Mesopotamia (modern-day Iraq and Iran). The resulting contrast works to make Agrippina's actions look like the petty, pathetic fussing of a foolish woman. While the actions of the men listed in the previous pages cause Roman power to spread and leaders to fall, the actions of Agrippina merely take down other women for ridiculous reasons. The sneer is Tacitus's voice as he relays this to us is almost palpable.

But when we actually look at Agrippina's role in the running of the empire and try to dodge the repulsed misogyny that fuelled our sources, we mostly see a competent woman getting shit done. Sometimes she won, sometimes she lost but she kept going. We see her doing things like joining Claudius with the people of Rome when a fire broke out, helping out like no imperial woman had ever done before her or after. We see her sitting in public listening to cases and receiving delegations and dealing with the boring politics when she could be spending her days having her hair done and eating and receiving much less hate for it. We see her taking an interest in foreign affairs in minor provinces and getting involved with the administration of the empire.

When you sit down and read Tacitus or Dio or even Pliny the Elder, and look at what she actually did in public, you get the impression that Agrippina as an empress was incredibly hardworking. She was involved in every aspect of domestic and foreign affairs, popping up all over the place to be disapproved of. She is portrayed as being single-mindedly dedicated to making sure that Nero became emperor over Britannicus, but that actually doesn't seem like it was a particularly hard thing to persuade Claudius on, as Nero was a much better option that Britannicus. She was a wicked stepmother, yet she never tries to harm Britannicus or kill him, as Livia is accused of doing to Nero's spiritual ancestors Gaius and Lucius Caesar, so she obviously wasn't that dedicated to the cause. Bumping off Britannicus would have solved all her apparent problems persuading people to accept Nero in a second but she didn't even try. Instead she spent her time worrying about who was going to be the next quaestor. She didn't even seem all that interested in domestic family matters beyond ensuring that Nero would be a legitimate successor and there would be no fighting or uncertainty when the time came. Given that Claudius was in his mid-fifties and had a serious illness during their marriage, and Britannicus was about 13 by the time Claudius died, this doesn't seem like a concern that was particularly out of place. It seems pretty damn pragmatic and sensible to me. Especially when we remember that both Claudius and Agrippina, and all their advisers, had lived through the uncertain and bloody successions of both Gaius and Claudius. Neither transition was smooth or assured; both were accompanied by a lot of death that would ideally be avoided next time.

Agrippina also comes across as thoroughly enjoying her status as empress and acting as though she truly believed that she was special, special in a sacrosanct kind of way, and that she deserved to be treated as such. She rode in her *carpentum*, behind by her lictors and wore men's cloaks covered in gold, and sat next to the emperor and was happily treated as a person who was straight up better than everyone else. There are two possible readings of this kind of public behaviour. The first is that she had fully internalised her mother's belief that their family just was better than everyone else, that their blood relationship to Augustus, to Julius Caesar and all the way back to Aeneas and Venus meant that they were in fact inhabiting a space that meant they deserved to rule, to be treated as demi-gods.

This would mean that when her slaves pinned her *chlamys* to her shoulder or helped her into her *carpentum*, when crowds parted for her to pass through and cheered for her and men bowed to her, she felt that this was her right. Like Louis XIV, the Sun King, she believed she had a divine right to rule over the other families, and so did her son. This would mean that she demanded these things to meet her ego's expectations of what was correct and what she deserved. This is certainly what Tacitus suggests when he says that she became obsessed with the enhancement of her own status and with eliciting awe and reverence from the Roman people. He acknowledges, though, that she already inspired admiration, even to his day, remaining 'unparalleled as the daughter of an Imperator, and the sister, wife

and mother of emperors'.[3] I quite like this image of Agrippina cours-
ing with indignant arrogance and iron-clad self-belief that comes
from an image of herself as literally carrying sacred blood; a kind of
vigorous, burning indignation as she claims the things she thinks she's
owed: not jewels and banquets and luxury, but reverence and respect.

Of course, there's another way of reading Agrippina's alleged
obsession with her public status and making people revere her, and
that is to see it in the vein of Augustus's public relations campaign
to have himself become the object of religious awe. Having his name
changed to Augustus was the cherry on top of this. It means essentially
The Most Religious One, or the most spiritual one. Augustus's genius
was to give up a good deal of his legitimate powers as a magistrate or
consul or whatever, but build up his personal authority so everyone
semi-voluntarily agreed that he could do what he liked because he was
so brilliant as a person. His difficulty came with passing that onto his
successors, but that's a difficulty for another book. He spent decades
building a system of government from the outside in until he was the
sole ruler of the Roman Empire and no one could quite remember
how they'd all agreed to it, but they did think he deserved it.

This second option is that Agrippina was attempting the same
thing, but with slightly different motives and much, much less time.
It was a propaganda campaign. Her aim was to legitimise the idea of
the emperor's wife as a public and political presence and to minimise
backlash against her. She presented herself in public as masculine and
arrogant so men would not have ammunition for attacking her femininity and femaleness. She carefully cultivated the image of herself as
a member and primary representative of the most distinguished, most
holy, most respected family and reminded everyone constantly that
she was imbued with a kind of supernatural specialness as a result so
that men would struggle to articulate criticism of her without com-
mitting treason or blasphemy. She deliberately, but somewhat incau-
tiously, constructed her public image to be as untouchable as she
could so she could get away with having a public, political life and
have the actual power, in contrast to influence, that she so wanted.
Like Margaret Thatcher, who refused to see herself as a female prime

3. Tacitus, Annals, 12.42.

minister, Agrippina tried to minimise her femininity as much as possible, to be a woman without having the perceived 'flaws' of women. At the same time, she used her family history and reputation as armour against the world that was appalled by her gender. She used her motherhood as a weapon to force her way into public spaces. The arrogance and austerity, the self-discipline and focus were all protection against men who did not want her in their sphere, so she could create an entirely new office for imperial women: the Augusta.

To me, this is who Agrippina was and what she wanted. She wanted an equal partnership with her husband and then with her son. She wanted to be a politician and to have genuine, active power. She simply did not want to be a passive, decorative wife, she wanted to be in the history books, and to represent her family. So she did what was necessary to make that happen. She got to be her husband's partner, not his consort. She had a tangible effect on the Roman world, its politics and its landscape and those effects were positive. She made Claudius more popular, more effective and less likely to be killed by a rival. She set up a clear path of succession that would eliminate potential power struggles without murdering a single stepchild. As ruler of the empire, her influence was pretty damn good. But it wasn't good enough.

The Murderer

None of these good things are what people think of when they think of Agrippina, though. What they think of is murder. In 54CE, Agrippina was accused of murdering two people: her former sister-in-law Lepida and her husband Claudius.

Lepida was first and it's a confusing murder. Firstly, there's some confusion over who was actually murdered because Domitius had two sisters, and both of them were called Lepida. The Roman practice of giving everyone the same damn name is just cruel sometimes. Because Lepida had the same name as her sister, Tacitus gets confused. He claims that Lepida and Agrippina were the same age, though Agrippina was 39 in 54CE and Lepida was about 15 years older. He then claims that they argued over who got to be closer to Nero, with Lepida enticing him with kindness and treats, while Agrippina was 'grim and menacing', which sounds like a definite confusion with his actual close aunt Domitia Lepida who took him in when he was semi-orphaned.[1] Tacitus then insists that Lepida was destined to die at Agrippina's hands because she was basically too similar to Agrippina: they were both as 'unchaste, as disreputable and as violent as each other'. The actual charges levied against Lepida are a little strange. She is accused of doing magic and trying to curse Agrippina, and allowing massive regiments of her slaves to rampage across Calabria and cause trouble. One of those is provable and it seems weird that Agrippina would make such a tangible claim, if it was a personal vendetta, rather than just magic or adultery or one of the easy ones. Modern historians have tended to emphasise the fact that Lepida was Britannicus's grandmother, and herself a descendant of Octavia, and suggested that Agrippina was very sensibly murdering someone who might cause trouble when Nero took the throne, but the charges bother me. I think it is possible – not likely, but possible – to believe that Lepida wasn't failing to discipline some rowdy slaves, but was maybe training up a slave army to cause some genuine trouble. The magical curses

1. Tacitus, Annals, 12.64.

against Agrippina, which everyone believed were a real and effective thing, remember, are just a bonus. It does seem that, like Lollia Paulina, she was trying to weaken Agrippina. The fact that it seems like a strange and murky story just emphasises how little we really know about the elite world outside of the Senate. Lepida was tried and executed. Nero testified in the trial against her.

The narratives all say that it was this murder of Lepida that tipped Claudius off that Agrippina was up to something. Somehow in the previous five years he had failed to notice his wife doing business in public and sitting next to him, or forgotten that he had adopted Nero, raised him to consular rank, had his own daughter adopted so he could marry her to his adoptive son and repeatedly presented him as his successor. Everything that had happened had just slipped his mind and this one case was such an eye-opener for him that he suddenly remembered that he had a biological son he could have as an heir! And where did that bio son go, actually? Tacitus gives us a brilliant portrayal of Narcissus having the same awakening moment and suddenly feeling really bad. His Narcissus starts spending his days clutching Britannicus to his breast while crying and giving really abnormal speeches full of plot exposition, and wishing that he'd never had Messalina killed because at least an ex-slave knew where he stood with a prostitute empress. Tacitus's Narcissus doesn't miss the opportunity to remind Britannicus that his stepmother is a whore, too. Poor Britannicus, who had had a very sheltered childhood, presumably endured this sudden outpouring of Greek emotion as Narcissus entreated him to kill 'the slayers of his mother', which was, of course, Narcissus. Or at least he would have, if this had ever actually happened.[2]

Suetonius and Dio prefer a narrative in which Claudius does the maudlin hugging of Britannicus. In Suetonius, he starts clinging to Britannicus and urging him to get older, as if that is something Britannicus can control, and mumbling Greek epigrams at him. He also starts insisting that Britannicus is the only true Caesar, which would contradict his every action and statement in the previous years. Both Dio and Suetonius say that Claudius suddenly realised that his wife was wicked and had decided to give Britannicus the *toga virilis* and do

2. Tacitus, Annals, 12.65.

something non-specific about Agrippina that would definitely mean that Britannicus would be emperor and not Nero. At the same time, in the sources, informers were starting to emerge; perhaps they had heard that Agrippina's star was about to fall and wanted in on it, and were accusing her of all kinds of crimes. Agrippina got wind of Claudius's plans and decided to make the ultimate move and cut him off before he could undermine her terrible plan to deprive Britannicus of his rightful inheritance. The narratives now converge into a remarkably consistent ball of inconsistencies. They go like this:

Narcissus was out of Rome, either because he was so stressed by fear of Agrippina that he went to visit some medicinal springs, or because Agrippina had insisted that Narcissus go and seek treatment for his gout and sort of forced him into a carriage like in a bad sitcom. The moment Narcissus was safely out of the way, she then got the very famous poisoner Locusta (who is considered to be involved in every high-profile poisoning from Tiberius onwards) to produce something that would be slow-acting but effective. Locusta provided her with a powder, which either Claudius's official taster Halotus or Agrippina herself sprinkled on a particularly delicious looking mushroom. Claudius then either felt nothing or immediately felt pain, either did a massive poo or threw up or neither, either died swiftly or had to be administered a second dose while he was in pain, the second dose, if it was given, was administered by a doctor who was now somehow in on the plot, either by syringe or on the tip of a feather that was put down his throat to induce more throwing up, or in some gruel that was given to him after he threw up.

There are baffling contradictions at every stage of the stories of Claudius's death and in the end it becomes a bit of a choose-your-own-regicide. Do you want a version in which Agrippina applies the poison herself, but Claudius pukes before any effects kick in so she gives him poison in gruel? Or one where Halotus applies the poison and Claudius immediately becomes speechless with pain, but is given a second dose in syringe? Or any other combination of potential events. And one has to wonder, why wouldn't Locusta just give him a poisonous mushroom instead of mucking about with doses? Maybe it isn't even worth asking such questions when the sources can't even get the omens of Claudius's death straight, which is quite good fun. Tacitus has the omens as a swarm of bees landing on the Capitol, fire from heaven dancing around some soldiers' tents, and the births of a hermaphrodite and a pig with the talons of a falcon, the last of which is genuinely horrifying, Suetonius has a new comet appearing in the sky, Claudius's father's tomb being hit by lightning, and several magistrates dying in the year 54CE. Dio has a shower of blood, the doors of the temple of Jupiter Victor opening by themselves, the standards of the Praetorian Guard being hit by lightning, plus the comet and Tacitus's bees, which he puts in the praetorian camp. God knows where they got this stuff from (okay, we do know. It was contemporary sources who were randomly collating stuff).

The only thing that can be said for sure is that Claudius died on 13 October 54CE. He was 63 years old and he had been sick. It's impossible to say whether Agrippina murdered him. On the one hand, Claudius had been very ill the year before, ill enough that Nero had made public promises about his wellbeing, and in the year 54CE there had been some kind of illness going around that had managed to kill a lot of senators including one from each of the four magistracies. A satire published in Nero's reign by an anonymous writer imagined Claudius in heaven being laughed at by the gods and claimed that he had died of fever. And poisoning is a suspicious trope. It's what Livia was accused of, it's what Tiberius was accused of, and it's particularly associated with stepmothers in Roman fiction. The idea of an empress killing an emperor just feels a bit too overblown to be real, and the notion of her using poison just makes it all the more overblown. On the other hand, every single written source that isn't anonymous is clear and consistent on one specific point: Agrippina murdered Claudius with a mushroom. The specifics of the murder vary, the omens vary, but that point that she did the murder stays the same. Even our one contemporary source, Pliny the Elder, says twice that Claudius was knocked off with a poisoned mushroom.[3] As ancient historians, we do not often get several sources saying the exact same thing, and we certainly don't get too suspicious about lots of sources saying the exact same thing. But there is a deep reluctance

---

3. Pliny the Elder, Natural History, 11.73; 22.46.

to believe that Agrippina really poisoned her uncle and husband, and I understand it. I don't want her to be a woman who murdered her husband and neither does anyone else. Historians have come up with all kinds of causes of death for Claudius that don't include poison including gastroenteritis, malaria and heart failure caused by the stress of arguing with Agrippina over Britannicus, all of which are bizarre. A slightly more convincing one is that he might have accidentally eaten a death cap mushroom but really only slightly more convincing, and they all feel like desperate grasping at straws because, really, it is too dramatic and ridiculous for the empress to actually murder the emperor. That happens in fairy tales, not real life. But that's not really a good argument. I have a card on my desk that was produced by the artist Isabella Streffen for a piece.[4] It reads 'Truth is structured like a fiction' and I keep it there for times like this. Fairy tales originate somewhere, and that somewhere is reality.

The other evidence against Agrippina is in what happened next: she sprang into action. She shut down the palace and immediately identified where everyone was and kept them there. Britannicus was confined to his room while the Senate was secretly convened. She made an official announcement that Claudius was picking up, well after he had actually died, to keep everyone calm while she got agreement from everyone that Nero would be emperor and there would be no problems. All this was fairly pragmatic and sensible. It's what I would expect Agrippina to do even if Claudius had died in the most unsuspicious of circumstances: smooth everything over, quietly negotiate in private, keep everything calm and unveil Nero as a *fait accompli*. Of course, this was how Agrippina reacted to everything. She was never a ditherer. She was always decisive, effective and strong. But there's one more damning thing. She spirited away Claudius's will, and it was never officially read or seen again. And that was extremely suspicious behaviour that casts a little doubt over everything. It makes it far more plausible that Claudius and Agrippina had had some kind of falling out, and that maybe he had planned to elevate Britannicus to heir or co-heir. One of the last things Claudius did in public before

4. Isabella Streffen, Whores, 2001. The cards were hidden inside Streffen's favourite books in bookshops in England for readers for find.

dying was have his will sealed by all the magistrates and filed away, according to Suetonius, and this, combined with its disappearance, is information that definitely does not work in Agrippina's favour.

In situations like this, you can only go with your gut feeling and acknowledge that's what you're doing. The sources are too biased against Agrippina as a woman, too traumatised by the experience of Nero, and too Roman to be totally trustworthy, and there's no such thing as an objective, scientific capital T Truth in history anyway. But at the same time, they are all in agreement and that is pretty rare. So perhaps all that matters in reality is that literally everyone believed that Agrippina planned and executed the murder of her husband to protect her son. Not one writer believed that she was innocent either during her lifetime or after. In my heart, I don't know. I waver back and forth. Right now, I think she did it. The disappeared will damns her. I can never prove it, I can never tell you that this is definitely what happened, but I can't do that for anything in Roman history. I can just tell you what I believe based on what I know from the sources and from what comes next. I think she killed him. I don't think that killing him was the plan from the beginning, I think she was expecting their relationship to remain cordial and in concert until he died naturally in a decade or so, and that she would have Nero so firmly in place as a successor by then that there would be no problems with the transition. But I think there was a problem, and that was Britannicus growing up.

When Britannicus was a small child and Nero was a teenager, it was easier for Claudius to rationalise making Nero his sole heir to the throne. But Britannicus had turned 13. Maybe he'd had a growth spurt or hit puberty and started growing a fluffy moustache. He was starting to look like a man to his father. And I think Claudius started to raise uncertainties about what Agrippina thought was their agreed plan, started to wonder out loud about Britannicus as a co-emperor, started to think about things that would cause strife and acrimony and possibly even wars if he was allowed to live until both Britannicus and Nero were in their twenties. I could make a pathetic argument that Agrippina was sacrificing her husband for the good of peace in the empire, a mid-century Brutus doing an honourable thing, but we'd all know that would be risible. I think she decided that Claudius could no longer be trusted to do what she believed should be done, what her son deserved. I think she was extremely reluctant to cede a drop of her position or power to Britannicus and knew that having a second adult heir hanging around would dilute her strength. But she didn't want to hurt the child. So I think she decided to kill Claudius. That she planned it with Locusta and that she waited until the right moment, when Narcissus was away on a wee holiday for his health, and she added the poison to his mushroom and then when he said it tasted a little funny, she ate a bite herself and laughed. I think she did it in cold blood but maybe with a touch of regret.

I think that whatever happened next, she was there when he breathed his last and stood for a second in stillness because, for just a minute, she was the most powerful person in the entire Western world. Until she made the official announcement, she was empress and there was no emperor. And I wonder if, for a heartbeat, she considered taking it for herself. Just a single heartbeat, because she was too pragmatic and sensible and aware of the realities of the world to really try it, but just for that heartbeat, do you think she was tempted? Her husband lay dead on the bed. Her son was just 17. She was 39 and widowed for the third time. She had been a sister of the emperor, hailed by him and adored, and she had been an exile. She had been terrified for her life so many times, terrified her son would not see adulthood. She had been worshipped in Asia and adored in Rome. She was the daughter of Germanicus, the great-granddaughter of Augustus. She had her divine blood. She had ruled the empire like no woman before her. She was Agrippina Augusta, the first and last. But it was just a heartbeat. A single breath maybe. And then she snapped into action – close the gates, where is Britannicus, call the Senate – quietly, bring me Seneca and Burrus. And it was done.

A few hours later, Tacitus says at midday, the Praetorian Guard lined up outside the palace. Something was about to happen. The gates of the palace opened. There were crowds outside, anxious to hear about the health of their emperor. Claudius wasn't enormously popular, but he was still their emperor and his health mattered. The gates opened and out stepped Nero, with Burrus by his side. Burrus nodded and the Praetorians hailed Nero, little 17-year-old Nero with a little bumfluff neckbeard and blank eyes blinking in the sun. They hailed him as Imperator. The crowd hesitated for half a second, wondering what was happening. Where was Claudius? Where was Britannicus? But Romans catch on quick and they raised their cheers as the teenage emperor climbed into his waiting litter to be carried away. The Senate immediately issued a decree formally announcing Nero's ascendance to the throne and not one province or legion protested as the news spread. It was 13 October 54CE. Claudius was dead and Nero was emperor. Agrippina was no longer the emperor's wife; she had gone one better. She was the emperor's mother.

Chapter Five: Mother

The Empress Regent

'Agrippina could tolerate giving her son the empire, but not him being emperor.'[1]

If Agrippina did murder Claudius and her aim was to increase or maintain her own power, her triumph was short-lived. The change of emperor in the Roman world meant that everything changed within the palace; power structures shifted invisibly but were immediately felt and Agrippina almost immediately lost a gamble she had made many years before.

But before things started to slip away, Agrippina got to enjoy the apotheosis of her ambition, in the public eye at least. On Nero's first day as emperor he did as he was told and, undoubtedly under Agrippina's guidance, handled the balance of power between the Praetorian Guard and the Senate well. You'll remember that when Claudius ascended to the throne, it had been pretty much a military coup. He paid off the Praetorians and the Praetorians menaced the Senate for two days until they backed down. This was one of the reasons why the Senate spent half their time plotting against Claudius and the other half making rude gestures behind his back until Agrippina got involved. Agrippina made sure that Nero paid his respects to both the Praetorians and the Senate and that they both felt they had an equal say in Nero becoming emperor. Nero popped up first at the praetorian camp and promised them a bonus thank-you payment that matched what Claudius had given them: 15,000 sesterces each. He then nipped immediately over to the Senate where he gave another speech saying thanks and in return the Senate spent the entire afternoon voting him honours. He refused the title 'Father of the Country' because he was still a teenager but accepted everything else. The full list of honours and titles that made up the Principate is long and exhausting. It had taken Augustus decades to build them up, but from Gaius onwards they were pretty much granted en masse by a Senate

1. Tacitus, Annals, 12.64.

195

that didn't have much choice in the matter. It says something about how in denial the Romans were about having a monarch that they maintained the fiction that these were separate honours and powers that could be parcelled out or individually denied if they felt like it and it just so happens that they never did. When the voting and honouring was finally over, Nero returned to the palace that was now his and agreed a password for the day with his guards. His first password was *optimam matrem:* the best mother.

Agrippina, the best mother, had spent the day hanging around the palace with Britannicus and Octavia, and of course Pallas, Seneca and Burrus. She was ostensibly comforting her stepchildren, but in reality she would have been working. There was an imperial funeral to organise and getting the optics right was vital. There was a eulogy for Seneca to write for Nero to deliver, and that had to be perfect. Claudius would ideally be deified and that would involve some negotiation with the Senate. In Agrippina's mind, too, there was imperial business to deal with. She had been Claudius's junior partner in the empire and as far as she was concerned she had just been promoted to senior partner. Tacitus claims that in this regard she made a swift and disturbing decision to protect Nero, and, without her son's knowledge, she ordered that Junius Silanus be executed. Silanus was the proconsul of Asia at the time and was apparently poisoned by an equestrian and a freedman on Agrippina's payroll. Silanus was dispatched because he was a potential rival to Nero. He was the brother of Octavia's first fiancé, the one who killed himself after being accused of incest, and had the same claims to the throne: he was the grandson of Julia the Younger, great-great-grandson of Augustus, and was considerably older and more experienced than teenage Nero in a world that saw male youth as an affliction to be gotten over, a bit like acne. So he was cleared out of the way as quietly as possible. Next to go was Narcissus, a dispatch so speedy that one wonders how long Agrippina had been secretly dreaming of doing away with him. Narcissus could have stayed away and lived a happy retirement with his ill-gotten billions, but, in a fit of misplaced loyalty to a corpse, he returned to Rome. His reward was to be instantly put under guard and a few months later he was either killed or committed suicide.

The death of Narcissus was the first sign that the power structures in Claudius's court had been dissolved. Narcissus had previously been untouchable. He had practically drowned the entire imperial family and got away with a stern look, but without Claudius around he was stripped of everything that protected him. He really should have stayed by the medicinal springs and found a nice partner. The second sign came during Claudius's funeral, which also brought some of Agrippina's most dramatic and impressive public moments. This was the first proper imperial funeral since Tiberius in 37CE. Tiberius's had been a bit of a farce, marred by people shouting 'throw Tiberius in the Tiber' and everyone getting all fanboy over how much they loved Gaius, and then Gaius had never had a proper state funeral due to being murdered horribly. So Agrippina decided that it would be appropriate and fun to have Claudius's funeral imitate Augustus's 14CE funeral. Claudius admittedly was the most successful and popular emperor since Augustus half a century earlier, but that really says more about how bad Tiberius and Gaius were than how great Claudius was. The funeral began with five days of Claudius lying in state, although I don't know if people could visit him like you can visit Lenin's body, or Romans used to be able to visit Alexander the Great in Egypt (fun fact: young Augustus once visited Alex's body and accidentally broke his nose off). After the five days, on 18 October 54CE, the proper funeral happened. It contained all the bits that we saw when Passienus died, but turned up to eleventy-stupid.

Claudius's body led the procession from the Palatine to the Campus Martius, and then around a couple of times. The body was in a coffin, which was on top of a catafalque, which is a fancy word for a fancy platform. This one was made of gold and ivory and must have been unbearably gorgeous and unbearably heavy. Behind the body walked the consuls, praetors and so on who carried a life-sized wax figure of Claudius dressed in triumphal gear. Behind them walked the rest of the Senate, carrying another figure of Claudius, this time made of gold, and behind them was a triumphal chariot in which yet another wax figure of Claudius stood. Do feel free to do this for me when I die because, to a modern eye, it's unbelievably creepy to have this many effigies around and I like that. The next part was even creepier:

a collection of actors wearing the wax death masks of Claudius's ancestors. These would presumably be Claudians, so Claudius's father Drusus I, his grandfathers Tiberius Claudius Nero and Mark Antony and so on, back as far as you can imagine. The Claudians were an ancient, venerable family and the procession would be long and full as a result. Dozens of death masks walking through the streets of Claudians no one thought would ever be forgotten, but not a single former emperor. Halfway to the Campus Martius would be the eulogy at the Rostra in the Roman Forum and this was given by Nero, but written by Seneca as the sources are very keen to emphasise. Getting someone else to write your speeches was considered to be very bad form and a sign of intellectual weakness. Even Gaius managed to write his own eulogy for Tiberius, Tacitus notes with an arched eyebrow and a sneer. Seneca's speech did not diverge from the traditional sentiment that nothing ill is ever spoken of the dead. It celebrated his Claudian heritage and his literary achievements, his colonisation of Britain and his political prowess and wisdom. This latter section drew laughter from the crowd, which was awkward. Following the eulogy, the procession did a couple of laps of the Campus Martius, while the pyre was lit in the centre by centurions and Claudius was cremated.

At Julius Caesar's funeral, the onlookers and participants were so anguished they tore off their robes and the triumphal ornaments they had received from the great general and cast them into the burning pyre as offerings to him, while women and children threw in their jewellery and clothes. Augustus's death prompted a similar response. This is the Roman equivalent of bystanders burying the car that transported Princess Diana's body during her funeral with flowers, and leaving a seemingly random array of offerings at Kensington Palace: an act that feels impotent for the individual but, en masse, becomes a potent sign of public grief. There is, however, absolutely no sign that Claudius's death prompted such a reaction. His funeral passed without either abuse or any great sign that he ever emotionally impacted anyone, which is rather sad really. His funeral was much more about what Nero and Agrippina could make of it than it ever was about mourning, or even celebrating, his death. As was traditional, once his body was gone and the fire died down, the pyre was left for five days. When Augustus died, as a sign of devotion Livia stood for the entire five days with some prominent equestrians and then personally gathered his ashes and interred them in the Mausoleum of Augustus. Claudius did not inspire such devotion in Agrippina.

Only Nero received such fierce attention from Agrippina, and this was Nero's time to step into the spotlight. As the flames died down, the senators and Nero retired to the Senate house, where Nero gave another speech written by Seneca, this time focused on himself and laying out his policies for the new administration. The speech contained things to delight Agrippina and lines that would, if she were paying attention, have sent a little chill through her. The former was the deification of Claudius. All the sources pass this over in a single line as if making a man a god were an act that didn't demand too much thought, and by the time they were all writing between 50 and 200 years later it wasn't. Even Tacitus had lived through Vespasian being made a god. It was essentially nodded through, which speaks to Agrippina's excellent groundwork among her senatorial allies. Before Agrippina entered public life in 50CE, Claudius stood more chance of spontaneously turning into a pumpkin than he did of being deified on his death. Half the Senate had been trying to speed along the death part for the better part of a decade. At the very least, Claudius was looking at a Tiberius situation, where Gaius casually brought up the whole deification issue to a distinct lack of enthusiasm and it was swiftly dropped. That would be no good for Agrippina, though, whose primary claim to power, rather than prestige, was that she was Claudius's wife. She was helped along significantly by her being Augustus's great-granddaughter and Germanicus's daughter, but these were bonuses. It was her marriage that granted her access to actual politics rather than just nice dresses and people being nice to her. Being a god's widow was important. So she smoothed the way, and Claudius was officially made a god. She must have found someone willing to say that they had witnessed some sign of Claudius being accepted into the heavens, but to my great dismay it isn't recorded. When Julius Caesar was deified, they found someone to say that they had seen a comet and that the comet was his soul entering heaven.

The Romans were not a subtle people. When it was Augustus's turn, an ex-praetor showed up to tell everyone that after the cremation he had seen Augustus's ghost on its way to heaven; even Drusilla, with her extremely short-lived deification, had a senator claim that he'd seen her on her way to hang out with the other gods. So you'd expect Agrippina to have found some dude to do the same for Claudius, or maybe everyone just nodded it through without worrying about things like the gods' approval anymore. Agrippina was also immediately made the head priestess of her husband's cult; she was given an official public role as part of a state-sponsored cult with official public duties.

That was the high point of the speech for Agrippina. The low point came a little later when Nero started to outline his plans for his reign, and began to heavily emphasise that he would separate the palace and the state: 'there would be no more venality, no loopholes for intrigue.'[2] This was a very clear warning to the freedmen, and to Agrippina, that their power was about to be curbed.

These were Seneca's words and Seneca's sentiments, and the clash between Seneca, who allied with Burrus, and Agrippina would come to characterise the early years of Nero's reign. But for now, Agrippina still had some glory days to enjoy as the emperor's mother, a role she apparently considered to be a regency. All the sources say that she effectively took over the actual running of the empire, the day-to-day administration and boring bits of being emperor. Nero and Agrippina were mostly seen in public together, rather than separately, which was an innovation even from Claudius's time. Mother and son were sometimes seen with her being carried along in a litter and Nero walking beside her, a pretty spectacular show of devotion from the young emperor to his mum and an unmissable signal to the watching populace that Agrippina was still holding the power in her hands. And, when Agrippina went out in public alone, she now had two lictors rather than one. These lictors in front of her, carrying their *fasces* and clearing everyone out of Agrippina's way, left the indelible impression that Agrippina was a part of the state of Rome. Nero was constitutionally unsuited to the job of emperor. He didn't even seem to

2. Tacitus, Annals, 13.4.

particularly want to be emperor for large swathes of his reign, and at 17 he was in the thrall of more powerful personalities, of which the most powerful was his mum. The height of her power is presented by Tacitus and Dio as being her new desire to almost participate in senatorial debates by listening in instead of having to rely on second-hand accounts from men. She encouraged the Senate to hold their meetings at the palace, or at the Library of Apollo which was next door, instead of in the Senate house that she was legally unable to enter. This bit wasn't so unusual; though if we only had Tacitus's account of the situation you'd think she'd done something truly wild. The Senate met in various places, and regularly popped up to the palace so that the emperor didn't have to strain his wee imperial legs going down a hill. Agrippina's innovation was the listening in. She would stay hidden, behind a curtain in a vestibule where she presumably sat and made mental notes about who to reward and who to punish. Her presence would have been well known among the Senate themselves and I rather like to imagine her doing well-timed coughs to remind her pals to get on with things or keep Nero doing as he was told.

These early days of Nero's reign also gave Agrippina the chance to get yet more firsts in the realm of numismatics. She was a multi-generational numismatic trailblazer. On her coins with Claudius, she appeared on the same side as her husband but his face is laid over hers or hers over his (this is called jugate) and these coins appear only to have been produced in the east. Now that she was the mother of the emperor, she got her first coins minted in Rome in which she shared a side with the emperor. This time, Nero and Agrippina are facing one another and the legend reads 'Agrippina Augusta, wife of the Divine Claudius Nero Caesar, mother of Nero Claudius...' and then all of Nero's new and extensive titles (Augustus Germanicus Imperator with Tribunician Power). This is perhaps the best evidence that Agrippina saw herself as a co-ruler in these early months, and that Nero wasn't disagreeing. She is presented, tangibly, on gold and silver coinage that would pass through the hands of everyone in Rome, from consuls to sex workers, as the emperor's equal. No woman before her had appeared on a coin in the city of Rome sharing a face with the reigning emperor and no one in Rome would be able to deny her position when they held this coin in their hands. Agrippina started to appear in her son's inscriptions, too, because she was not content with just smashing traditions around coins. Nero became the first emperor to start including his maternal descent as part of his inscriptions. He described himself as the son of the Divine Claudius and the descendant of his mother's relatives: Germanicus, Tiberius and Augustus. Like the coins, this was the kind of thing that was unmissable to a Roman onlooker used to the tedious formality of a list of paternal ancestors and suddenly confronted with a deviation from that. In yet another way, Agrippina demanded respect for herself as a person in her own right.

The most extraordinary sign of Agrippina's power, though, is back in Aphrodisias, where they had already popped up a relief of her wearing a diadem and were unabashed die-hard Agrippina Augusta fans. They were there from the start and they were there at Nero's ascension, with a giant stone slab and a chisel, carving out another adoring relief in the hope that she'd look at them. In this case, they broke the mould again with how far they could go. The relief shows a little Nero, so young and fresh-faced, no trace of his later blubber and neckbeard, with Agrippina next to him. She is dressed as the goddess Demeter, in sweeping gauzy material that falls low and leaves her belly and hips bare, all fertile and sexy. She's holding a massive cornucopia, half her height and overflowing with grapes to emphasise her fertility, and she's wearing a diadem. So far so average (for Aphrodisias). But with her right hand she is doing something quite extraordinary: she is crowning Nero, making him emperor. In every other similar relief and representation from every other reign, the emperor is crowned by a personification of the people and Senate of Rome: the goddess Roma. The general agreement is that the emperor rules because the Roman Senate let him rule and the imagery of the ascension goes along with this. Except here. In Aphrodisias in Anatolia, Agrippina holds the power to grant the throne and shares it with her son.

These days were Agrippina's most glorious as an empress. They were the days in which she seemed to stand as an equal to her son. Her only limit was her inability to cast a vote, a limit that does not seem to affect her much though it must have infuriated her. As she lay in a litter being carried through the Roman streets, with her son, the emperor, walking beside her, she must have felt that her time had come. In the play *Octavia*, written, as we have seen, by an anonymous Pseudo-Seneca after Nero's death, Agrippina describes 'the Empire which I, in my foolish love, gave to him' and this must be how at least a little of her felt:[3] she had worked and worked to remove herself and Nero from the safe anonymity of near-exile she had retreated to after her sister's execution. She had dragged them back to where they, as Julians, belonged. She had honoured the memory of her mother and father who had been deprived of their perceived right to rule the empire, and fulfilled the family name. She was the mother of the emperor and she was outshining even Livia.

Livia was the original mother of the emperor. She was Augustus's third wife, and his best wife. They married when he was in his twenties and she was 19, and were together until he died aged 75. Tiberius was Livia's oldest son from her first marriage and was adopted by Augustus as a kind of last resort because everyone else Augustus marked as an heir dropped dead. Like Agrippina's uncles Lucius and Gaius. The unlikeliness of Tiberius being Augustus's heir, lacking as he was charm, charisma and any desire to hang out with senators, led to ongoing accusations that Livia had poisoned all the other heirs so her son would be the only one left. And then poisoned Augustus for good measure. Livia then became a thorn in Tiberius's side, forever telling him off, reading aloud to him from letters Augustus wrote to her about how much of a dick Tiberius was, getting her mates off murder charges and generally being a pain. She was also richer, more popular, more experienced and better connected than her son, and had, on top of it all, been adopted posthumously by her husband, making her her own husband's daughter and also a Julian (because apparently the relationships in this family weren't gross and complicated enough already for Augustus). In short, she thought she'd be a bit of a backseat driver in the Principate.

3. Pseudo-Seneca, Octavia, 612.

In all these ways she was the proto-Agrippina. She was generally, however, considerably better at hiding what she was doing, in that she tried to behind a semblance of traditional, Republican womanhood. She wasn't trying to hang out in the Senate behind curtains for a start. She also had a son who was much older and less patient than little Nero. Tiberius cultivated an image that was somewhere between bluff old soldier and distracted academic and, in both guises, he was extremely conservative. One of the biggest complaints of his reign was that he demanded that the pretence of democracy continue in the Senate, while accepting no deviation from his own desires. So he'd not tell anyone what he wanted, then punish anyone who voted the wrong way. It was very stressful. His conservatism was even stronger when it came to his mother's role in public life, to which he immediately put a stop. She had been granted the right to a lictor, so he curbed the times she was allowed to use it;[4] he instantly shot down anyone who thought that Livia becoming an Augusta meant that she would receive concrete privileges. Tiberius treated his mother's new title as you might treat a celebrity's honorary doctorate. He did everything in his considerable power to stamp out any attempts by sycophantic senators, who reasonably thought that he would welcome people giving his mum cool things, to honour her. When they tried to name the month of October 'Livius' he practically fainted with horror. Tiberius had extremely clear ideas about his mother's role, very traditional ideas, and he had absolutely no hesitation in making sure that she stayed exactly where she should be: in the private, domestic realm, and in his shadow.

This was the traditional place for Roman mothers. As their sons grew up, they were expected to take a step back into an advisory role. There was an unspoken social convention that when men reached adulthood they made the active decisions in their lives and their mothers merely advised and gently suggested things, or offered their resources to help their sons' plans along. They were only allowed to influence their sons if the boys were doing something really, really bad, like trying to take an army into Rome. Coriolanus, for example,

4. She was only allowed it when she was acting explicitly as a priestess of the cult of Augustus, because she was also the head priestess of her now divine husband–father's cult.

was persuaded by his mum to stop attacking Rome and this was generally considered to be excellent maternal influencing. But after Julius Caesar, practically everyone had tried to march an army into the city so that didn't matter so much anymore and there wasn't much at all that a mum was needed for once her son grew up. She was instead supposed to sit at home and weave and chat to other ladies and say 'that's nice, dear' or, at worst, 'are you sure, dear?' Everything else was overstepping. This is where Tiberius made Livia stay, which presumably infuriated her but which she was powerless to prevent.

Agrippina apparently did not feel powerless at all. Nero was too young and weak even to begin to have opinions of his own about the proper place of mothers and certainly could not have enforced them if he had. So it was Agrippina who lay in the litter while Nero walked in the dust and it was Agrippina who saw ahead of her many years of shared rule of the most glorious empire on earth and maybe even thought she could relax. There was just one problem, a problem that Agrippina was perhaps just a little aware of, one that she assumed she could control. That problem was the men she had employed to be Nero's tutors: Seneca and Burrus. Agrippina believed that they owed her; they owed her their positions and, in Seneca's case, their lives. Agrippina believed this would keep them loyal, she gambled by trusting them with her son and she was about to lose.

The First Crisis

Let's recap: Seneca was a long-time friend, since the days of Gaius's reign. He was a stoic philosopher and playwright, and writer of moralising tracts to women about how great he was and he had been exiled by Claudius for banging Agrippina's sister Livilla. Agrippina's first act as Claudius's wife had been to rescue Seneca from exile (and presumably stop him writing letters) and install him as Nero's teacher. Burrus was a military man who everyone seemed to respect for great military prowess despite never actually achieving anything. He must have just had the right bearing. Agrippina liked him very much, to the extent that she promoted him to Praetorian Prefect out of, essentially, nowhere and then linked him up with Nero as a mentor and teacher. She was in practice, if not in name, patron to both men and therefore quite reasonably expected that they would do as good clients should, which is as they are told. Agrippina had done strategically the right thing: she had allowed other people unfettered access to her son and his education, but had ensured that they were people who owed her everything and would work with her. Unfortunately, Agrippina had underestimated just how much Seneca despised Claudius, Claudius's reign and everything Claudius had ever stood for. And Agrippina was a glowing beacon of everything Claudius had done wrong in Seneca's eyes.

One work that is ascribed to Seneca, and I do so hope he wrote it because it is so very mean, and so very funny, is the *Apocolocyntosis* (roughly translates as the pumpkinification, a play on the word apotheosis) of Claudius, which is a parody of Claudius arriving in heaven and the reactions of the other gods and it is one of the strangest and most cruel things to come out of Roman literature. It begins with Claudius dying and his last words being 'oh no, I've shit myself' to which the author replies, 'I don't know if he really did, but then he did always shit everything up.'[1] He then appears in heaven and is immediately mocked for his limp and his speech impediment and called a

1. Apocolocyntosis, 3.

monster that frightens all the gods. Everyone then takes the piss out of Claudius until Gaius turns up, claims him as his slave and then gives him away. The whole thing is preposterous and hilarious, absolutely full of bizarre and incomprehensible Roman proverbs like 'well, the knee is nearer than the shin' and 'you have come to the place where the mice nibble iron' and 'because the mice lick meal at Rome'. Whoever wrote it was definitely intimate with Claudius, and Nero was definitely emperor at the time because there's a strange bit where the god Apollo goes all misty eyed about Nero's pretty face and lovely hair that made everyone swoon, which is thigh slappingly funny in its own right. So there's a distinct possibility that Seneca wrote it to let out his burning hatred of Claudius, once his nemesis, with whom he'd been forced to regularly hang out for years, and who had finally died. One of the more subtle accusations in the piece is that Claudius was unable to control his wives and freedmen and their role in politics. He was careful, because Agrippina and Pallas were still powerful, and he only named the deceased Narcissus, but his feelings on the matter are undeniable: Claudius was a pathetic, weak man who let the people he was supposed to control walk all over him, while killing all his good friends. Which is also why Seneca wrote a treatise at the same time, addressed to Nero, about how important it was for emperors to be nice and not kill people. Especially not their close friends and advisers. That aside, he had clear ideas about what a good emperor did, and good emperors did not let women and people who were once owned like jugs are owned make the decisions.

I said earlier that the first clues that Agrippina's reign would not be smooth came in Nero's speech the day after Claudius's funeral, which was written by Seneca. When Nero said that his regime would separate the palace and the state, he was talking explicitly about the role that Claudius's private friends and family, his royal court, had had in ruling the empire during his reign, the direct impact his wives and freedmen had had on state policy, in founding cities and defining laws and running public projects. He was talking about the only two of those who were left: Agrippina and Pallas. When Nero spoke these words, they were a deliberate little stab at Agrippina and her best friend, a notice that a new reign meant new rules. We can but guess at what Agrippina might have felt when she heard what was said. Whether she laughed with derision at Seneca's gall, was offended by his suggestion that she was a mere wife who meddled – no different from Messalina – and not a true partner in Claudius's rule, or was furious at the slight, she certainly did not miss what Seneca was saying. But, as we have seen, Agrippina was undeterred. Presumably she thought that Seneca's words (in Nero's mouth) were merely the pretty words that emperors always used with senators. Certainly, they were exactly the kind of thing all three of the emperors so far had said at the beginning and so far every one of them had screwed this up. Agrippina was entering this new reign off the back of four years of smooth sailing and was not expecting much trouble now. Except then the Armenians started acting up again and the first major blow to Agrippina's reign came.

The Armenians have appeared regularly in Agrippina's life because Armenia was in an annoying place, right on the border between the Parthian Empire and the Roman Empire. Both sides wanted to control Armenia because both sides wanted it to be a safe buffer zone against the other empire. This meant that Armenia was never stable and was constantly being invaded by one side or the other, switching kings and generally being a headache. At this time, the king was Radamistus. The Parthians had invaded and, at the first sign of trouble, Radamistus had bolted for the hills. The Armenians, now kingless, sent a delegation to Rome to ask them to help in repelling the Parthians. When the Romans heard who was coming, they got a little anxious. Tacitus said they suddenly started wondering whether a 17-year-old kid with no military or diplomatic experience would be up to handling a complex negotiation with the Armenians and the Parthians, or the battles and sieges that would follow a Roman intervention. They also began to panic that Nero wouldn't be making any of the decisions. Agrippina might do it for him. The idea of a woman getting involved had the Romans (by which, of course, Tacitus means Roman senators) in a state of panic. 'What hope,' Tacitus's Romans ask, 'is there in a child led by a woman?!'[2] You can almost feel

2. Tacitus, Annals, 13.7.

the fear. And that fear was immediately realised in a devastating public incident in front of the Armenian delegation. The meeting began normally; everyone entered the room and took their seats. Nero was accompanied by Seneca and Burrus who went with him to his throne on his dais.

Before anyone could start, however, Agrippina entered the room. This wasn't unusual. She was used to meeting officials and delegations with Claudius by this point. It might have raised a few Armenian eyebrows, but no Roman ones were shocked. The fact that she hadn't entered with Nero would perhaps be the thing that they noticed; had she not been invited? Until she did something new. With Claudius, Agrippina had always sat on a separate dais. She maintained a kind of 'separate but equal' visual situation, which we all know never means equality for the separated party. At least everyone was mildly uncomfortable but willing to let it go. They didn't have to look in her direction if they didn't feel like it. Today, though, Agrippina stepped onto her son's dais. Today she was claiming true equality and these Armenians would look her in the eye. She would take her seat as the rightful partner in the empire, as her son's equal. Or she would have. If Seneca hadn't intervened.

The room was frozen in silent horror at what Agrippina was doing. She was violating every unspoken rule about her position and every very clear written-down law about what women were allowed to do. She had done some shocking things in her time, but this was a statement about her power that was intolerable. Seneca certainly couldn't tolerate it. He moved like lightning, and pushed Nero forward, hissing at him to stop her. Nero, as he always did, obeyed. He did the best acting of his life as he greeted his mother and guided her carefully away from the dais, though whether she got to stay or was embarrassingly escorted out of the room is not known. The scandal was averted. The meeting presumably went on, though I can't imagine the atmosphere was conducive to excellent negotiation.[3] This incident is treated briefly in Tacitus, as a sign that Agrippina was overstepping her mark. It is treated more seriously in Dio, who thinks that Seneca and Burrus

3. As it happened, things sorted themselves out in Armenia when the Parthians got into an internal leadership crisis and voluntarily withdrew.

conspired to make the moment happen so they could put an immediate and public stop to her involvement in public affairs. Whether this was a set-up to spite Agrippina and curb her power is impossible to know. If it was, she did not take the hint. But set-up or accident, it worked. Agrippina never again received imperial delegations with Nero. It was the first blow.

For the sources, this incident is one of many, but for Agrippina it must have been shattering and deeply humiliating. Had she not been cremated, the very fact that you are reading about it now would make her spin in her grave. In terms of the very public collapse of her plans, this was almost as bad as her trial in 39CE for adultery and treason. This was an absolutely undeniable statement by Nero and his advisers that Agrippina's status has irreparably changed, and the fact that they were able to make this statement to the woman who was currently acting like she was a regent highlighted something that Agrippina had thought she had moved past: her power was entirely dependent on the co-operation of the sitting emperor. It was closer to influence than she had realised.

Agrippina had begun to act as if, and possibly even believe, that she had transcended the legal and social limits that were placed on her in Rome because of her gender. She had done everything in her power not to appear in any way 'womanly' in public; she had moved into roles that were ambiguously gendered; she had refused to be put into the easy boxes of wife and mother and had taken on the role of Augusta and made it something unique. But none of it mattered because, to the male eyes that looked at her, she could never, ever escape her gender. She could never be trusted or respected or accepted. She could only ever be loathed and feared for her refusal to be a proper woman and stay behind her men. This moment, just a whisper and a couple of steps forward by her son, hurt more than a slap in the face. As it happened, her heart must have stopped, either with fear or rage. As the full implications of what was happening dawned on her, I'm amazed she went along with it and didn't start throwing chairs. It is testament to her self-control, her understanding of good optics and her desire not to fuck up that she neither started a scene nor had Seneca killed on the spot. The fact that she didn't try to take any action to reassert herself and her power after this incident is telling, I think. It shows that she was smart. A more impulsive person, like myself, for example, might have started beheading my son's advisers for daring to fuck with me. Agrippina was better at this than me, though, and she put on her good face and kept going.

This was the first tangible evidence of what Tacitus calls Nero keeping his word, and what others have considered to be an internal power struggle between Agrippina as the emperor's mother and Seneca and Burrus as his pals. This is always constructed in modern histories as if Nero was a passive player in this game between the good sensible men and the violent ambitious woman, and it's told as if the struggles of Claudius's day had been flipped. On the one side, next to the emperor, were Seneca and Burrus who had been moved into the same position that the three ex-slaves – Pallas, Callistus and Narcissus – had held in Claudius's court. They were his friends, his advisers and his mentors. He trusted them to look after him and to steer him right, by which we mean conservatively. They were ready to advise Nero on how to adhere to traditional Roman values and live up to conservative ideas of what Roman leadership is that still derive from the Republic. On the other side was Agrippina, his mother, a woman with unprecedented power who styled herself as an empress and covered herself in gold, who was believed to have murdered her husband for her own gain and who kept insisting on acting like a man, to the revulsion of actual men. In the middle was Nero, being pulled in two directions. The truth is, though, that neither side could win anything unless Nero picked them. This was a monarchy and Nero held supreme power in his little teenage hands. And the thing that probably chilled Agrippina's heart the most, that hurt the very most when Nero stepped to meet her and prevent her from taking her place, was that he chose to do so. He could equally have chosen to ignore Seneca, to invite his mother's partnership and accept her position and there was nothing Seneca or Burrus could have done about it, but he didn't. He picked the other team. In that one little moment, not only did Agrippina's supposed allies show their opposition to her public power, her son sided with them.

As 55CE dawned and Nero began to settle into his role as emperor and test the limits of his power and independence, we see perhaps why Nero decided to side with Seneca and Burrus over his mother. Nero began a relationship with an ex-slave named Acte. Normally, this wouldn't be an issue. Roman men having mistresses or concubines of non-citizen status was extremely normal. The problem is that Nero only had one. If he'd had 14 mistresses, it wouldn't have been a problem, but having one suggested that he actually liked her and that she might begin to have influence over him as a wife might. As indeed his actual wife Octavia might have had if she hadn't spent pretty much all her time as far away from her husband as she could get. The men in Nero's life all raised their eyebrows a little over the situation but decided that, on balance, there wasn't too much harm in it. Mostly there was a lot of relief that Nero wasn't going to steal any high-status citizen women and cause a fuss among the reputations of proper families. No one wanted to relive the Gaius years. Seneca and Burrus, however, seemed to actively indulge his passion for the girl; they carried messages back and forth between the lovers and helped him hide her from his mum. This is what Seneca and Burrus had over Agrippina and this is how they betrayed her: they indulged Nero. They were like lenient grandmothers sneaking him Haribo even though they know his mum doesn't let him eat sugar at home. They let him learn music and practise his dancing and sneak off to knob an unsuitable woman. They ruffled his hair and wrote long satirical poems about his rubbish adoptive father that contained unexpected digressions about how pretty he was. Agrippina did none of these things. Agrippina preferred the tiger mother method of parenting. Tacitus says she was grim and menacing with Nero. She had no time for his now 18-year-old bullshit or how much he thought he liked this foreign ex-slave. And she told him so.

Tacitus being Tacitus, he tells us that Agrippina reacts poorly to this affair because she was jealous and offended. He calls it 'feminine rage' because nothing is so diminishing as calling something feminine. This is a turning point in Tacitus's narrative of Agrippina. Up to this point, she had been extremely controlled and unemotional, and Tacitus has recited everything in the third person, which is a useful distancing technique: Agrippina did this, Agrippina did that. Here, though, Tacitus's Agrippina becomes extremely emotional, and remains so for the rest of the story. To highlight her emotional state Tacitus starts giving her long, first-person speeches. Obviously, this is fun, because the speeches are always angry and indignant, but they also need to be handled with deep suspicion. Tacitus rewrote public speeches that we have in other records so that they met his narrative needs, so we know he was telling a story and was happy to massage his sources to fit that story. And that's the stuff that was written down. These are the words of a woman which were exclusively spoken in a private context, being written by a man who hated her and saw her as a symbol of everything that was wrong with Rome 50 years after her death. Even if these words came from histories that were written in 55CE, we're still not going to treat them as any kind of record. Instead we are going to treat them as what they are: a version of a woman who was seen to be giving into her natural, female urges at the very first sign of trouble. There is universal agreement, however, that Agrippina did not like the girl her son had chosen to hang out with and wanted him to spend more time with his actual wife, ideally making babies. She was grim and harsh and the crosser she got about Nero's refusal to stop banging Acte, the more Nero insisted that he loved Acte. It's such a ridiculous teenage rebellion situation that it's a struggle to remember that this was an argument between the two most powerful people in the Western world. You can almost hear Nero screaming 'I hate you!' and slamming a door. At the very least, he told her that he might quit being emperor and go and live in Rhodes and be an actor which was both some brilliant trolling and probably what Nero would have been happiest doing. In Tacitus, who Dio is definitely copying in his version of this, Agrippina then did something extremely out of character: she started trying to flatter Nero and apologise to him. This is weird. Either she genuinely realised that she had messed this one up and wanted to make amends or she was behaving very oddly. Whatever it was, Nero apparently decided to go for a reconciliation and gave her a nice dress and some jewellery that had previously belonged to other imperial women; I'm guessing Livia. Nero seemed to think he was doing a nice thing for his mum. Agrippina took it as an outright insult.

In all the sources, this is treated as Agrippina being an ungrateful bitch, but I empathise with her. This gift said to her that she was the same as every imperial woman that came before her. It told her that she was decorative and sexy and nothing else. Agrippina had never been a woman who cared about jewels or clothes in a traditional 'feminine' way. She was renowned for her austerity and her refusal to spend her money on unnecessary luxuries. As this gift was given she was spending all her own cash on a temple of Claudius, a massive one. To be given dresses and necklaces was an insult; it was meant to show Agrippina her place and Agrippina was right to take it as such. Appalled, Agrippina spat at her son that this gift was merely a sign that he would keep the empire from her. 'I gave you the empire' is what Dio reports she said to him, and she is right.[4] She gave him the empire and in return he gave her fripperies. Dio makes a great point in his telling of this incident. He says that she had failed to realise that power given is not something that can be taken back. She thought she had given her son a gift that he would freely, and lovingly, share with her. Instead, Agrippina had handed her son a weapon, which he could now easily wield against her.

4. Dio, Roman History, 61.7.

The Second Crisis

Néro was becoming more comfortable with using his power as a weapon against his mother. These two incidents had been small in their physical reality but had resulted in huge psychological and political shifts. This was how court politics works: tiny incidents affected everything, and Agrippina had found no way to re-establish her position. Cracks were showing and showing fast. Unbearably, Agrippina was finding out that, with Nero, she had no power, only influence and, as Tacitus told us, influence rarely lasted. Nero was discovering this, too, and felt bold enough to make a concrete and political move against her by firing Pallas.

Pallas had retained his old position after the ascension because of his relationship with Agrippina. Callistus had died years earlier, and Narcissus had been immediately killed for being far too Team Claudius. Pallas was fully Team Agrippina and Nero, though. Or at least he thought he was. It turned out at the start of 55CE that there was no longer a Team Agrippina and Nero. There was a Team Agrippina and a separate Team Nero, and so Pallas had to go. There was, of course, a perfectly rational reason for Nero to fire Pallas and that was his promise to remove personal, domestic staff from running the state's institutions. Pallas, you'll remember, had been running the imperial finances for years and had received a lot of public honours that would later repulse Pliny the Younger, while being technically Claudius's ex-property, client and pal. His loyalties, therefore, were always to Claudius and the Claudian family before the Roman state and this was a problem that Seneca and Nero wanted out of the way. However, there was no way of firing Pallas without it being a crisis for Agrippina. This was something that was beyond her control: the nature of Claudius's rule had meant that she was forced to ally with people who would be unable to maintain their position after Nero took the throne unless Nero ruled in exactly the same way as Claudius had, and Nero had no plans to do that. Why would he? Claudius was not a popular ruler, and the adoptive father and son had nothing in common. Nero removed Pallas with the greatest of care. Had it been a true move

against Agrippina or attempt to take her down, Nero could have prosecuted Pallas or at least demanded a full audit of the previous few
years' worth of spending. As the imperial household, and indeed the
entire apparatus of the Roman Empire, was staggeringly corrupt and
self-interested there can be no real doubt that Pallas was doing some
skimming. But Nero magnanimously allowed Pallas to leave with full
acceptance of his accounts and a promise not to investigate him.

In Tacitus's account, however, Agrippina took this news as a personal attack and reacted poorly, by having a full screaming meltdown.
The meltdown was the kind of meltdown that both Claudius and
Gaius are said to have had in times of crisis, veering wildly between
fear and rage and desperation. The idea of Agrippina having some
kind of screaming, crying, terrified tantrum after she had politely and
coldly endured everything she had for the past 40 years feels very
unlikely. This Agrippina threatened to hit Nero, and then furiously
declared that she would side with Britannicus, that Britannicus would
receive his *toga virilis* soon and that she would make Nero's reign very
difficult indeed. Agrippina was popular outside the palace and Senate house, still had an awful lot of friends in the Senate and palace
and was spectacularly popular among the troops because of her dad,
so this was not necessarily an empty threat, and she knew it. Tacitus's
Agrippina, who had a wonderful line in bombast, declared that she
would take Britannicus to the praetorian camp: 'there let the daughter
of Germanicus be heard on the one side, and on the other the cripple
Burrus and the exile Seneca!'[1] Glorious, rousing stuff. If she decided to
join Team Britannicus, she could definitely cause a lot of trouble for
Nero and his team. Except her doing so would be bizarre. As she said
herself, her main claim to power was her bloodline, it was her Julian
blood as the great-granddaughter of Augustus and the daughter of
Germanicus. Nero had her Julian blood; Nero was her son. She grew
him and endured a breech birth and raised him. Later on, in another
crisis, she declared 'a mother does not change her children as easily
as a whore changes partners'.[2] Championing Britannicus would be a
repudiation of everything she had stood for, that her mother stood for.

1. Tacitus, Annals, 13.14.
2. Tacitus, Annals, 13.21.

And Agrippina deciding that she would turn against Nero in a tirade of abuse feels wrong. This whole situation is ridiculous and an obvious attempt to show her as the pathetic, weak and emotional woman that she 'really' was. The idea of her initiating some kind of military coup is hilarious and an overt attempt to make Roman readers think of a notorious Republican woman named Fulvia.

You might remember we mentioned Fulvia earlier as Mark Antony's third wife and a passionate defender of his. When his relationship with Augustus fell apart, Fulvia raised an army and started a war with Augustus. An actual Italian war. They were eventually defeated and then Augustus wrote a really mean poem about Fulvia in which he claimed that Fulvia started the war because she wanted to fuck him, but, because he'd lose his cock if he put it inside her, he fought her instead. Young Augustus was a mean little misogynist himself.[3] So this isn't the first time that Tacitus invoked the spectre of Fulvia as a comparison for Agrippina or forced Agrippina into an existing stereotype of bad womanhood, and it won't be the last.

Nonetheless, something happened with Britannicus because Nero seems to have decided that he had had enough of having someone who could have a valid claim to the throne around and Britannicus died in deeply suspicious circumstances in the early months of 55CE. The sources are all in total agreement that Nero murdered Britannicus using a poison that was once again sourced from Locusta. Tacitus paints Nero as being extremely cruel to young Britannicus, who was almost 14 and being bullied by an 18-year-old emperor. At the Saturnalia in 54CE (held in December), Nero had forced the poor kid to sing a song in front of braying drunk friends, only to find that Britannicus was good at it and that everyone thought he was adorable. It might have been this rather than anything to do with Agrippina that

---

3. 'Spiteful censor of the Latin Language, read six insolent verses of Caesar Augustus: "Because Antony fucks Glaphyra, Fulvia has arranged this punishment for me: that I fuck her too. That I fuck Fulvia? What if Manius begged me to bugger him? Would I? I don't think so, if I were sane 'Either fuck or fight', she says. Doesn't she know my prick is dearer to me than life itself? Let the trumpets blare!" Augustus, you certainly grant my clever little books pardon, since you are the expert at speaking with Roman frankness', Martial, Epigrams, 11.20.

pissed Nero off, given how precious Nero was about his singing. This is why you don't give teenagers the power of life and death over an entire continent. They're very impulsive.

They're also very dramatic and so Britannicus's death went down as a wonderfully theatrical scene. You can imagine it on film. It happened at dinner one day, where Tacitus tells us that children would sit with their family but at a kid's table, like at Christmas at your nan's house when you were little. Everyone, of course, had a taster, but Nero had found a way around this to avoid arousing Britannicus's suspicion. The taster tried a drink and declared it safe but made sure that it was too hot for little Britannicus. When Britannicus burned his tongue on it, the taster apologised and added a little cold water. Cold water laced with Locusta's poison. And so, in full view of the entire household and any guests, Britannicus began to gasp and clutch at himself before keeling over. Nero, full of youthful arrogance and insouciance, declared that Britannicus was having another one of his epileptic fits and asked for him to be removed until he was feeling better. The room was thunderstruck. Tacitus became capable of reading people's minds in the past, which is very impressive for a historian and a trick I wish I had. He tells us that Agrippina controlled her expression and managed to maintain a neutral face, or more likely a gosh-poor-Britannicus face, as he was carried out, but that underneath her veneer of control she was overcome with terror that she would be next. Tacitus likes to tease us with a little foreshadowing, but, honestly, anyone who had been made to watch a child die while being forced to pretend that it didn't happen and then continue eating dinner was going to be afraid. It was a terrifying thing. This was the Roman version of that *Twilight Zone* episode where the child forces the entire town to be constantly happy and hurts anyone that thinks a bad thought.[4] That moment of horrified silence was broken by someone with a quick wit and then the revelries started again with fixed grins and manic eyes. For Agrippina, the moment would have been even harder than for most, apart from Octavia who had just watched her little brother being murdered by her husband. But Agrippina had

4. It's called 'It's A Good Life' and you probably know it from The Simpsons' 'Treehouse of Horror II'.

just watched her son, the light and centre of her life, do something monstrous.

There is, of course, always a question hanging over any imperial murder: was it really murder? Some people have tried to argue that Britannicus really did die of epilepsy because his body turned dark after death, a sign of death by tetanoid epilepsy, and epilepsy was not uncommon in the Julio-Claudian family tree. Those arguments, however, tend to overlook the fact that tetanoid epilepsy is a model for inducing seizures in rats, not an actual form of epilepsy. Tacitus offers up another theory, that Nero had murdered Britannicus to cover up the fact that he had raped him the night before. This is definitely a story that developed much later, when Nero had apparently become quite the sexual adventurer, but its inclusion in a work as serious as Tacitus's means that it must have been everywhere. Anyway, as with Agrippina and Claudius, it does not really matter in the end whether Nero was actually responsible for poor Britannicus's death; what matters is that every single source and every single person says he was. Even Seneca said that Nero did it. And it was a remarkably convenient death, just a few months before people would start actively expecting Britannicus to take the *toga virilis* and engage in a public role; just when people had started to be openly sympathetic towards him. Certainly, there was a sense of genuine mourning over Britannicus.

In the play *Octavia*, every character openly grieves for Britannicus and curses Nero for murdering him. Even the ghostly form of Agrippina, who appears to give a monologue and then disappear, weeps for the child. During Claudius's reign, as we saw, she was pretty universally seen as his wicked stepmother, but his death seems to have wiped away any assumed resentment. Britannicus's funeral was held very shortly after he died, and without any imperial pomp. He was cremated on the Campus Martius in the pouring rain and I wonder, as Agrippina stood at yet another funeral pyre, saying goodbye to yet another family member, whether she remembered him and Nero playing together as children. There is an extremely charming domestic scene in Pliny the Elder's *Natural History* about Agrippina's fondness for birds. She owned several as pets and gave Britannicus and

Nero a starling and some nightingales that they tried to teach to speak both Greek and Latin, probably inspired by a bird Agrippina owned which could allegedly speak. Pliny says he remembered that the boys would sometimes spend all day on the task, laughing together in the early evening sun. This image of the two little boys playing in the sun with their pets, giggling in delight, is what comes to my mind when I imagine Nero, now emperor, and his mother in the rain watching Britannicus's body burn. This was not what Agrippina had planned. Everything was going very wrong.

After the funeral, Agrippina and Octavia suddenly became very close, while Seneca and Burrus began to try to distance themselves from advising Nero, according to Dio. The true nature of Nero's reign, which was to be impulsive and terrifying for anyone close to it, seems to have been revealed. Once again, it came as a surprise to people that giving a very young man huge amounts of power and then hoping that he would do what other people wanted him to do was a bad idea, even for mothers. Agrippina was furious about Britannicus's death and told anyone who would listen, which turned out to be quite a lot of people. Lots of members of old and very rich families turned up at her door, including magistrates and centurions. Tacitus openly claims that she was trying to build a faction within Rome that could take on Nero. Perhaps she thought he was still young enough to be threatened by a political faction; maybe she thought she actually could overthrow him, although this seems unlikely to many. Certainly, she was still supported by the Praetorian Guard and the armies and people that adored her father, and adored her. More likely to me, though, is the argument that she was trying to maintain her power through other means. The death of Britannicus was effectively an announcement that Nero was going to do what he wanted, to who he wanted and in front of everyone and there wasn't a damn thing anyone could do about it. Shoring up her allies in the Senate and Praetorian Guard would make sure that Agrippina could still influence what was really going on in the empire and work with the Senate around Nero. Certainly, if she knew one thing about her son it was that he had little to no interest in the diplomacy and paperwork aspects of being emperor, and hadn't had to do it so far. There's a chance that what Agrippina was doing was making sure that she would be able to actually get things done on the quiet while Nero pranced about being distracted by shiny things. Maybe she'd even wear the sparkly dresses he'd given her to keep him happy.

Nero, though, was not as oblivious or stupid as he looked and managed to notice that the constant stream of important men going in and out of his palace weren't all coming to see him. So he made a move that escalated the crisis between himself and Agrippina into something even more tangible: he kicked her out of the palace and removed her armed guard. He had her forcibly moved to Antonia's house on the Palatine. This all happened incredibly fast. This was less than a year after Nero had taken the throne, just a few short months since Agrippina had attempted to step onto the dais and Nero was walking beside her as she was carried through the streets in a litter. There was no slow, bitter decline in the relationship between Nero and Agrippina: it was fierce and it was swift. This forced move changed everything for Agrippina. It was a visible sign that she was out of favour with the current regime and that she, therefore, was powerless. The space one occupied in the Roman world was so important. Where one sat at dinner, where one stood and was seen, whereabouts in the house one was seen by their patron, all these were tangible signs of one's rising or falling status and they were in constant flux for everyone. Agrippina's place had remained relatively stable for the entire time that she was still in the palace because she was still living and working in the centre of power. Her closest predecessor Livia had never had this access, being forced to remain in her own house. When Livia tried to invite magistrates over to celebrate an image of Augustus in her house, it was such a big deal that Tiberius made the Senate debate it and then decided that men weren't allowed to go at all. Then he held his own party on the same night, like a dick. His point was pretty damn clear, though: his house was where the power concentrated and he wasn't going to let his mum have her house be a place where powerful people could go. Livia's house would have to always remain a female place for women's things. Nero kicking his mother out of his palace said the same thing, and gave the same brutal message as the dresses and jewels. It told her to step back into the female realm and get behind him.

The effect was immediate. Agrippina's door was suddenly empty. Just a few female friends came to visit. Powerful and influential men stayed far away. Gossip flew among the people of Rome about what was happening, but when people saw Agrippina walking without a guard, they were still shocked. For five years, Agrippina's position had seemed unassailable, and five years is a lifetime in politics. People were used to seeing her carried in litters or riding in *carpentia*, accompanied always by the imperial soldiers and often with the lictors in front of her. People were used to getting out of her way, or begging her guard for a minute of her time. Agrippina appearing in the streets was an event like the president coming to town. It was something special to turn and watch. But now, she was ordinary. Just her and her retinue of slaves and ex-slaves, walking alone like anyone else, holding her skirts out of the mud. According to Dio, her fall from the top was so brutal, and association with her so potentially toxic, that men practically flung themselves into the gutters to avoid being seen near her in case anyone thought they were hanging out. In previous years – in previous weeks – she would have been followed by a crowd trying to win her favour, flirt with her, make conversation, ask a favour. Now crowds were virtually fleeing in her path as if being chased by a wolf. They were avoiding eye contact and hiding behind pillars in case she tried to talk to them. This was a total abandonment by virtually all her friends. Even Octavia was gone. After years of being busy, wanted, competent, independent and in charge, Agrippina was very suddenly bereft of everything she loved. Her son had evicted her, had turned into a murderer; her friends and allies were all dead, unemployed or hiding from her; her job had been snatched from her. She was left as any other woman of the imperial family: all alone in a big, beautiful house. I imagine her a little like Susan Alexander Kane, the second wife in *Citizen Kane*, neglected, doing jigsaw puzzles, in an echoing, empty mansion.

The situation would not get better for Agrippina. As soon as her expulsion from the imperial court was known, she became hugely vulnerable and people took immediate advantage of that fact. They began to dredge up old slights and take their revenge. Suddenly, the empress who had been invulnerable to any attack, who had been able to exile anyone who even tried to step to her, was exposed and unprotected. No one in power fails to make enemies. It is telling, though, that Suetonius claims the lawsuits that Agrippina was pestered with were the result of Nero bribing people to sue her and piss her off, while Tacitus recounts just one major attack, which came from a very old frenemy: Junia Silana. They had remained close throughout the years of Agrippina's marriage and new role as empress and then mother of the emperor, as had Agrippina's ex-sister-in-law and Nero's aunt Domitia Lepida. Three women of the Julio-Claudian family of similar age and upbringing; they had things in common that most families would not understand. Unfortunately, Agrippina upset Silana. Tacitus makes this look like the pettiest, most pathetic fight you can imagine. In his version, Agrippina told a young man who Silana fancied that she was too old and too slutty for him and thus scuppered Silana's marriage plans. Can you imagine a more stereotypically female reason for a fight than over a stupid boy? It's possibly true in a way; when Agrippina was empress she would have had the ability to block marriages within the imperial family, and having the very rich, very connected Silana marry the rich, well-connected member of an ancient family would be bad for Nero. Domitia, meanwhile, had been a frenemy since Agrippina stole her husband Passienus and then inherited all his money. That would be annoying enough, but then a few years later Agrippina killed her sister. And all that after Domitia spent a couple of years looking after baby Nero.

Domitia Lepida and Junia Silana saw Agrippina's new vulnerability, saw that she was being abandoned by Nero and that he seemed to hate her, and decided to team up to take their revenge against Agrippina, a woman they had apparently only been friends with because she was empress and they sort of had to be. So they hatched a plot to destroy her once and for all. The plot was quite complicated and involves the participation of several other actors. First, Rubellius Plautus was dragged in. He was Tiberius's biological great-grandson, and Claudius's nephew, being the son of Drusus II's daughter Julia Livia (I swear, I will never forgive the Romans for their naming conventions). He was about 22 in 55CE and he'd spent his days hanging around, being quiet, going to family parties, reading stoic philosophy and hoping that no one would notice or kill him. Unfortunately, as a member of the family, the sole living relation of a former emperor and Nero's second cousin, that wouldn't last and he got tangled in this. Essentially, Domitia Lepida and Silana identified him as one of the only remaining credible threats to Nero's throne. Being Tiberius's great-grandson wasn't a brilliant claim, but it was better than most people had. So, the two women concocted a story in which Agrippina and Rubellius were having a torrid affair and plotting a rebellion. They then got two clients of Silana's to make the official accusation. Instead of taking it public, though, the two men grabbed two ex-slaves, one of whom was also a favourite actor of Nero's, and persuaded them to get Nero drunk and then relay the accusation. Quite why they decided to do this is unclear, but possibly they hoped that Nero would be so drunk that he'd react impulsively and have Agrippina immediately executed without having to risk the fuss of a public trial.

Tacitus, unusually but pleasingly, cites his sources for the scene that follows: Fabius Rusticus, Cluvius Rufus and Pliny the Elder, all of whom were contemporaries of Nero. Fabius is described as 'the most graphic of the historians' and whenever his name comes up it's in relation to the most salacious and horrible stories of death and incest and drunken debauchery, so it's a bit devastating that his histories are lost.[5] At least we have him here. All three sources describe the actor, whose name was Paris, waiting until Nero was nice and drunk before going over to his house. Apparently, it was Paris's habit to roll up in the late evening when everyone was flagging and get the party started again, so he's basically everyone's loud university friend who drinks alone and then gets nude on a table at every single house party. But this time he turned up doing the performance of his life, feigning great distress about what he had to tell. He made Nero bully it out of him in a 'what's wrong?' 'nothing' 'there is something wrong, I can tell' sort of way, so it looked convincing, and then dropped accusations: Agrippina was planning to overthrow her son and put Rubellius Plautus on

5. Tacitus, Agricola, 10.

the throne, and she was sleeping with Rubellius and might even marry him. Paris lavished the story with the detail until little drunk Nero was a wreck. It seemed at first that the plan to rely on Nero's impulsive nature might work; he started screaming that he was going to kill them both, and that Burrus had to go, too. It's interesting that he thought Burrus might side with Agrippina in a fight, because that was exactly what happened. Burrus heard the fuss, came to see what was up and found Nero in a state of high anxiety, demanding that someone murder his mum immediately. Burrus tried to calm him down, and told him that he was drunk and tired; it was dark and he was being rash. He sat Nero down, gave him some water and persuaded him to take a deep breath, talk to Agrippina and find out what was happening. If the accusations turned out to be true, he promised Nero, then we can murder your mum, which was a pretty horrible bit of reassurance to have to give.

Agrippina woke up the next day unaware of the chaos that had unfolded the previous night until Burrus, Seneca and a collection of Nero's freedmen turned up. Much like a phone call in the middle of the night, or a surprise knock on the door from the police, Burrus and Seneca turning up was never going to bring good news. They told her about the accusations that had been made, with Burrus playing bad cop and Seneca playing good cop. Agrippina's response was furious, and really undermined the idea that she was throwing weeping tantrums over Acte. Tacitus provides her with a long speech, presumably modified from the sources he mentioned, in which the overall tone was cold anger mixed with overt disgust. You can feel the disdain dripping off her words and it is this Agrippina that forms the very core of the Agrippina in my imagination. This grim, furious woman who was shocked that anyone would dare try to attack her, who was full of rock-solid self-belief and a desire to crush these other women with her disdain for them. She began with that line I mentioned earlier and it is chilling: 'I am not surprised that Silana, who hasn't got children of her own, doesn't know what it's like to be a mother or she would know that mothers do not change their children like a whore changes partners.'[6] That line makes me want to scream with delighted

6. Tacitus, Annals, 13. 21. Translation mine.

horror. It is brutal. The whole speech is brutal. She went on to call Silana old, and her clients pathetic slaves. Domitia she sneered at for sleeping with a freedman and being too interested in frippery and luxury. A bit of her speech is worth quoting in full because it is ferocious, sharp and makes me want to leap up and applaud, but it is written by Tacitus to make his readers loathe her. It is, to Tacitus, a confession of all her crimes against the state and her female weakness of being a mother:

> 'While my advisers were arranging Nero's adoption, and his proconsular powers, and preparing his future consulship and making all the other preparations for his ascension, [Domitia] was tending her fish-ponds in Baiae...'[7]

Notably, Agrippina did not deny the charges. She dismissed the very possibility that they could be believable. She swept them aside with an imperious disdain, stepped over them and demanded that Burrus and Seneca take her to her son. The men, presumably awed into submission, led her to the palace where she got to have a private chat with Nero. No one reports what happened in that room but, by the time she had finished, her accusers were to be punished and her remaining friends were to be given powerful positions in the imperial administration. Whatever happened between Nero and Agrippina, it was somewhat transformative. A tentative agreement seemed to be reached between mother and son, in which she stopped making official public appearances and he stopped trying to humiliate her. We see some of her allies get nice jobs, like being in charge of the corn supply and overseeing Egypt, both jobs that could starve Rome if they were mishandled, while another got to be governor of Syria. Agrippina, as always, gave great advice and all these men did their jobs well, leaving positive impressions in their wake (more evidence that Agrippina had influence in eastern politics). While it would be nice to think that Agrippina and Nero had a tearful heart to heart full of apologies and hugs, this doesn't seem like something Agrippina would do. It seems somewhat more likely that she scared him into admitting that he had been horrible to her, but we can never know. Maybe it was a beautiful moment between mother and son. You can imagine your own scenario.

The results of that night were immediate. Agrippina stopped harassing Nero, and Nero stopped harassing her. And that's how things stayed for a while. Or at least, we assume so because, all of a sudden, Agrippina disappears from the record.

The Disappearance

All the events in this chapter so far occurred within the first year of Nero's reign. Between October 54CE and October 55CE. By the time Agrippina celebrated her fortieth birthday on 6 November 55CE, the crises were over and Agrippina had vanished. We can perhaps assume that she retired into a private role and stopped fighting for a public one. She became what she had never really wanted to be: just the mother of the emperor. Suetonius says that she retired to the country, where Nero paid people to drive by her house and shout insults through the window. While that is a very funny image, it's also a strange lie because we know that Agrippina was knocking about in Rome and regularly turning up at special events. She was also still appearing on coins, though she never again appeared on a coin minted in Rome. All we know for sure is that from the end of 55CE to early 59CE, she was around but quietly.

She appears in the textual record just once, in the year 58CE when she was brought up in an accusation against Seneca by a guy named Sullius Rufus, who was corrupt and nasty even for the Romans. Sullius was having some troubles of his own when he suddenly and for no real reason came out fighting against Seneca. Among other things, he accused Seneca of shagging both Agrippina the Elder and Younger, the former while Germanicus was alive. This was quite the accusation and thrilling for all onlookers. Seneca had now been accused of banging a mum and two of her daughters, which would make him quite the lothario and a lot more charismatic in life than he comes across in either writing or statuary. Dio adds his own little commentary here and includes a list of all the ways in which Seneca's life deviated from what he taught in his writings, which is brutal and hilarious. He says things like, 'though finding fault with the rich, he had a fortune of 300,000,000 sesterces; and though he censured the extravagances of others, he had five hundred tables of citrus wood with legs of ivory'.[1] He also accuses Seneca of having homosexual relationships

1. Dio, Roman History, 60.10.

231

with older men, a practice the Romans considered to be appalling, and of teaching Nero to do the same thing. It's an unexpectedly violent attack from Dio, which makes it even better. Unfortunately, Sullius was a terrible, corrupt and violent man who made no effort to hide his own corruption and brutalities, so his attempt to distract everyone by pointing at Seneca went nowhere but he got to be exiled to Majorca. It's useful for us, though, as it seems that Agrippina was around in 58CE and in close enough proximity to Seneca that she could be accused of adultery.

The main reason that Agrippina disappears from our surviving record is that Tacitus decided not to include her anymore. He instead switched his narrative focus to other things, and because Dio relied quite obviously on Tacitus, and Suetonius reduces the entirety of Agrippina's life to about three paragraphs, and Pliny only mentions her when there is a particularly bizarre natural history-related story about her, she doesn't appear anywhere else either. As a result of Tacitus's irritating narrative decisions, we can only work on those few clues we have to try to speculate about how she spent her time. I am pretty confident in speculating that she was in Rome and actively involved in politics for this entire time for two reasons. First, because there was an even more serious relationship breakdown with Nero in 59CE that wouldn't have happened if she was quietly retired in the country. Secondly, the empire and city ran really well for these years and fell into a nightmare after she died. That second point is a somewhat controversial one and it's not one that I can point to any concrete evidence for, other than the impression that Agrippina's death comes immediately before Nero's worst excesses begin. Tacitus's account of these years is exceedingly boring, containing only dry accounts of senatorial debates and yet another tedious skirmish in Armenia. Nero's appearance in all of them, though, is sober, careful and broadly disinterested. Nero maintained a hands-off approach to governing that Tacitus briefly praises as a 'shadow of the republic' because Nero let the Senate sort out their own disputes about who had jurisdiction over what and only appeared once in a while to advise on what he would like. When, in 57CE, someone suggested that it might be a nice idea to let slave owners have the right to re-enslave freedmen who weren't grateful enough for their freedom, which is obviously horrifying, Nero deliberated with a series of advisers, of which I think Agrippina was certainly one, and rejected the case. He was consul in both 57CE and 58CE and did nothing that seems to have bothered anyone during that time. He just turned up and nodded, or at least didn't outrage anyone. His outrages were kept in the private sphere during this year, where they were politely overlooked.

He liked, for example, to dress up as a slave with his best mate Otho and then go rollicking around the streets, bars and brothels of Rome causing trouble. He was a one-man stag party that never ended, rolling around the streets of Rome with his terrible sidekick stealing bottles of wine, and beating people up for fun. The attitude of the sources, though, is that he wasn't hurting senators or equestrians so it didn't really matter. In his public, political life Nero was doing fine. And I think at least part of that was because Agrippina, probably with Seneca and Burrus, was secretly behind the scenes, very, very quietly doing his job for him.

So here, in this book, that's what we're going to say. Other books can and will say other things and I won't pretend this is any kind of iron-clad argument because it is absolutely speculation. But I think Agrippina and Nero reached an agreement after the crisis with Silana and Lepida and I think that agreement was that she was to back the hell off from the limelight and, in public, accept her proper place as a woman and as the mother of the emperor and stop telling him what to do. In return he wouldn't worry too hard about what she was doing chatting to senators in the Forum. One slim piece of evidence for this is Tacitus's slip when talking about Nero's plans for her; he says that every man wanted the mother's power to be broken, and uses the word *potestas*. This is in the context of 59CE, three years after she apparently vanished, and I think it speaks volumes. However, the events of 59CE would suggest that the agreement was uneasy and that neither side was particularly happy. Agrippina maybe felt humiliated and scorned, being forced to act like a woman of no consequence, and couldn't hold her tongue, while Nero apparently hated that she continued to try to boss him about. She certainly did not really become the passive mother he wanted.

This was also the time when weird rumours started to emerge about the nature of their relationship. None of them are consistent in any aspect except the accusation that there had developed some kind of sexual relationship between them. In Dio's account, Nero had a mistress who looked exactly like his mother, who he liked because he fancied his mum so much. He liked to display this mistress to his friends while pointing out that shagging her was exactly like shagging his mum. Suetonius also recounts this story, but says that Agrippina's enemies kept him from actually shagging his mum because they thought it would give her more power. Dio adds the similar accusations that Agrippina attempted to seduce her own son because she thought that he was slipping away from her again, but admits he doesn't know if they were true. Suetonius is never that careful and he sniggers that, in the early days of the reign when Agrippina and Nero would ride in a litter together, you could tell that they were shagging in there because Nero would emerge with cum stains all over his toga. Even Tacitus gets involved, though he admits that his sources weren't in agreement and that it might be a story but that it did seem like something Agrippina and Nero might do. He claims that two of his sources agreed that Agrippina tried to seduce Nero, and one outlier stated that Nero tried to seduce Agrippina. Interestingly, Tacitus also directly equates incest with sleeping with an ex-slave, which is just about everything you need to know about how Romans felt about freedmen. Much like the accusations that Gaius raped all his sisters, these stories are generally treated just as stories. The kind of stories that are told about literally every unpopular man or woman in power for centuries. The David Cameron Fucked a Pig stories. They are stories that are useful in telling us that Agrippina was still spending plenty of private time with Nero, though, perhaps more than people were really happy with, and that she still had influence, if not power, in Rome.

I have one other theory about this time in Agrippina's life: I think this is the time when she wrote her memoir. In the modern world, where it seems everyone has a ghost-written autobiography by the time they are 24, this doesn't seem like much of a muchness. In the ancient world, it was a different thing altogether. A Roman woman writing a memoir was a woman saying that her life, her actions, were worth remembering and that was a punch in the face to the Roman establishment. We have just a few mentions of her memoirs in the ancient literature, in Tacitus and in Pliny. Tacitus describes them as a *commentarium*, which was a very specific genre of Roman writing. It is what Julius Caesar wrote about his Gallic Wars, and what Augustus wrote about his life. Tiberius and Claudius both wrote lost *commentarii*. You see where this is going. They were a genre of writing that was about war and politics and the deeds of exceptional men. And Agrippina wrote herself one. This wasn't a 'musings on my life' memoir; it wasn't an extremely political act. By writing and publishing them, she was telling the world that she was just as important as any man. The inclusion about her experience of childbirth in her memoir is a particular fuck you that I love because it is a female act, an act that had never been included in a *commentarium* before. This is a book that can only have been written when Agrippina was empress, and when she felt that she had achieved enough to make such a statement about herself, her power and her position. Even better, all the men who read it and quoted it were implicitly agreeing with her that her life was worth recording.

That doesn't mean that any of them were willing to explicitly agree with her, though. And it was not until another woman entered the scene in mid-58CE that Nero's personal life began to become a problem for Tacitus again and therefore Agrippina reappeared, in the worst possible way. That new woman was Poppea Sabina who, despite being later kicked to death by Nero while pregnant and therefore definitely a victim, has a terrible reputation. She first appears as Otho's wife. He had wooed her away from her first husband, who was an equestrian, by being young, hot, rich and friends with the emperor. Otho was so taken with Poppea, who was apparently extremely beautiful, that he kept bragging about her to Nero. His most common trick, according to Tacitus, was to get up from the dining table early with a big theatrical yawn and declare that he had to get home to his wife who was, dontcha know, very beautiful. Nero was charmed by the sound of this woman and essentially stole her from his friend by sending Otho to Lusitania (modern Portugal) and not letting Poppea go with him. To Tacitus, and therefore to Dio, this was the first trigger for the end of the good times for Nero. Like any woman, Poppea was a bad influence in Tacitus's eyes and he saw her as encouraging Nero's worst excesses and impulses. That bad times were coming is obvious to Tacitus, who recounts the most terrifying portent so far. Opposite the Senate house there stood an 830-year-old tree, the tree which was believed to have sheltered Romulus and Remus as infants suckling on the wolf. It was a symbol of the city's foundation, of its divine roots and its antiquity. As 58CE came to an end, that tree withered and died.[2]

2. Don't worry, it came back to life again later.

The Murder

'Let him kill me, so long as he reigns.'[1]

Early in 59CE, when Nero had just celebrated his twenty-second birthday, shortly after Agrippina had celebrated her forty-fourth, Nero decided to kill Agrippina. No one knows what triggered Nero's decision, but everyone has a theory. Each of our sources has a different one. For Suetonius, Nero was afraid of his mother, who was a violent woman prone to constantly threatening her son, and this drove him to murder. For Dio, the reasons are sexier: Nero had a concubine who looked like Agrippina and this was making Poppea jealous. So Poppea encouraged Nero to kill his mother. Bizarrely, Dio also accuses Seneca of wanting to eliminate the accusations of his adultery with Agrippina and encouraging the murder. He really did not like Seneca. Tacitus has the most detailed account. In his version, Poppea wanted to marry the emperor but Nero was too afraid of Agrippina to divorce Octavia. Rather than have another confrontation with Agrippina (apparently, for Tacitus's Nero, that one in 55CE was enough for a lifetime), he decided to kill her so he could freely marry whoever he wanted. The notion that it was actually Poppea's idea to kill Agrippina, or that he did it to please her, is the earliest of the theories. In the contemporary play *Octavia*, the title character declares that Nero committed matricide to gratify the 'whims' of 'that insolent whore'.[2] The murder, as we shall see, was incredibly complicated and took a very long time and a lot of money to plan and execute so Nero must have been wholeheartedly behind the idea. This wasn't a case of a woman forcing him to do something he didn't want to do. There were numerous occasions when he could have backed out but instead he doubled-down and ploughed ahead, even as his plans collapsed.

The true reason for Nero's dedicated desire for his mother to die a violent death is lost to history. There is one line of Tacitus's that might

---

1. Dio, Roman History, 61.34.1; Tacitus, Annals, 14.9.
2. Pseudo-Seneca, Octavia, 12–128.

237

give a little hint. He says that Nero decided not to kill her the clean and traditional way (by sending an assassin to run her through with a sword) because he feared that the assassin would not carry out the orders. Right at the end of this story, the same worry was voiced by Burrus who would refuse to send any Praetorian Guards against her because he thought they would refuse to hurt Germanicus's daughter. Tacitus hid Agrippina from us for four years, but there are enough clues to strongly suggest that she was still a force in the Roman state who held a terrifying amount of power over the army and the guards. And if she ever wanted to flex that power, Nero might not win. We can see this power also in Nero's desire to have the murder look like an accident. He very much wanted the reality of his mother gone so that he could exploit her popularity and her prestige without interference.

The motive is, however, the only significant detail on which the sources disagree, and, even then, there is a vague consensus on Poppea being involved. When it comes to the details of the murder itself, every source is astonishingly consistent and the story is bizarre. The first plan, say all the sources, was to poison Agrippina. This was too soon after the death of Britannicus for them to risk another suspicious death at the emperor's dinner table so they attempted to infiltrate her household. Suetonius says they tried this three times and were foiled, Tacitus says that she was well prepared against the possibility of someone trying to infiltrate her staff and had plans in place to stop them. All three of the sources agree that Agrippina regularly took antidotes and had immunised herself against poisons, an act of such brilliant forward planning and judgement that it makes me fall a bit in love with her. Agrippina was too prepared for sneaky poisons. She had seen too many in her family die, she had possibly been on the delivery end of a poison to a man who was much less well prepared than she was, and she trusted no one. Both her immune system and her household were loyal. Both Dio and Tacitus state that the next option was the classic stabbing, but that Nero was too afraid that this might backfire horribly. There were multiple ways this could go wrong, and no way to pretend that Nero wasn't involved and reap the glory from deifying his mother if it did. If the assassin refused to hurt Agrippina, and then the Praetorian Guard sided with her, the consequences could be very bloody indeed. There is then a very strange plan that only appears in Suetonius and doesn't seem like it could possibly be real. He claims that Nero designed and installed a machine in her bedroom ceiling that would drop roof panels on her bed while she slept, making her death by crushing look like an accident. The plan was leaked and never carried out, possibly because it was completely stupid. Who knows where Suetonius got this story from; even as gossip it is weird. But it is only marginally weirder than what actually happened.

Where Nero heard of the idea of a collapsible ship is a matter of minor debate. Dio says he saw it in the theatre, when a boat opened up to let some beasts out and then closed again, but Tacitus says that an ex-slave named Anicetus, who loathed Agrippina for unknown reasons, came up with the idea having heard of such a thing while overseeing the navy. The broad idea behind the boat is that part of it could detach or fall away or open up, plunging some of the occupants into the sea. It could then somehow be reassembled seamlessly and sail away from the scene of the crime, claiming that the victim had merely fallen overboard and that the death was a tragic accident. Nero would be able to mourn his mother extravagantly and put up temples to her and maintain the support of the people who loved her, while not having to put up with her. Nero was delighted. Even a cursory consideration of this boat makes it clear that the design made absolutely no sense. Tacitus tried to give an account of how it worked and ended up making the description even more confusing and ridiculous. And how would Nero, or the ship's crew, make sure that Agrippina was in the right bit of the boat at the right time? Would they wait until she stood there and then pull the lever? Would they pull a strange 'Hey, Augusta, come and look at this here on the floorboards' trick? It's a huge, silly risk. Yet every single description of Agrippina's murder states that this collapsible boat was at the centre of it. The play *Octavia* gives the most convincing explanation: the boat was not a trick boat, built with some kind of complicated mechanism, but was merely an unseaworthy boat that would be unable to survive a trip and would spring a leak. Even that seems somewhat unconvincing. It relies on every member of the crew being either willingly suicidal or not in on the plan. Both of those options are big risks. The play *Octavia,* in fairness, does state that the situation was a massacre and that many people died, but none of the other sources agree. What we can agree on is that something happened on a boat and Nero seems to have planned it. But it didn't work.

Here's how the story goes: Nero needed to get close to Agrippina in order to lure her onto his boat set-up, so he invited her to spend a festival with him in Baiae. She was staying in her villa in nearby Bauli, which is about four kilometres away by road, and was apparently thrilled to be asked to join her son. Tacitus has to get in one last dig at her for being a woman, saying that women are always inclined to believe good news. It was 19 March 59CE, and the festival was sacred to Minerva. When the time came for Agrippina to leave for her son's villa, though, someone told her that he was planning to kill her that night. She hesitated. He had sent a special and newly refurbished boat to collect her rather than let her use her usual trireme. What had looked like a kind gesture suddenly looked suspicious. She refused to use the boat and travelled to her son by land instead. Maybe she hoped that the reconciliation he offered was real, and that she was being foolish and bitter and suspicious in refusing his boat. When she arrived at Baiae, she was greeted by an effusively affectionate Nero. He gave her a seat of honour, above even his own, and spent the evening talking just to her. They kissed and giggled, and talked about serious business and ate good food and drank good wine and celebrated Minerva with apparent familial love.

Did Agrippina suspect something in this demeanour of Nero's? Did she wonder what he wanted, what he was doing? Did she see through his insincere laughter and false proclamations of affection? Or was she just happy, with her only son on a calm night in March, toasting the gods? If only I had Tacitus's mind-reading trick and could know what she felt and thought that night. What I wouldn't give to know how she felt as, late in the night, a tipsy Nero led a tipsy Agrippina to the shore and helped her aboard the boat he'd prepared for her, the boat she now trusted. The sources all agree that on the dock Nero clasped his mother to him tight and kissed her eyes gently. He knew that this would be the last time he would see her alive. This woman who had dedicated half her life to him, who had swaddled him and cared for him, who had taught him and watched him train birds to speak and learn to act and sing, who named him Domitius and then made him Nero, who gave him an empire of his own. It is impossible to think of this final moment between them without knowing that this is the last time they will be together, and that Nero knows this, and not wonder how he does it. He must have truly hated her.

Eventually, Nero led her aboard the boat and it sailed away across the bay. Tacitus says that the night was clear and full of stars, and the sea was calm and softly lapping at the sides. He paints us a happy domestic scene of Agrippina and her two friends Crepereius Gallus and Acerronia Polla lounging on the deck, idly chatting about the evening, pleasantly drunk on expensive wine and rich food. Here, the sources diverge on what exactly happened.

In Tacitus, a canopy was dropped on the trio, killing Gallus instantly. The rest of the mechanism, however, failed to deploy and those members of the crew that were in on the plot tried to capsize the boat by all running to one side. The situation in Tacitus's telling rapidly became a farce as those who didn't know that this was an assassination attempt saw the boat tipping and ran to the other side to stop it. They were too late to save Agrippina and Polla, though, and the women slipped into the sea. Polla panicked and screamed that she was the emperor's mother. The assassins responded by beating her to death in the water with their oars. Dio has a slightly different set of events. In Dio, the ship parted successfully and flung both Agrippina and Acerronia Polla into the sea, and Polla died in the same dreadful circumstance as in Tacitus, but here there was no falling canopy or strange chaos. Suetonius offers no detail at all because he's never been knowingly useful. In *Octavia* the boat was rammed by another, causing it to fall apart and sink, taking down the entire crew.

In each of the stories, though, Agrippina did what she did best: she kept her head, she held her tongue and she swam for her life. Agrippina was not going down like this and she was not allowing anyone to pretend her death was an accident. Agrippina Augusta was not going to die in an accident. So she kicked off her clothing, she remembered her years in exile and she swam.

Here our stories diverge a little more. In Tacitus's, she was picked up by some boats, who conveyed her back to the shore of the Lucrine Lake, while in *Octavia* the crew of the original ship took pity on her and saved her, but in the others she swam to the shore and arrived safe in Bauli, alone, injured, exhausted. She then walked back to her villa, dripping wet and causing an extraordinary stir. She was tended to by a flurry of slaves bandaging her injured shoulder and drying her hair and giving her wine and she was able to sit and think for the first time. Agrippina was not a hysterical person. She was careful and sensible and planned, and so far in her life this had worked out most of the time.

She did two things. First, she sent a messenger to Nero to tell him she was alive. Then, she sent someone to find Acerronia Polla's will. Tacitus, using his mind-reading skills again, has his Agrippina reflecting on all the reasons why her accident had not been an accident, which centre on the fact that something fell on her from above. As that isn't in any of the other accounts, and Tacitus is mind-reading a dead woman again, I think we can safely disregard it. It's a nice bit of theatre from Tacitus, though. His Agrippina understood immediately that this was no accident, that it was an elaborate set-up, but she decided to fake ignorance and play for time. The messenger was sent to tell Nero that there had been an accident, that Agrippina was injured, but that he wasn't to come to her. She then sat and waited passively to see what would happen next apparently. I struggle to imagine that this woman who had just fought against the sea for her life, who believed that her own son had just tried to murder her, would sit and wait and twiddle her thumbs. The only time Agrippina ever sat and waited for anything was when she was stuck on an island as an exile. Without doubt she was sending other messages and making plans, working out what could be salvaged from this disaster.

Really, Agrippina surviving the boat was the worst possible outcome for everyone: she now knew that her son hated her so much that he was willing to go to these bizarre and extraordinary lengths to kill her, but she was also currently powerless in a holiday villa in the middle of the night. This must have been infuriating on multiple levels. The Agrippina in my head was furious that anyone would dare to think that she was killable. The Agrippina in *Octavia* obviously went full tragedy: she wept and rent her clothes and tore her hair and shouted at the gods. She did this in the sea as well. There's a lot of rending in tragedy. Anyway, whatever she was doing, she certainly wasn't relaxing and she wasn't waiting passively. Meanwhile, word had spread about the incident and the people of Bauli were beginning to react. The accident would have been a massive event in the area: the Augusta's boat had sunk and bodies were washing up. At least two named people died in the incident, so who knows how many anonymous people lost their lives and were then lost to history.

People began gathering outside Agrippina's villa early, desperate for news about her health. Boats were lining up and the crowd was soon so thick that men were clinging to the sea walls and standing waist deep in the water lamenting Agrippina's misfortune and praying for her good health, offering vows to the gods for her recovery and generally panicking a bit. It's hard for us now to understand what the imperial family meant to Romans, how entangled their person was with the stability and success of the state and how potentially frightening the idea of Agrippina being hurt was. Hard, but not impossible. Remember the numbers of people who waited outside hospitals desperate for news about Kate Middleton when she had her children – perhaps you were one of them, or maybe you watched the BBC livestream of the hospital door. Remember the millions who mourned genuinely and personally for Princess Diana. It's not quite the same, but many, many people are very attached to their heads of state, and these Romans were very attached to Agrippina. Rumours and gossip spread around the crowd, until the news came that Agrippina was safe and well, when they erupted with congratulations and joy. It was at this moment that a column of soldiers arrived, ended the celebrations and crashed into Agrippina's house. This was Nero's reply.

While Agrippina was waiting in her villa, four kilometres away Nero had spent the night anxiously awaiting the news that his mother was dead. The second he had sent her away on the rigged boat, his fear of the consequences of her survival had massively outweighed any other feelings he might have had about the murder of his mother. When Agrippina's messenger arrived with the news of her accident and minor injury, he collapsed with terror. On the one hand, he expected her to burst through his door blazing with fury, like a vengeful goddess ready to destroy him with her own bare hands. On the other, he thought she might march straight to Rome and rouse the armies, Senate and people of the city behind her to charge him with attempted matricide. He dragged Seneca and Burrus, who were apparently ignorant of the attempt on Agrippina's life until this point, out of bed and demanded that they fix this for him somehow.

The men responded with a long, painful silence. It was Seneca who broke it, and finally betrayed Agrippina totally, asking Burrus whether an official order could be given to kill the Augusta. Burrus, displaying the loyalty of the troops and their love for Agrippina to the end, replied that it could not. The troops, he said, had sworn to protect all the Caesars and that included Agrippina. More importantly, Burrus did not believe that the guard would obey an order to hurt Germanicus's daughter. Agrippina's aura, and the power of her father, were such that even now, on the orders of the emperor and at her lowest moment in the dark of the night, they would not hurt her. So Nero turned to Anicetus, the ex-slave who had come up with the boat idea, to finish the job unofficially and Anicetus was more than enthusiastic. They met Agrippina's messenger again, as if to send a message back, but – in possibly the most ridiculous bit of this entire farce of an assassination attempt – Nero flung a dagger at the messenger's feet and then started shouting that Agrippina had tried to kill him. One can only imagine the astonished faces as the realisation of what was happening dawned on everyone. But it was action and no one stood in Anicetus's way as he played out this pathetic charade and went to gather his own men to march to Agrippina's villa.

Four kilometres is about forty-five minutes walking at a reasonable pace, probably less at a marching pace. At a broad estimate, then, maybe two or three hours had passed between Agrippina's messenger leaving for Nero's and Anicetus arriving back at her gate. In that time, Agrippina had apparently retreated, exhausted, to her bedroom. Dawn was just beginning to break when Anicetus kicked her front door in and marched his column of men into her atrium. His men grabbed her slaves and dragged them outside, while Anicetus himself went looking for the Augusta.

He found her in her room, with a single female slave, awake and anxious. Three men entered the dark room – Anicetus, Herculius, the captain of one of Anicetus's triremes, and Obaritus, a centurion – while another dragged the slave out. They surrounded Agrippina on her couch. Agrippina loathed Anicetus as much as he loathed her and there was no doubt now about what would happen. She was never a coward, though, and would never beg for her life. Faced with three men towering over her, she didn't shrink back and she didn't lose her head. She sat up and spat at them: 'If you've come to visit the sick mother, tell him I'm fine. If you are here to murder me, I refuse to believe that this is my son's orders. Nero did not order his mother's death.'[3]

The reply was the first blow. Herculius hit her on the back of the head with a club. Although already injured and exhausted, Agrippina didn't go down. She drew herself back up, blood on her face, locked eyes with Obaritus as he drew his sword, and tore away her dress to reveal her stomach. Then she spoke her last words, defiant and fighting and Nero's mother to the last breath. Gesturing to her womb she demanded 'strike here'. Obaritus obeyed and the other blades followed. Julia Agrippina Augusta died at the point of a centurion's sword as dawn broke on 20 March 59CE. She was 43.

3. Tacitus, Annals, 14.3.

Afterwards

When Nero heard that his mother was dead, he sat motionless and silent. He only reacted when the centurions took his hand and congratulated him on surviving the danger of the night before. When it became clear that the Praetorian Guard would not turn against him, he began to cry. No one believed that he mourned his mother. Both Tacitus and Suetonius record that he rushed to inspect her body, stripping her naked and taking his time manhandling her and commenting on her features. Though both ascribe the story to someone else, they are equally keen to make sure that Nero comes across as a murdering pervert and emphasise the falseness, in their eyes, of his grief. Nero withdrew from Baiae, unable to handle the site of the murder, and wrote to the Senate that his mother had sent a freedman to kill him and had killed herself when it failed. In the letter he said, 'She had hoped for a partnership in the empire, for the Praetorian Guard to swear allegiance to a woman and for the Senate and people of Rome to submit to the same ignominy', which was, to be fair, probably true.[1] But is not much of a reason for a woman to die.

Agrippina was cremated the same day she died, in the grounds of her own villa, as the sun set that evening. Her body was placed on a dinner couch and that was placed into the pyre in her own grounds. As the flames rose, one of her ex-slaves, named Mnester, drove his own sword into himself, refusing to live in a world without her. Nero refused her a burial or a tomb. Only her own slaves publicly mourned her, and they buried her on the road between Misenum and Baiae. Stories circulated about her for years. Some claimed that they could hear trumpets calling from Agrippina's grave, and others that Agrippina's ghost haunted Nero's dreams, with the Furies at her back, for years. Immediately portents were reported: a woman gave birth to a snake, another woman was hit by lightning and killed while she was in her husband's arms, more lightning struck the Capitoline in 14 places. A much-believed story was that Agrippina had consulted

1. Tacitus, Annals, 14.11.

astrologers when Nero was born and been told that he would become emperor but that he would kill his mother. 'Let him kill me,' she replied, 'as long as he reigns.'[2] The death of Agrippina shook Rome and the quake was felt across the empire. The woman who had stood at the centre of the imperial family for a decade was suddenly gone.

Nero didn't return to Rome for several months, but the Senate did their obedient job. Thanksgivings were given for the emperor's survival of a terrible plot and Agrippina's birthday, 6 November, was added to the list of unlucky days. Just one senator, Publius Clodius Thrasea, walked out. In the middle of one of these thanksgivings, as the Roman elite gave blasphemous thanks to the gods for protecting an emperor who was a matricide and preventing a plot that never existed, the sun suddenly went out. It was a partial eclipse, and was seen as disapproval. In Nero's reign, this was a turning point. Whether it was the fact that he got away with the horror of matricide and realised he could do anything, or whether he had been genuinely kept in check by the presence of Agrippina, after 59CE Nero went off the imperial rails. His evening frolics in wine bars magnified to become a full-blown lifestyle. His reputation as a matricide never died and was compounded by his poisoning of his aunt Domitia Lepida in the same year.

When Nero eventually returned to Rome, he had a final blowout festival for Agrippina, a decision that was awkward in light of the fact that the Senate had spent days taking down her statues and denouncing her in anticipation of an expected *damnatio memoriae*. Instead, showing the confusion of his feelings, Nero decided to celebrate her. The festival was huge, Dio says, spanning several days and several locations. Apparently, an elephant walked a tightrope. I'm not sure whether I want that to be true or not. Dio also says that this festival marked the beginning of one of the social horrors of the era: senators acting, fighting as gladiators and otherwise violating the social code, many under duress. For Dio, the death of Agrippina meant the end of Nero's ability to control himself. That was the last that Agrippina was

2. Dio, Roman History, 61.34.1; Tacitus, Annals, 14.9.

mentioned. It was in everyone's interests in the short term to pretend that she had never existed.

Nero's reign lasted another decade. Things got bad. He eventually poisoned Burrus and forced Seneca to kill himself, eradicating virtually everyone from his childhood. He wanted to be an actor and singer and insisted that the entire empire pander to this ambition. He would probably have been happier if he had never been emperor at all. When a large part of Rome burned to the ground, he took the opportunity to build himself a palace that spanned an enormous section of the city and was coated in gold on the outside. He managed to do everything wrong. Eventually, several legions simultaneously rebelled against him and began to march to Rome. In terror, Nero fled with just a few friends to a villa where he eventually stabbed himself in the throat. He was buried by his old girlfriend Acte in the tomb of his biological father's family, rather than the Mausoleum of Augustus, marking his symbolic expulsion from the Julio-Claudian family in death. His death marked the end of the first and longest dynasty of Roman emperors. The Julio-Claudians had managed to wipe themselves out. The year of brutal civil war that followed is known as the Year of the Four Emperors, which is a story for another book.

Agrippina was born one year after her great-grandfather Augustus died. She lived through the reigns of Tiberius, Gaius, Claudius and Nero. As the daughter of an Imperator, the sister, niece, wife and mother of emperors, she was never paralleled. She pioneered a new role for an imperial woman, an active, powerful role that stepped outside of the boundaries of acceptable female behaviour. For a brief flicker of time, she succeeded, ruling with her son, by his side as the empress of Rome. In return for her moment in the light of history, she was abused, humiliated and eventually hacked to death. She stood as an example and a warning to Roman women for centuries. In the grand span of history, Agrippina's 43 years are a blink. Male historians have argued that even to the Romans she meant nothing. But no woman tried what she had tried for another century. And 40 years after she died, after the civil wars that followed her son's rule, after his golden house was torn down, his statues were destroyed and the

Colosseum was built where Nero once built a golden statue of himself, a new colossal statue was erected by Trajan in his new forum. It was of Agrippina. She lived again to oversee Rome. The first empress of Rome.

Extra Bits
Family Tree

The Julio-Claudian Family
44BC–AD69

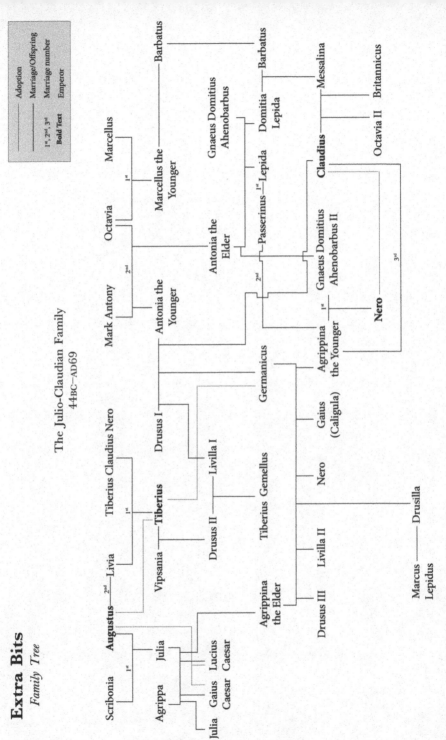

Dramatis Personae

Agrippa (Marcus Vipsanius)	Roman general in Augustus's army. Close friend of Augustus. Husband of Julia I, father of Agrippina the Elder and Julia II. Died 12BCE.
Agrippina the Elder	The granddaughter of Augustus, wife of Germanicus and mother of Gaius (Caligula) and Agrippina the Younger. Died 33CE.
Agrippina the Younger	Great-granddaughter of Augustus, daughter of Germanicus and Agrippina the Elder, sister to Gaius (Caligula), niece and wife of Claudius, mother of Nero. Died 59CE.
Antonia the Elder	Daughter of Mark Antony and Octavia I, wife of Gnaeus Domitius Ahenobarbus I, mother of Gnaeus Domitius Ahenobarbus II, Domitia Lepida and Lepida, grandmother of Messalina, first mother-in-law of Agrippina the Younger. Died 32CE.
Antonia the Younger	Wife of Drusus I. Mother of Germanicus, Claudius and Livilla I. Sister-in-law to Tiberius, grandmother of Agrippina the Younger and Gaius (Caligula). Died 37CE.
Augustus	First emperor of Rome (31BCE–14CE). Adopted son of Julius Caesar. Husband of Livia, father to Julia I, grandfather of Agrippina the Elder, great-grandfather of Agrippina the Younger, Gaius (Caligula), adoptive father of Tiberius. Died 14CE.
Britannicus	Son of Claudius and Messalina, great-great-grandson of Mark Antony and Octavia I, adoptive brother of Nero, stepson of Agrippina the Younger. Died 55CE.
Burrus (Sextus Afranius)	Praetorian Prefect under Claudius and Nero. Close friend of Agrippina the Younger and adviser to Nero. Died 62CE.
Claudius	Fourth emperor of Rome (41CE–54CE). Son of Antonia the Younger and Drusus I, brother of Germanicus and Livilla I, husband of Messalina and Agrippina the Younger, father of Octavia II and Britannicus, adoptive father of Nero. Died 54CE.

Domitia Lepida	Daughter of Antonia the Elder, sister of Gnaeus Domitius Ahenobarbus, sister-in-law of Agrippina the Younger, aunt to Nero. Died 59CE.
Drusilla	Sister of Agrippina the Younger and Gaius (Caligula), daughter of Agrippina the Elder and Germanicus, great-granddaughter of Augustus, wife of Marcus Lepidus, alleged lover of Gaius (Caligula). Died 38CE.
Drusus I (Nero Claudius)	Son of Livia and her first husband Tiberius Claudius Nero, brother of Tiberius, father of Germanicus, Livilla I and Claudius. Died 9BCE.
Drusus II	Son of Tiberius, adoptive brother of Germanicus, father of Tiberius Gemellus, husband of Livilla I. Died 23CE.
Drusus III	Son of Agrippina the Elder and Germanicus. Brother of Agrippina the Younger and Gaius (Caligula). Died 33CE.
Gaius (Caligula)	Third emperor of Rome. Son of Germanicus and Agrippina the Elder, adoptive son of Tiberius, great-grandson of Augustus. Died 41CE.
Gaius Silius	Roman senator and aristocrat. Lover of Messalina. Died 48CE.
Galba (Servius Sulpicius)	Sixth emperor of Rome (69–69CE). General under Nero. Died 69CE.
Germanicus	Son of Antonia the Younger and Drusus I, grandson of Mark Antony, adopted by Tiberius, husband of Agrippina the Elder, father of Agrippina the Younger and Gaius (Caligula). Died 19CE.
Gnaeus Domitius Ahenobarbus	Son of Antonia the Elder. First husband of Agrippina the Younger and father of Nero. Died 41CE.

Lepida	Daughter of Antonia the Elder, sister of Gnaeus Domitius Ahenobarbus, sister-in-law of Agrippina the Younger, aunt to Nero. Mother of Messalina, mother-in-law to Claudius, grandmother of Octavia II and Britannicus. Died 54CE.
Lepidus (Marcus Amelius)	Husband of Drusilla, close friend of Gaius (Caligula), alleged lover of Agrippina the Younger. Died 39CE.
Livia	Wife of Augustus, mother of Tiberius and Drusus I. First woman to take the title Augusta. Died 29CE.
Livilla I	Daughter of Antonia the Younger and Drusus I, sister of Germanicus and Claudius, wife of Drusus II. Died 31CE.
Livilla II	Sister of Agrippina the Younger and Gaius (Caligula), daughter of Agrippina the Elder and Germanicus, great-granddaughter of Augustus, alleged lover of Seneca. Died 41/42CE.
Lucius Junius Silanus	Son of Amelia Lepida, great-great-grandson of Augustus. Betrothed to Octavia II but accused of incest with his sister. Died 49CE.
Lucius Vitellius	Prominent Roman senator under, and close friend of, Claudius and Agrippina the Younger. Consul and censor of Roman Senate. Father of Vitellius, who became eighth emperor of Rome. Died 51CE.
Marcus Junius Silanus	Son of Amelia Lepida, great-great-grandson of Augustus. Died 54CE.
Messalina (Valeria)	Daughter of Lepida, grand-daughter of Antonia the Elder, paternal cousin of Nero, wife of Claudius and mother of Octavia II and Britannicus. Died 48CE.
Narcissus	Greek ex-slave owned by Antonia the Younger. Trusted freedman of and adviser to Claudius. Unofficial responsibility for emperor's correspondence and for matters of state. Notoriously one of the richest men in Rome. Alleged enemy of Agrippina the Younger. Died 54CE.

Nero (Lucius Domitius Ahenobarbus)	Fifth emperor of Rome (54–68CE). Son of Agrippina the Younger and Gnaeus Domitius Ahenobarbus. Adoptive son of Claudius, husband of Octavia II. Great-great-grandson of Augustus. Died 68CE.
Nero I	Son of Agrippina the Elder and Germanicus. Brother of Agrippina the Younger and Gaius (Caligula). Died 31CE.
Octavia II	Daughter of Claudius and Messalina. Stepdaughter of Agrippina the Younger. Stepsister, adoptive sister and wife of Nero. Died 62CE.
Otho (Marcus Salvius)	Seventh emperor of Rome (69–69CE). Close friend of Nero. Second husband of Poppea Sabina. Died 69CE.
Pallas	Greek ex-slave owned by Antonia the Younger. Trusted adviser to Claudius with unofficial responsibility for the imperial finances. Close friend and alleged lover of Agrippina the Younger. Recipient of unprecedented honours during his lifetime. Died 62CE.
Passienus (Gaius Sallustius Crispus)	First husband of Domitia Lepida, second husband of Agrippina the Younger. Close friend of Tiberius, Gaius (Caligula) and Claudius. Consul twice and procurator of Asia. Died c. 44CE.
Pliny the Elder	Prominent Roman natural philosopher and natural scientist. Author of *Natural History*, an encyclopaedia of natural phenomena. Died 79CE.
Pliny the Younger	Prominent Roman senator during the reign of Trajan. Author of ten books of letters. Nephew and adoptive son of Pliny the Elder. Died 113CE.
Poppea Sabina	First wife of Otho and second wife of Nero. Died 65CE.
Sejanus	Praetorian Prefect under Tiberius, alleged lover of Livilla I, alleged murderer of Drusus II. Political rival of Agrippina the Elder. Died 31CE.

Seneca (Lucius Annaeus)	Prominent Roman senator, author and stoic philosopher. Adviser to Nero and close friend of Agrippina the Younger. Author of numerous essays, letters and plays. Died 65CE.
Tiberius	Second emperor of Rome (14–37CE). Adoptive son of Augustus, son of Livia, adoptive father of Germanicus, father of Drusus II, second husband of Julia I. Died 37CE.

Timeline

19 August 14CE	Augustus dies
6 November 15CE	Agrippina the Younger born
26 May 17CE	Germanicus's triumph
Autumn 17CE	Germanicus leaves Rome
10 October 19CE	Germanicus dies
Winter 19CE	Agrippina the Elder returns to Rome
26CE	Confrontation between Agrippina the Elder and Tiberius Tiberius leaves Rome
28CE	Agrippina the Younger marries Lucius Domitius Ahenobarbus
29CE	Livia dies Agrippina the Elder and Nero are exiled
18 October 31CE	Sejanus is executed
32CE	Year of Lucius Domitius Ahenobarbus's consulship
18 October 33CE	Agrippina the Elder dies
16 March 37CE	Tiberius dies, Gaius ascends to the throne
15 December 37CE	Agrippina the Younger gives birth to Nero
Winter 39CE	Agrippina the Younger and Livilla are exiled
Winter 40CE	Domitius Ahenobarbus dies. Agrippina the Younger is widowed

January 41CE	Gaius assassinated. Claudius ascends to the throne
Mid-41CE	Agrippina the Younger and Livilla return to Rome Britannicus is born
Late 41CE	Livilla and Seneca are exiled Agrippina the Younger marries Passienus
42CE	Agrippina the Younger and Passienus are in Asia
Early 44CE	Passienus is consul Passienus dies
47CE	Agrippina the Younger and Nero return to Rome
48CE	Messalina dies
1 January 49CE	Agrippina the Younger marries Claudius
49CE	Lollia Paulina dies Seneca is recalled from exile
50CE	Agrippina the Younger becomes Agrippina Augusta Nero is adopted by Claudius Cologne is founded
51CE	Nero receives *toga virilis* Dismissal of Praetorian Prefects Burrus becomes Praetorian Prefect Death of Vitellius Capture of Caratacus
52CE	Investigation into Judea Draining of the Fucine Lake
53CE	Nero begins overseeing cases Nero becomes prefect of Rome Exile of Titus Statilius Corvinus Death of Lepida Nero and Octavia are married

54CE	Claudius dies
	  Nero becomes emperor
	  Claudius is deified
	  Reception of Armenian ambassadors

55CE	Nero and Agrippina fight over Acte Pallas is fired Britannicus dies Agrippina is removed from the palace Accusations against Agrippina
57CE	Accusation of adultery between Seneca and Agrippina
19 March 59CE	Agrippina is murdered

Glossary

Arval brethren	A college of priests in Rome based in a sacred grove. There were twelve priests. They are mostly known for their extremely detailed records relating to the emperors and their focus on praying for the imperial family.
Claudian family	The Claudians were a patrician family of ancient and enormously prestigious lineage. A large number of Claudians obtained military and political success at almost every point of Roman history and they were considered one of the most distinguished and impressive families in Rome.
Consul	The highest political position in Rome, and the highest official rank in the Roman class structure. Two men were selected by the emperor to be consul annually, although the position was originally elected. The consuls had *imperium* but, by the time of Tiberius, the office was primarily honorific, a representation of the emperor's favour.
Equestrian	Equestrians (also known as knights) were the second highest class in Roman society. They formed the highest business class and membership to the equestrian class required the ownership of 400,000 sesterces. Equestrians had significant social capital, but had limited access to politics.
Fasces	Bundles of sticks, approximately 5ft in length, of elm or birch, tied around a single-headed axe and carried by lictors. A symbol of the power of the state of Rome. Those carried before emperors and imperators were crowned with laurels.
Freedman	Freedmen (and freedwomen) were emancipated slaves. As part of their manumission they were usually granted Roman citizenship but were bound by ties of obligation and formal gratitude, and sometimes affection, to their former owner and their families. In the early imperial period, they formed an informal nouveau riche business class.
Imperium	Authority or the right to command others. Deriving from military command, it refers to a person's formal ability to rule others. It is what is represented by the *fasces*.

Julian family	The Julians were a patrician family who claimed direct descendance from the goddess Venus and the Trojan founder of Rome, Aeneas. Until the successes of Julius Caesar, the family was not politically prominent.
Julio-Claudian	The Julio-Claudians were the ruling family of Rome from 14BCE, when Augustus took full control of the Roman state, to 68CE when his great-great-grandson Nero was overthrown. The extended family was in fact two lineages joined by marriage: Augustus's Julian lineage and his third wife Livia's Claudian lineage. Hence, Julio-Claudian.
Lictor	Attendants to the representatives of the state who had *imperium* who were responsible for carrying *fasces*. They accompanied the representative at all times, walking in single file in front of them. Their number varied according to the rank of the representative. The highest number was 12.
Patrician	A privileged class of Roman citizens; the most revered of the senatorial class. Patrician status could originally only be inherited, not conferred, and they were perceived to be the most ancient of Roman families. Patrician families dominated the priesthoods in Rome and highest offices of the Senate. However, it is estimated that only 14 patrician families remained by the time of Augustus, of which the Claudians were one.
Plebeian	Any Roman citizen who is not a member of one of the small number of patrician families. The differentiation between plebeian and patrician was primarily important in the early Republic and, by the time of Augustus, 'plebs' was a term applied to those who did not belong to the senatorial or equestrian ranks.
Pontifex (Pontiff)	A Roman priesthood, of which there were multiple pontiffs with different but related religious responsibilities. Pontiffs were responsible for the state religion, and also oversaw family law, adoptions, most of the major festivals and sacrificial observances in the city and the care of the eternal flame.

Pontifex maximus	After Augustus, the pontifex maximus was the high priest of Roman state religion; the most prominent representative of Roman religious practice and belief. It was a position held only by the reigning emperor.
Potestas	Loosely translated as 'power', it is an active power to control another. *Potestas* requires someone to be subject to it and it is particularly used in the contexts of slavery and of political rule.
Praetor	The second highest office/magistracy in the Roman Senate, just below consul. There were 16 praetors in the Senate in both military and political roles.
Praetorian Guard	The personal bodyguard of the emperor consisting of nine cohorts of 500 (or 1,000) men. Three cohorts were permanently stationed in Rome by Augustus. Their responsibility was purely to the emperor and his family.
Praetorian Prefect	Instituted by Augustus, the Praetorian Prefect was the commander of the Praetorian Guard, the emperor's private bodyguard. They were selected by the emperor and were usually of equestrian rank. The Praetorian Prefect was also a member of the emperor's advisory council and had significant personal influence.
Princeps	The closest thing to a formal title for the emperor, meaning First Citizen.
Principate	The system of government instituted by Augustus in 14BCE. An informal monarchy where supreme power is held by the emperor.
Province	An overseas territory under permanent Roman control.
Senate	An official group of 600 men who met the financial and moral requirements to be members of the senatorial class (see Senator) which formed the formal ruling body of the state. Magistrates and priests were chosen from among their number. The Senate's official role was to debate motions, advise the magistrates and, later, the emperor, and vote on decrees.

Senator	In order to be a senator after Augustan reforms, a man had to be 17 years old and in possession of one million sesterces. There were also nebulous moral requirements, which were occasionally checked by a censor. Until Claudius, senators had also to be Italian, but Claudius introduced Gauls into the Senate. Senators were responsible for advising the emperor, the magistracies of the state and for the day-to-day running of the empire. They wore a particular form of toga and special shoes as marks of their rank but were not allowed to engage in business.

Further Reading

These are the main books and translations I used to write this book. They are mostly academic in nature, I'm afraid, because that's how I roll. You can't take the academy out of the girl.

Primary Sources

I used multiple translations of almost all the sources because it's useful to check one's own reading of a text against others'. You'd be surprised at how much difference there is between translations.

I used two translations of Tacitus's *Annals*, as well as the Latin text. They were the Penguin translation by Michael Grant (2003), and the three-volume Loeb Classical Library translation by John Jackson (1937).

For Suetonius's *The Twelve Caesars,* I used Michael Grant's Penguin edition (1979), the revised Penguin Robert Graves translation (2001, revised by James Rives), the Catherine Edwards translation for Oxford World Classics (2008) and the Latin text and Loeb Classical Library translation by J. C. Rolfe (1914). I used John Bostock's translation of Pliny the Elder's *Natural History* from 1856 and the H. Rackham translation and text from the Loeb Classical Library (1938). I don't read Greek, so for Dio's *Roman History* I relied on Earnest Cary's Loeb Classical Library translation (1914).

Bill Thayer's LacusCurtius website hosts public domain translations of these and it's a brilliant resource if you want to read some good translations of Roman texts.

Secondary Sources

There is only really one other biography of Agrippina in English (plenty in German, though), and that's Anthony Barrett's *Agrippina: Mother of Nero* (1996), later republished as *Agrippina: Sex, Power and Politics in the Early Empire* (1998). It's a great work of scholarship and contains comprehensive lists of all the evidence for Agrippina's life, which was invaluable.

Judith Ginsberg's *Representing Agrippina: Constructions of Female Power in the Early Roman Empire* (2005) was also brilliant.

I won't bore you with a full bibliography, but useful works I consulted more than once or cited are as follows:

Barrett, A. A., 1996. *Agrippina: Mother of Nero*, London: B. T. Batsford.

Barrett, A. A., 1989. *Caligula: The Abuse of Power*, 2nd edn, Abingdon: Routledge.

Barrett, A. A., 2001. 'Tacitus, Livia and the Evil Stepmother'. *Rheinisches Museum für Philologie*, 144(2), pp. 171–5.

Barrett, A.A., 2002. *Livia: First Lady of Imperial Rome*, New Haven, CT: Yale University Press.

Carlon, Jacqueline M., 2009. *Pliny's Women: Constructing Virtue and Creating Identity in the Roman World*, Cambridge: Cambridge University Press.

Champlin, E., 2003. *Nero*, Cambridge, MA: The Belknap Press of Harvard University Press.

Gallivan, P., 1978. 'The Fasti for the Reign of Claudius', *The Classical Quarterly*, 28(2), pp. 407–26.

Gibson, A. G., 2013. *The Julio-Claudius Succession: Reality and Perception of the 'Augustan Model'*, Leiden: Brill.

Ginsburg, J., 2006. *Representing Agrippina: Constructions of Female Power in the Early Roman Empire*, Oxford: Oxford University Press.

Griffin, M., 1987. *Nero: The End of a Dynasty*, London: Routledge.

Harlow, M., and Laurence, R., 2002. *Growing Up and Growing Old in Ancient Rome: A Life Course Approach*, London: Routledge.

Hemelrijk, E. A., 1999. *Matrona Docta: Educated Women in the Roman Elite from Cornelia to Julia Domna*, London: Routledge.

Joshel, S. R., and Joshel, S. R., 1995. 'Female Desire and the Discourse of Empire: Tacitus's Messalina'. *Signs*, 21(1), pp. 50–82.

Keen, T., 2005. Claudius, Nero and the Imperial Succession. Available at: https://www.preteristarchive.com/2005_keen_claudius-nero-and-the-imperial-succession/.

Kersch, K., 2010. *The Roman Wedding: Ritual and Meaning in Antiquity*, Cambridge: Cambridge University Press.

Levick, B., 2015. *Claudius*, 2nd edn, London: Routledge.

Levick, B., 1986. *Tiberius the Politician*, London: Routledge.

Laurence, R., 2009. *Roman Passions: A History of Pleasure in Imperial Rome.* London: Bloomsbury.

Rupke, J., 2016. *On Roman Religion: Lived Religion and the Individual in Ancient Rome*, Ithaca, NY: Cornell University Press.

Seager, R., 2005. *Tiberius*, 2nd edn, Oxford: Blackwell.

Shotter, D. C., 2005. *Nero*, 2nd edn, Abingdon: Routledge.

Wilkinson, S., 2004. *Caligula*, London: Routledge.

Wilson, E., 2014. *The Greatest Empire: A Life of Seneca*, Oxford: Oxford University Press.

Winterling, A. 2015. *Caligula.* Trans. D. Lucas Schneider, G. W. Most and Paul Psoinos. Berkeley, CA: University of California Press.

Woodman, A. J., 2009. *The Cambridge Companion to Tacitus*, Cambridge: Cambridge University Press.

Acknowledgements

First, thank you to everyone whose name is at the back of this book. This exists because of you and I appreciate and am awed by every single one of you.

The following women are my rocks and my difficult aunts and had my back every step of the way: Alice Tarbuck, Anna Scott, Eley Williams, Marika Prokosh, Ella Risbridger, Sara Guilick, Isabella Streffen, Sarah Perry, Sarah Phelps, Livvy Potts, Kate Young, Fiona Zublin, Janina Matthewson, Phoebe Bird, Sian Hunter, Hannah Reynolds, Amy Jones. To Helen and John for just being the best. To John Underwood, always the best of us.

Thank you to Gerard and Margaret Sally who let me repeatedly use their lovely holiday home to write without distractions, where I got an awful lot of this written.

No thanks to Livia who tried to eat my notes, sleep on my books, pissed on a copy of *The Twelve Caesars*, tried to delete my words and repeatedly sat on my keyboard while hitting me in the face. She was an adorable distraction.

Thank you to Scott, who saw something in a hundred-word pitch written on a whim, and everyone at Unbound. They are all good people who will go to heaven. As is Oliver Kealey, who made the family tree and was remarkably calm in the face of the horrors of the Julio-Claudians.

As always, Conor Sally was here for every word, every comma and every sulk. I can never thank him enough for taking the internet away from me, for the relentless belief in me, and for every holiday that was really a writing retreat. He is my heart and my world.

Finally, to Mum and Tony, Dad and Karen, Katie and Dave, Lucy and Michael and all my niblings for putting up with me being like this, and still being proud.

I've wanted to write this book since I was an undergraduate at the University of Birmingham, where Dr Mary Harlow in particular shaped me as a historian. I am so grateful that I could learn from her, and that I could bring Agrippina to readers. I hope I have done her justice.